AF516494

MEDIA EDUCATION

MEDIA EDUCATION

Dr. Shanmukha Rao Padala
Dr. N.V.S. Suryanarayana
Mrs. Goteti Himabindu

A P H PUBLISHING CORPORATION
4435-36/7, ANSARI ROAD, DARYA GANJ
NEW DELHI-110 002

Published by
S.B. Nangia
A.P.H. Publishing Corporation
4435–36/7, Ansari Road, Darya Ganj,
New Delhi-110002
Phone: 011–23274050
e-mail: aphbooks@gmail.com

2026

© Reserved

Typeset by
Ideal Publishing Solutions
C-90, J.D. Cambridge School,
West Vinod Nagar, Delhi-110092

Printed at
DIVINE DIGITAL PRINTERS
Ansari road Daryaganj Delhi-110002

Contents

ABOUT THE BOOK

Media is the means to achieve Excellency in all walks of life. Everyone should realize its importance in this millennium and make the best utilization of all components of media technology for the development of humankind and better living. This book contains nine interesting chapters covering all the areas of media and education. It is very useful for Students, Teachers, Parents, Administrators, Researchers, Policymakers, as well as Youth and for the performance enhancement of the Media.

ABOUT THE AUTHORS

Dr. SHANMUKHA PADALA : The author is a well qualified with M.Com (Accountancy), M.B.A (Human Resources Management), M.Phil and Ph.D in Management. He posses Vast teaching experience in Degree and PG level Teaching. He has great interest in the field of Human Resource Management and Accountancy. Now he is working as Faculty in the Department of Commerce and Management Studies, Andhra University Campus, Vizianagaram. He participated in National and International Seminars, Workshops, Symposias, FDP Programmes and published rich number of articles in reputed journals.

Dr. N.V.S.SURYANARAYANA : The author is an eminent person in the field of Education. Presently he is working as Faculty in the Department of Education, Andhra University Campus, Vizianagaram. He has rich experience in the field of Teacher Education about a decade at Post Degree and PG level. He is having so many degrees and Diplomas like M.Sc (Applied Psychology), M.Sc (Chemistry), M.Sc (Geology), M.Sc (IT), M.A. (Philosophy), M.A (English Literature), M.A (Telugu Literature), M.A (Child Care and Education), M.Ed, M.Phil (Education), and Ph.D in the Field of Educational Psychology. He also Posses PGDCA, PGDEPM, PGDIPM, CFA, CPFN, Certificate in Guidance and Counseling through IGNOU. He is very much fascinated to Psychology and very much interested in Educational Psychology and Guidance & Counseling. He participated in so many National and International Seminars, Workshops, Refresher Courses, Symposia's and published so many articles in reputed Journals. He produced a number of M.Ed and M.Phil Dissertations. He wrote so many books on recent trends in education and innovative Psychological concepts. He is leading the Vizianagaram Unit as **General Secretary** of Andhra Pradesh Progressive Psychologists Association. And Honorary advisor for various Schools and Colleges. For any quarries/suggestions you may contact the author through.

Mrs. GOTETI HIMABINDU : The author is a well qualified Teacher having so many Degrees like M.A (Politics), M.A. (Public Administration), M.A. (Education), M.Li.Sc, M.Ed., M.Phil (Political Science), and now she is doing her Ph.D. She posses good experience in the field of teaching and Research. She has great interest in the field of Education/Psychology/Politics and Contemporary issues and she is doing Educational/Career Counseling. Now she is working as a Faculty in the Department of Political Science, Andhra University Campus, Vizianagaram. She conducted so many Pre service/in-service Training Programmes. She participated in so many National and International Seminars, Workshops, Refresher Courses, Symposia's and published so many articles in reputed Journals.

1

Introduction

The concept of the media center or learning resource center provides for integrated use of all media. In education, the secondary schools have led the way in this approach to learning. Many of the community colleges are moving towards the concept of integrated media use, but he four-year program is changing more slowly, and in many colleges the audio-visual department is entirely separate from the library.

Media literacy education is at watershed moment around the world. A growing number of countries are developing media education programs in their schools. Media educators from around the world are meeting more often to share curricula, research and strategies. Representatives from nearly 60 countries attended, make this the largest gathering of media educators in history in 2000. Media education is the entitlement of every citizen in every country in the world to freedom of expression and to information and is instrumental in building and sustaining democracy. Media education should be introduced whenever possible within national curricula as well as in tertiary, non-formal and lifelong education. Many positive media literacy developments of today are worth nothing. In addition to new organizations promoting media literacy, a growing number of states have added media literacy goals to their education standards. The considerable presence of media analysis goals in the areas of health and consumer skills also surprised us.

A great deal of publicity is being given to high technology in education, particularly micro-computers and video-discs. There is a danger though that these developments are diverting attention away from the effects of equally powerful low-cost technology. Audio recording is not new education, nor glamorous, but the development of cheap, easy-to-use audio-cassette equipment has already had a major impact on the use of educational broadcasting, both in schools and adult education.

Most of the media program will be implemented outside the center itself, to facilitate and enrich the instruction in the classroom. 'The educational program of the school is strengthened in direct proportion to the quality of the school's library service,' said the 1960 Pennsylvania Governor's Committee on Education. The statement is as valid today as it was then. Today, the media specialist is a teacher in the best sense organizing and maintaining a materials collection. He works directly with teachers and students to achieve educational excellence.

The call fro media education in the United States dates back to the 1950s and the 1970s, when many critical viewing programs were developed, if not back to 1916, when psychologist Hugo Munsterberg called for the serious study, in schools, of the new medium of film, which he called 'The Photoplay'. One of the significant developments in the history of US media education occurred in December 1992 when the Aspen Institute brought 25 educators and activists together for a National Leadership Conference. The group established a definition of media education and a vision for developing it in US education, stating that a media-literate person should be able to access, analyze, evaluate and produce both print and electronic media.

A good background reading before progressing to other books in the bibliography is Robert M.W. Travers' Essentials of Learning: An Overview for Students of Education. An excellent book of background readings which analyse selected factors underlying the process of individualized learning is R.A. Weisgerber's Perspectives in Individualized Learning. An excellent film – which shows the work of Howard kindler or New York University, Tracy Kendler of Barnard College, Kenneth Spence of the State University of Iowa, Harry Harlow of the University of Wisconsin and B.F. Skinner of Harvard is Learning about learning.

Here we discuss about the past research literature concerned with the impact of the media on children and young people. While, there is a particular focus on computer games and the internet. The research on these issues is set in the context of a broad account of research relating to older media, particularly television. In line with the remit of the Byron review the focus here is on negative effects i.e., on the potential harm to children. However, attempts to address negative effects e.g., through various forms of regulation or intervention may also have consequences for positive effects. The report therefore also seeks to address some of the research into the beneficial effects of these media.

Ofcom and other s funders have recently sponsored a comprehensive review of research on harm and offence in media content and an update of that review is currently in progress. Ofcom's review focuses on a broader range of media and is not confined to children and young people. Meanwhile, other more or less definitive reviews specifically relating to games and the internet have also have been produced in recent years. This report does not attempt to duplicate these, but rather to build upon them and to provide a more general commentary on the field of research that will be accessible to the intelligent lay reader. This is not therefore a first hand review of all available studies, although it does incorporate a more original review of emerging developments in the field.

This report seeks to be cautious and even-handed, but it does adopt a rather critical stance towards research, both about the negative effects of these media, and about positive ones. It must certainly prove frustrating to the general reader and indeed to policy-makers seeking to develop an evidence-based approach that research in the field appears so inconclusive and so fraught with disputes and disagreements. Our aim here is partly to explain why that should be the but also to suggest some ways of moving ahead.

The discussing about this attempt is made that the broader social and historical context of research on children and media. It then moves on to outline a possible typology of media effects and to discuss the contribution of two main research traditions in the field. Also review previous research on computer games and the internet, while another issue is new and emerging aspects of these phenomena and their implications for young people. Finally concludes the roles of media literacy both in schools and in the home.

The film is available from State University Film Service, 1400 Washington Avenue, Albany, New York. It shows the different strategies employed by these men in developing new theoretical concepts about man's ability to learn and demonstrates the effect of their theories work upon methods of instruction in schools and colleges. Instruction and learning encompass many processes, many that are not included in learning theories specifically. Instruction involves such considerations as stimulating recall, guiding the learning, gaining and controlling attention, aiding remembering, providing feedback and assessing outcomes. Ultimately, it is the learner who performs such functions. Carefully designed combinations of media best serve the teacher and the school to achieve the kind of learning that is most effective. Robert Glaser, in a number of reports issued through the Learning Research and Development Center, University of Pittsburgh, stressed the concept of learning as education for individuals. The University of Pittsburgh Learning Research and Development Center is an important source for up-to-date information on individualized instruction and learning. In this bibliography, basic background readings on learning are included to provide students of education with an overview of current knowledge.

The Aspen Group also proposed the following precepts:

- Media are constructed and construct reality.
- Media have commercial implications.
- Media have ideological and political implications.
- From and content are related in each medium, each of which has a unique aesthetic, codes and conventions.
- Receivers negotiate meaning in media.

Media literacy involves critically analyzing media messages, evaluating sources of information for bias and credibility, raising awareness of how media messages influence people's belief, attitudes and behaviours and producing messages using different forms of media. Children throughout the world spend an average of three hours each day watching television. At this rate, by the time they reach age 75 they will have spent nine years watching Television. In the US they will have spent two of those nine years watching television ads. When we add the number of hours young people spend watching movies, listening to music and radio and surfing the Internet, they easily devote one-third to one-half of our waking lives to electronic media. Yet many schools still treat poetry, short stories and the novel as the only forms of English expression worthy of study. As a result, most children are not media literate, so they are poorly equipped to engage actively and think critically about the very media that most affect their lives.

Although schools systems throughout the United States are mandated to teach critically thinking, if the schools are not linking this skill to the media world in which so many students are spending upwards of six hours a day, they leaving a potential gold mine unexplored. Most anyone who has engaged in media literacy instruction knows that, before long, parents will report that their children are no longer watching television in the same way they did before. Indeed, parents often remark that after instruction in media literacy, their children constantly point out things while they watch movies or TV programs. They identify jump suts, fades and voiceovers. They detect bias and the power of words to shift meaning and of music to alter the viewer's mood.

Television viewing – which formerly involved relatively passive reception– now involves much more mental activity. Willingly, although without knowing it, the student is now spending a good chunk of those three hours of daily television viewing engaged in critical thinking. The same thing can happen when they are surfing the Net, listening to radio, watching movies, reading the newspaper or playing video games. This is not to say that they will be engaged in critical analysis every moment, but they will be using their higher critical faculties much more if they have been given some of the basic to old of media literacy, of media analysis, than if they have not. We know of no evidence that more critical appraisal undermines one's enjoyment of television or film. To the contrary, understanding how television shows and film are made enhances enjoyment. In some cases, one's tastes may eventually run to less obvious or more sophisticated material, but there is no reasons to expect that a media literate person can't still enjoy the media and derive pleasure and information simultaneously. If schools want students to spend more time thinking critically and practicing critical thinking skills, then they are missing the boat if they are not teaching media literacy and using the media as a site for this critical analysis.

Edgar Dale has said that 'every classroom can have the best in instructional materials now produced' but even if the schools instructional materials are less than excellent, they must be well-organised and administered for effective use.

The library is the center of the program and must lead the way to effective use of educational media. A fine, attractive learning resources center is not the only answer. Teacher must be led to, informed about, and must make use of book and non-book resources to be found in the center. The program of the media center must be planned also to meet the varying and different needs of students. It is the responsibility of the school librarian or media specialist to formulate the objectives of the specific media program, the sum total of all services and learning involved in the center. This must be based upon full and effective participation in the school's curriculum planning. One objective must be to stimulate and guide students and teachers in the uses of media. Another of the opportunity for creative uses of media, to recommend and suggest to students appropriate uses of all media as they work in the center or library. It is necessary that teachers be involved in the selection of media as well as in utilisation. To effectively use media as in integral part of the classroom instruction, teachers must know what is available, have previewed the materials, and have access to the needed equipment and materials.

The Presidential Commission on Instructional Technology offers the following: 'Educational technology is a systematic way of designing, carrying out and evaluating the total process of learning and teaching in terms of specific objectives, based on research in human learning and communication and employing a combination of human and non-human resources to bring about more effective instruction'. Whichever definition is chosen, the important aspect is that education is a systematic process within the framework of educational technology or educational media, a process with a purpose. The purpose of curriculum design is to bring about more effective learning, to solve educational problems, to design effective instruction.

There is a variety of definition of educational technology or educational media. The Random House Dictionary defines Technology as 'the application of knowledge to practical ends, as in a practical ends, as in a particular field: established a National Center for Educational Technology. In our schools and libraries we are most concerned with media, many resources which are used in teaching and learning. Hence, the name educational media, the Department of Audiovisual Instruction Commission on definition and terminology has this definition: 'Educational technology is that field of educational theory and practice primarily concerned with the design and use of messages which control the learning process.' The term audiovisual communication was the label formerly used.

Curriculum development must be systematic if students are to learn to the maximum. We are a goal-oriented society. Whereas most curriculum planning has traditionally been concerned with concept, design for learning in the classroom and school to day is based upon objectives. Educational technology is concerned with curriculum design emphasizing objectives, as well as with methods, materials and evaluation. A Maugham Lee, writing in Audiovisual Instruction, states that 'instructional development seems to hold the greatest promise yet for a way to improve instruction and promote more efficient learning in our increasingly complex and technological society and without compounding the very problem that we are trying to solve'. The purpose of design as a function is to translate general education technology theory and research, as well as subject-matter content, into specifications for learning resources.

Design is not as broad a term as development; development includes production and evaluation functions as well as design.

Students enjoy mediated instruction, they do learn and their varying needs can be met through the use of many media. But media must be a part of planned instruction, and we must have clearly stated objectives. This bibliography emphasizes the importance of design in the curriculum, and the place media has in learning in our schools. We will 'manage' learning as we consider planning controlling, organizing and uses of media. It is the teacher and his new concept of teaching and learning that will change education. It is not the machine but how and why media are used that is important.

Librarians and teachers work together when selecting resources to support the program of the school. A librarian must be knowledgeable of the educational program of a school this is a time-consuming task but important as one aims to provide educational media for the total school program. He must consult with the administration as well as with individual teachers; he must analyse course content and know textbooks well, and must analyse course content and activities to be included in each unit plan. He must know his students, their needs, interests, goals, abilities and concerns. He must match materials with needs; offer services designed to make those materials effective teaching resources in the school. Evaluation involves definition decision-making, values and criteria, administrative levels and the research model.

The items listed in this chapter deal basically with education and learning as related to educational technology. There are references which discuss the major theories of learning in the twenty-first century. Emphasis is upon books which attempt to answer the question of what is known about the process of learning which can be used to design better education in our schools and for individual students.

The winter 1974 issue of School Media Quarterly introduced, in its current Research Column, a listing of 'School Media Dissertations in Progress'. The idea for this came from the Journal of Education for Librarianship, which lists 'Doctoral Dissertations Topics Accepted in Library and Information Science'. The editors of School Media Quarterly hope to develop a listing of school media, dissertations which will tap non-library/information science programs and isolate the school media dissertations found in the JEL list. This current-awareness listing of dissertations on the school library media program is a step toward creating more interest in media research. Much more research in educational media and technology is needed to define and implement solutions to the needs in education today. In research, media is defined broadly as including all print and non-print aids to instruction. Research is needed, in both education and librarianship, on educational media and technology, its uses, preparation, selection, distribution, research, preserves and in-service education, design and evaluation. Good's Dictionary of Education 'study and investigation in the field of education or bearing upon educational problems'.

A more specific one is 'an inquiry-oriented activity employing an objective, empirical and controlled methodology, the findings of which must be replicable when subjected to scrutiny by other investigators, must instill a high level of confidence and must be generalized beyond the local setting in which they are obtained'. The systems approach is a methodology which shows promise in research in new classes of education endeavors. Systems technology has strengthened educational research, and research can make a contribution in educational systems, engineering: the two, in a sense are complementary. The systems approach as research methodology denotes a collection of procedures directed toward realistic effects. Systems, methodology may enable the researcher to focus on larger phenomena and hence produce findings of broad significance. The value of a research study or a systems design, however, depends always upon the researcher's ability ro abstract effectively from the 'rich complexity of reality'.

Application of Media Education

Promoting Democracy

Research has shown that media literacy activities in social studies classes significantly promote civic participation and increase regular newspaper readership among teenagers. With the incredible rise of the internet and the unedited nature of many websites, students need more than ever to learn how to assess the validity and credibility of the information to which they exposed. Our political life became increasingly mediated in the middle of the last century, and now certainly in campaigns and elections, and in day-to-day governance– the media could hardly be more crucial to how we view politicians and our leaders, and how we think about the critical issues of the day. Should we go to war? How will we protect the environment? Will we be taxed more or less? These and every other vital question in our democracy are raised and debated, often superficially, in the nation's media.

Politicians have become extraordinarily adept at using the media to their advantage. If their interests are in line with the nations, this can result in effective government. But as often as not, well-intended or not, vast distortions take place in our public life that are partly a function of how our media systems operate. To the degree that the media are used to propagandize or manipulate and therefore interfere with the public being well informed, we need media education to be part of our schools' civics and social studies classes. No student should leave high school without knowing the classic techniques of persuasion and propaganda, many of which have been taught for decades, but not to all students. Students should be able to recognize 'name-calling', 'bandwagon' and 'glittering generalities' in the arguments they hear and read. But this is only the most basic of beginnings.

Promoting health

Media literacy techniques are also being used increasingly in programs designed to promote health and prevent substance abuse among young people. Indeed, the education represents 'a simple, effective approach to combating the myriad of harmful media messages seen or heard by children and adolescents'. Media literacy approach can also be used in programs focused on conflict resolution and the reduction of aggression and violence. Middle or high school students can be asked, for example, to view part of a film depicting a growing conflict between two rival gangs in a school. The film is stopped, and the students are then assigned to groups to write the next scene, wherein the characters resolve the conflict through talk, rather than with fists, knives or guns. The assignment prompts students to think through how a conflict might be peaceably resolved. Then, in sharing their solutions, the class has the opportunity to hear a variety of solutions. This increases the like hood that some of these solutions will be mentally available should students become involved in a similar conflict.

With the rise of the internet, access is more important than ever, not only should students be able to access the World Wide Web, they should also receive instruction in how to assess the value and validity of websites in all areas, whether medical, political or educational. Now that most anyone can create their own website, a great deal of freedom has been accorded citizens who comes a new and increasing demand on our educational systems and on caregivers to help young people use the internet and all other media-critically and thoughtfully.

One way to integrate media literacy with traditional literacy is to emphasize writing skills in students' scripts and in their critical reviews of films, TV programs, advertising and websites. One way to increase students' interest in literature is to help them recognize that many of the same storytelling techniques used in the classics is also used in the popular programs and films with which they are already familiar. Students already respond to foreshadowing in a television series like Malcolm in the Middle or a movie like Spiderman; they are often simply unaware that foreshadowing is a deliberate technique used to heighten suspense, drama and irony. Knowing the terms and being able to apply them is more important than some might think. Knowing about foreshadowing, symbolism, character development and other techniques used in literature and in film and television permits greater appreciation of the art forms.

Prevention of public health problems

Today most prevention practitioners and researchers, as well as concerned teachers and parents recognise that many of the messages we get from the media are risk factors for numerous public health problems. From the time we wake up to the radio alarm clock to the time we fall asleep with the TV on, we live in a media culture. We cannot escape the media's influence on either our healthy or unhealthy behaviours. Numerous studies over the past five decades have examined the impact of media on children, with regard to such risky behaviours as violence, alcohol, tobacco and other drug abuse, poor body image and eating disorders, precocious, unsafe sexual activity and teen pregnancy. More than 1,000 studies have looked at the effects of violence in television and movies, including the three-year National Television Violence Study completed in 1998. Most of these studies conclude that children who watch significant amounts of television and movie violence are more likely than children who see media violence to exhibit aggressive behaviour, attitudes and values.

The pervasiveness of the media, there are neurological reasons that we do not perceive the influence of the media. Brain research demonstrates that we respond to images differently than we respond to print. When we read books, we process the text in the neocortex and the process is slow and thoughtful. When we process images, we do it in the limbic system and the process is very rapid through instinct, impulse and emotion. This is the same part of the brain that produces the fight or flight response, which gets our adrenalin pumping without our conscious thought. Critical thinking is necessary to media literacy as a prevention strategy. The goal of media literacy in prevention is to move our responses to media images out of the limbic system and into the neocortex, where we can respond more thoughtfully and carefully to the messages the images are giving us. Media literacy allows youth to reflect on important life choices and make decisions about their health behaviours. It allows young people to control the influences of media messages instead of controlled by them.

Emerging development of Mass Media

The mass media reader edited by Wardrip-Fruin and Montfort defines new/mass media by using eighth simple and concise propositions.

1. *New media versus cyber culture:* cyber culture is the study of various social phenomena that are associated with the internet and network communications, whereas new/mass media is concerned more with cultural objects and paradigms.

2. *New media as computer technology used as a distribution platform:* new/mass media are the cultural objects which use digital computer technology for distribution and exhibition. E.g., internet, web sites, computer multimedia, blue-ray disks etc. The problem with this is that the definition must be revised every few years. The term 'new/mass media' will not be new anymore as most forms of culture will be distributed through computers.
3. *New media as digital data controlled by software:* The language of new media is based on the assumption that, infact, all cultural objects that rely on digital representation and computer-based delivery do share a number of common qualities. New media is reduced to digital data that can be manipulated by software as any other data. Now media operations can create several versions.
4. *New meida as the mix between existing cultural conventions and the conventions of software:* new media today can be understood as the mix between older cultural conventions for data representation, access and manipulation and newer conventions of data representation, access and manipulation, e.g., in film, software is used in some areas of production, in others are created using computer animation.
5. *New media as the Aesthetics that accompanies the early stage of every new modern media and communication technology:* while ideological tropes indeed seem to be reappearing rather regularly, many aesthetic strategies may reappear two or three times. In order for this approach to be truly useful it would be insufficient to simple name the strategies and tropes and to record the moments of their appearance instead, we would have to develop a much more comprehensive analysis which would cooelate the history of technology with social, political, environmental and economical histories or the modern period.
6. *New media as faster execution of algorithms previously executed manually or through other technologies:* Computers are a huge speed-up of what weere previously manual techniques. E.g., calculators. Dramatically speeding up the

execution makes possible previously non-existent representational technique. This also make possible of many ne forms of medi art such as interactive multimedia and computer games. On one level, a modern digital computer is just a faster calculator, we should not ignore it's other identity, that of a cybernetic control device.

7. *New média as the encoding of modernist avant-garde, new media as metamedia*: Manovich declares that the 1920s are more relevant to new media than any other time period, Meta media coincides with postmodernism in that they both rework old work rather than create new work. New media avant-garde is about new ways of accessing and manipulating information. Meta-media is an example of how quantity can change into quality as in new technology and manipulation techniques can recode modernist aesthetics into a very different postmodern aesthetics.

8. *New media as parallel articulation of simlar ideas in post-world war II art and modern computing*: post world war II art or combinationtorics involves creating images by systematically changing a single parameter. This leads to the creation or remarkably similar images and spatial structures. This illustrates that algorithms, this essential part of new media do not depend on technology, but can be executed by humans. Moreover, the emerging trends of mass media is numerous, heterogeneous and multifaceted. We the communication specialists have named the all the emerging mass media trends as new media. It is a term meant to encompass the emergence of digital, computerized or networked information and communication technologies in the later part of the 20th century. Most technologies described as new media are digital, often having characteristics of being manipulated, networkable, dense compressible, interactive and impartial. Some examples may be the internet, websites, computer multimedia, computer games, CD-Roms and DVDs.

Negative effects of Media

Looking across the research literature, one can see that a very wide range of potentially negative effects of media have been identified and discussed. These would include effects relating to:

- Violence contenty including imitation in the form of aggression or anti-social behaviour, desebsitisation and fear.
- Sexual content includes imitation in the form of promiscuous or unsafe practices, arousal and shock or disgust.
- Advertising in relation to misleading claims as well as consumerist or materialistic atttudes more broadly.
- Inappropriate or unwanted contract with others for example in the form of stranger danger or bullying.
- Health e.g., to do with smoking, alcohol and drug-taking .
- Eating behaviour– in relation to both obesity and eating disorders
- General personality disorders, such as low self-esteem, identity confusion or alienation.
- Physical effects of excessive use e.g, RSI type conditions and eyesight problems relating to computers.
- The undermining of children's imagination and free play.
- The physical development of the brain and disorders such as attention deficit and hyperactivity.
- Sleeping problems and other behavioural difficulties reduced for family interaction or relationships with peers
- Reduced levels of educational achievement or reading more specifically.
- Mistaken values, attitudes or beliefs e.g., in relation to gender or ethnic stereotyping.

While there is clearly a danger here of generating an endless litany of the evils wronght by the media. It is important to recognise that different types of potential effects are frequently confused or conflated often in quite contradictory ways. This is perhaps clearest in the case of debates about media violence. Researchers in this field have explored a very wide range of potential effects of media violence and generated some very different theories to explain how these ocuur. A short list of such theories are:

- Imitation: people identify with attractive role models they encounter in the media and learn specific patterns of aggressive behaviour from them.
- Arousal: people are emotional and/or physically aroused by media in general and this increased level of excitement can lead to aggressive behaviour.
- Desensitisation: repearted exposure to media violence dulls people's responses to the effects of violence in real life and thus leads them to regard it as acceptable.
- Catharsis: viewing violence can reduce or even purge aggressive tendencies or psychological tensions that people already possess.
- Cultivation: the media portray violence in systematically distorted ways e.g., in terms of its frequency or who perpetrated it, which leads people to have distored beliefs about the real wold.

Again, this list is not exhaustive. Even so, just in this one area we find a range of competing and potentially contradictory hypotheses. Different theories propose different mechanisams through which such effects might be assumed to occur and behind this there are potentially quite different ideas of what would count as violent or aggressive in the first place. In broad terms, it would be helpful to distinguish here between three potential types of negative effects. We could illustrate these with examples relating to the effects of sexual content:

- Behavioural exposure to sexual content might lead people to copy what they see, to seek out situations in which they might be able to copy it, or alternatively to avoid it.
- Attitudinal: such exposure might lead people to develop particular beliefs e.g., about the situations in which sexual activity is appropriate or morally acceptable or about the desirable behaviour of men and women.
- Emotional: people might obviously become aroused by sexual content, but they might equally be shocked disgusted or even traumatised.

These three types of effects are clearly not mutually exclusive. They might well reinforce each other, although equally they might contradict each other. For example emotional effects might have behavioural consequences. Disgust at sexual images might lead one to avoid potential sexual encounters, just as feelings of fear aroused by media violence might lead people to avoid conflict in real life. In addition, it is important to make other types of distinctions among potential media effects. These would include:

- Short-term and long-term: some types of effects might build up over a long period, last a long time and be hard to displace while others might be more immediately intense, but might fade more quickly.
- Individual or social: some types of effects might apply primarily to individuals, while others might apply more to particular social groups than others or function on a more general societal level.
- Direct or indirect: some effects might be direct and of a stimulus-response variety, while others might work through other factors rather than immediately on the individual.

These different hypotheses and approaches also translate into different research methodologies e.g., in the case of violence, laboratory experiments are typically concerned with measuring relatively short-term effects on behaviour. They do not in themselves provide sufficient evidence about long-term effects e.g., that watching violence at one point will result in violent behaviour at some later point. Researchers concerned with the impact of violence on attitudes or beliefs are more inclined to use surveys in which people report their own media use although these often have difficulty identifying the specific contribution of the media to the formation of such beliefs. Researchers looking at shorter-term emotional responses may sometimes employ physiological measures these typically provide very little evidence about the meanings people attribute to the media or the reasons why they respond in the way they do.

Media is quite useful in fostering development. In the past it has been seen that media has not played its role in accelerating development. Only recently some sections of the media have tried to bring out deficiencies in achieving millennium development goals. Media has not able to drive into the minds of the ordinary people – what is millennium development goal? People at large, particular the poor do not understand human development index. It is necessary to make people aware about their role in improving their own quality of life and Human Development Index. All development programmes of the central and the state government are not known to the people for whom these programs are meant. They do not know the purpose of different schemes launched to improve the quality of lives of poor people in particular. Such ignorance leads to information blackout for the poor. Government functionaries at the grass root level deliberately conceive such information from the target group beneficiaries. The poor man is required to pay information brokers to get information about the schemes. There after the poor has to pay the power brokers moving around the power centres in rural areas to get their legitimate rights like old age pension, India Awas Yojana, NRHM, SC & ST scholarship, opportunities to work public distribution system etc.

Now-a-days media is increasingly becoming commercial in nature leaving little space for vital information meant for the poor. Being the fourth pillar in functioning of democracy media should be responsible to disseminate vital information to the poor by devoting adequate space for the purpose. With the advent of technology and mobile connectivity it is also necessary to collect information from the poor regarding their miserable plight. Media houses should create voice mail based blogs to enable the poor to air their views regarding the benefits reaching them or otherwise. It is possible to create facilities to get public feedback through mobiles which can be collated to generate interest in news items for the benefit of government functionaries and public.

The youth people of our country are enthusiastic and can be encouraged to act as citizen reporters on developmental issues concerning the lives of the poor. The role of the youth in generating awareness about anti-poverty programmes and employment opportunities is of paramount importance. Young people should come forward to collect and pass on to the media in relevant news on improvement of deficiencies in implementation of welfare programmes concerning human development indexes.

2

Media Education in Indian Society

In last 50 years the media influence has grown exponentially with the advance of technology, first there was the telegraph, then the radio, the newspaper, magazines, television and now the internet. We live in a society that depends on information and communication to keep moving in the right direction and do out daily activities like work, entrainment, health care, education, personal relationships, traveling and anything else that we have to do. A common person in the society usually wakes up checks the television news or newspaper, goes to work, makes a few phone calls, eats with their family when possible and makes his decisions based on the information that he has either from their co-workers, news, TV, friends, family, financial reports etc.

What we need to be aware is that most of our decisions, beliefs and values are based on what we know for a fact, our assumptions and our experience. In our work we usually know what we have to do base on our experience and studies, however, on our daily lives we rely on the media to get the current news and facts about what is important and what we should be aware of. We have put our trust on the media as an authority to give us news, entertainment and education.

The media makes billions of dollars with the advertising they sell and that we are exposed to. We buy that we are told to be good, after seeing thousands of advertisings we make our buying decisions based on what we saw on TV, newspapers or magazines to be a product we can trust and also based on what everyone else that we know is buying and their decision are also base on the media. These are the effects of mass media in teenagers, they buy what they see on TV, what their favorite celebrity advertise and what is acceptable by society based on the fashion that the media has imposed them.

Here is a positive influence example, if there is a sport that getting a lot of attention by the media and gains popularity among your friends and society, you will more likely want to practice the sport and be cool with all your friends. The result is that you will have fun with your friends and be more healthy because of the exercise your doing. Recent example is world cup hockey being watched by millions due to the advertisement and publicity in media which also increased TRP and desire of many people to watch our national sport.

However a negative influence in teenagers is the use of cigars by celebrity movie stars, the constant exposure of sex images, the excessive images of violence and exposure to thousands of junk food ads. Young people are in a stage of life where they want to be accepted by their peers, they want to be loved and be successful. The media creates the ideal image of a beautiful men and women and tells you what the characteristics of a successful person are; you can see it in movies and TV. It's a subliminal way to tell you that are not like them you are not cool yet so its time to buy the stuff they buy and look like they look.

Another negative influence in teenagers that has grown over the years are anorexia and obesity. There are millions of adolescents fighting obesity, but all the same time they are exposed to thousands of advertisements of junk food, while the ideas image of a successful person is told to be thin and wealthy. Also more women are obsessive with losing weight even they are not obese, these are many thin women that want to look like the super models and thin celebrities so they engage in eating disorders which leads to severe health issues and even death.

Radio and television has been the most economical, long-standing and the most widely used among various electronic media. Despite the arrival of various media options, radio continues to remain as one of the dominant media among the public. Radio and television as a medium for information and communication to the masses is predicted to retain its relevance and potency. In particular its reach and efficacy as an educational medium is finding increasing relevance to students in recent times. It is the most extensive network. Radio and television signals cover almost the entire country. A parallel development sweeping the field of electronic audio media is a successful introduction, meteoric rise and spread of FM radio channels run by both public and private initiatives. Community radio is now booming through out India. Reports confirm that it has supported educational programs in a wide range of subject areas in many different countries.

Review of Media Literacy

The Byron review is assessing a range of potential measures that might be taken to ensure children's safe and productive use of the internet and computer games. These are included regulatory strategies and interventions of various kinds. These possibilities will be carefully evaluated in the light of growing international experience in the field. This final section of the report considers one such strategy, namely the promotion of media literacy. This issue has been addressed extensively in our earlier review for Ofcom, so this section will provide a brief overview of the rationale for this approach and some of the questions that it raises.

Both in the UK and Internationally, media literacy has become an increasingly significant dimension of cultural policy. According to the former Culture Secretary Tessa Jowell, media literacy is an essential component of contemporary citizenship that will eventually become as important skill as Math's or science. Ofcom has a statutory responsibility under the 2003 Communications Acts to promote media literacy, though supporting research, educational and networking activities. The BBC, the film Council, Skill set and the British Film Institute are leading a media Literacy task Force that has produced a media Literacy chapter, which currently has more than 120 institutional signatories. Meanwhile, the European Commission has established a media literacy expert group and will shortly be issuing an official communication on the theme and UNESCO has launched a new policy statement on media literacy following a high-profile meeting in Paris in 2007.

The growing interest in media literacy reflects a new emphasis in regulatory policy. While it is by no means incompatible with content regulation or with government intervention more broadly, the focus here is on empowering consumers to make informed choices and judgments about media on their own behalf. This is a broadly educational strategy, which includes work in schools as well as in the home and in other informal settings. Media literacy is generally conceived as a partnership between government, the media industries, teachers, parents and children themselves.

Ofcom defines media literacy as the ability to access, understand and create communications in a variety of contexts. Media literacy is partly able to locate and use media, but it is also about critical understanding evaluation and judgment and about creating media for the purpose of communication and self-express. Promoting literacy is therefore about addressing basic inequalities in people's access to media not only the so called digital divide, but also divides in relation to other media as well. Ultimately these divides are not simply about access to equipment, they are also about cultural capital about the skills and understanding that people need in order to use and interpret what they see and hear and to create their own communications.

Beyond extending access, a basic first step in media literacy is informing consumers, in case of the concerns of this review, this point to the crucial role of content labeling. Much of the democratic potential of the modern media derives from the fact that gatekeepers or intermediaries are no long have such powerful control, yet it is also from this that much of the risk and potential for harm derives. In this new environment, there is an increasingly important role for labeling and classification systems that inform parents and children about what they are likely to encounter. This should be seen not only in negative terms as a matter of warnings or guidance but also more positively, as a matter of alerting people to content that they might find particularly valuable. The contemporary proliferation of media has generated new risks, but it has also led to the production of a great deal of positive material that could never have been created or distributed before some of it made by children themselves. One of the key challenges that parents and children face is simply finding out what is available and knowing where to locate it.

There is a long tradition of media education in UK schools, although it has remained fairly marginal to the mainstream curriculum, particularly in primary schools. Paradoxically, media literacy has not been a significant element of the National Literacy Strategy and the National curriculum for information and communication technology currently focuses primarily on technical skills rather than on the evaluation of digital content. By contrast, media educators have a well-established conceptual framework and a developed set of classroom strategies, that increasingly need extended to digital media such as computer games and the internet. Media education involves understanding the processes by which media are produced, analyzing the verbal and visual languages' they use to create meaningful judgment about how media represent the world and understanding how audiences are targeted and how they respond. These approaches generally involve both critical study and creative production of media. As digital media have become more and more accessible and easy to use, teachers have found that children can develop critical understanding in a more engaging, hands-on way by making media themselves. While there is a considerable body of professional know-how among specialist teachers in this field, there remains a need for in-depth evaluation of the effectiveness of media education and for a more systematic approach across the age range.

I relation to new media, there have been several educational initiatives addressing aspects of online risk. There is now a plethora of websites and educational resources in the field produced by a wide range of voluntary sector and industry bodies as well as by government agencies. Evidence of the effectiveness of these initiatives is rather limited and somewhat mixed; much depends on the training of teachers and on the involvement of parents. Some research suggests that a greater awareness of risk does not necessarily lead children to adopt less risky behaviour and this in turn points to the need for approaches that connect more effectively with children's everyday experiences of these media. In the light of contemporary developments of the kind strategies also need to adopt broader approach; children need to be aware of stranger danger, but they also need to understand the commercial strategies that are being used online and develop skills in critically evaluating online content. Here again, the experience on such issues could usefully be drawn together and evaluated at this stage and more coherent strategic devised.

The new media pose much wider challenges for educators. In addition to addressing inequalities in access to technology and in the competencies that are required to use it, educators also need to be exploring some of the new ethical issues posed by new media and the ways in which online content needs to be assessed and evaluated. In this respect, they will need to look beyond narrow conceptualizations of digital literacy that see it simply in terms of safety or technical skill and to address much broader questions about how these media are produced, circulated and consumed. Such approach would need to address issues of trust and credibility, but it would also need to analyze the social, political and economic dimensions of technology. Further it should be emphasized that media literacy is not simply concerned with information, but also with media as art forms with intrinsic and lasting value. Many computer games and online worlds offer rich and complex symbolic environments; and the experience of play is often very emotionally intense. Likewise, some forms of online communication and the creation of user generated content can involve profound issues of identity, self-representation and personal investment. Media literacy also involves reflecting on these cultural experiences and the pleasures that they entail, here again, addressing the risks that may be at stake in young people's use of media must involve an understanding of the reasons why they often deliberately choose to take them.

Parents can clearly play a key role in developing media literacy. However, we should be way of assuming that parents necessarily possess such skills and knowledge themselves, particularly when it comes to new media, media literacy is an issue for adults too, as Ofcom's report on this issue makes clear. Regulatory devices such as filters or age verification systems or legislative constraints such as those introduced in the US under the children's online protection and privacy act are unlikely to be effective if parents are unable to operate the technology are unaware of what their children might be doing online. Research suggests that parental monitoring and involvement can make a difference to children's awareness of issues such as safety, but this need to be handled sensitively, in a way that respects young people's right to privacy and does not place an undue burden on parents themselves.

Simply sharing and discussing experiences of game-playing and online participation can be a valuable starting point. Here too, there is a need to develop constructive approaches that are positively child centered and in tune with the realities of everyday family life, and the basis for this should be dialogue with parents and children themselves. Finally, it is important to emphasize that media literacy is not an alternative to regulation as is sometimes implied. People who are more media literate are not necessarily immune to harm or to media influence more broadly. The primary aim of media literacy education is not to reduce the influence of the media, any more than the aim of literacy education is to reduce the influence of books. Rather, it seeks to enable children to make informed decisions on their own behalf and thereby to make the most of the opportunities that the media can provide.

In 1956, India was site of the famous Pune Radio Farm Forum Project. The United Nations Educational Science and Cultural organization (UNESCO) sponsored 'Pune' Project it was inspired by Canada's experience with radio farm forum in the 1940s. the Pune project was a field experiment to evaluate the effects of radio farm forums, each consisting of several dozens of villagers who gathered weekly to listen to a half-hour radio program and then to discuss its contents.

The All India Radio development programming range is use of entertainment-instruction serials. As defined previously, entertainment instruction was the process of purposely designing and implementing a media message to both entertain and educate, in order to increase audience's knowledge about an educational issue, create favourable attitudes and change overt behaviour. Entertainment-education seeks to capitalize on the popular appeal of entertainment media, in order to show individuals how they can live safer, healthier and happier lives. Since 1987, the Central Educational Broadcasting Unit (CEBU) of All India Radio has produced several entertainments – education.

The National Broadcasting Company transmitted the experimental program from the third floor of the Radio Corporation of America building to 25 receivers watched by the students in 1938. The show was 45 minutes long and students asked questions via a two-way radio communication and were answered by the instructor on the screen. With the expanding and enormous capacity of radio to deliver their goods to the people many new channels have emerged. Moreover, they are working for round the clock in a day. This has encouraged the authorities to start Gyan Darshan on television and GV for radio. These channels are dedicated to transmit educational programs. As per planning of GV in future to start more than hundred FM educational radio stations would come up in the country. In the later planning more FM stations are expected to be allowed for the purpose of education and development.

A study tried to gauze the situation pertaining to radio listening and number of FM sets. It also includes the concept of educational programs on radio. The study having sample of 100 FM radio household in urban area and equal number in rural was recently conducted by All India Radio, Ahmadabad. This suggests that in urban areas there was higher listening compared to rural area. The average listening among total respondents was 85 per cent. Another study was conducted by Kumar, A. (2002) it was found that 15 per cent of academic counselors in the Indira Gandhi National Open University have been using radio programs including GV for their core academic activities. Computers and Internet have started influencing the way we learn. Radio is still a dominant medium with wide access, all these media are very powerful to reach teach and enrich. Basic tips to learn from broadcast and non-broadcast media have been provided.

Reports are confirmed that it has supported educational programs in a wide range of subjects in many different countries. In Thailand, the radio is used to teach mathematics to school children and for teacher training and other curricula. Swaziland, for public health purpose, Columbia for various programs, Nicaragua, for health education and Philippines uses the radio for nutrition education, Sri Lanka, for family planning and health, South Korea, in support of family planning, Botswana for civics education, the Dominion Republic in support of primary education and Paraguay to offer Primary school instruction. The above review suggested that there are number of educational courses that rely on educational radio, more so in case of distance education. Education was become technology and media enable worldwide.

Public Opinion influenced by Media

As we have said above, the media has a huge impact on society and also in public opinion. They can shape the public opinion in different ways depending of what is the objective. For example, after the attacks of 9/11 the media gave a huge coverage of the event and exposed Osama guilty for the attack as they were told by the authorities. This shaped the public opinion to support the war on terrorism, the same happened with the war of Iraq. The problem is that if media received inaccurate information then the public opinion supported a wrong cause, this is the power of public opinion influence.

Other ways to influence are with polls and trends, especially in political campaigns. The candidates that can pay more TV and media exposure have more influence on public opinion and thus can receive more votes. The media shape our attitudes about everything from soap to politics. It's important for us to be aware of the impact the mass media has on each and every one of. We need to be vigilant and ask ourselves to look for opposing opinions and evaluate the facts for ourselves rather than blindly accepting the media's version of the 'truth'.

Everything has been changed due to change in technology and globalization. New media effect and also affect the social behaviour of the people. Basically youth behaviour and their relationship with parents, brothers' sisters and other relatives are being influenced by Mass Media. Today television and internet have become a part of the life of adolescents. Media factionalize people with its mixture of technology. So, electronic media has tremendous impact on youth compared to print media.

Mass media may be defined as any form of communication which effect large number of people at the same time directly in a uniform manner. The mode of communication may be through TV, radio, print media, internet etc it I not consider as a tool of marketing or advertising drive but an instrument to influence the behaviour of mass. Basically it is termed as word-of-mouth channel. So, mass media is considered as a technology tool for masses for providing every type of education to change the life style of the people.

Keeping in mind the above issues, the media should not help to raise crime, vandalism, alcoholism, sex, teenage pregnancy etc. Media plays a very important role in creating awareness. Certain issues which are untouched must be highlighted. The anxieties to know something should be protested in a decent manner. Decency is always praise worthy. It develops peace and brings happiness among various communities which ultimately leads towards the improvement of quality of life of the human beings. Therefore, the role of media should be bring peace and happiness among the audience and try to develop the human values.

Media role to development of India

Media is the means of support to the people in the world which shapes their attitude, opinion and makes them to think before they start doing a particular work. The most beautiful is it helps the people to know about different religions, places, languages important things to do about the past and the future.

Had it not been the media or publicity, Taj Mahal would not have become one of the seven wonder of the world. Had it not been the media we would not be able to see our real heroes, the NSG commandos who saved us from the terrorist attack in Mumbai. Who would have cared or even think of saving our national animal whose count is decreasing day by day to 1411 only for the audience mass media is source of entertainment, for journalists media is source of prestige and salary and for the owner media is source of profit and political influence! It is because the media possesses so much power to influence, that those in the media must be feel their duty about delivering news in a balanced manner that brings the story to the consumer with all sides fairly represented.

All the mediums like the radio, the newspaper, magazines, television and now the internet are bringing the updates of each and every bit of news that is available round the world and now you can also actively take part in the discussion or give your comments by polling, blogging or sending SMS. Certain issues which needs to be discussed or certain questions which needs to be answered by the authority can now are easily done with the help of different media.

Media plays a very important role in creating awareness. There are certain issues which remain untouched among youngsters as they feel guarded concerning it. Media helps in providing information regarding such topics. There are many such topics that are highlighted by the media. The current one that can be talked about is the quota system in colleges. Media created awareness that how injustice was being done with deserving candidates due to reservations in colleges. There was procession taken out by students in order to object regarding this bias discrimination.

One other such issue is the debate carried on regarding sex education. Media was trying to highlight both the aspects of the matter that whether sex education must be allowed in schools or not. There were a group of people who were all for it and there were people who considered it a taboo. Even though we are heading towards westernization, our roots still remain Indian and that is the reason why we fell anxious discussing such issues with young ones. But if we think practically then there are so many instances where children head the wrong way just in the anxiety of knowing certain issues. So, the only acceptable approach in which we can guard our child from choosing the wrong path is by talking to them and educating them about the issues that need to be learnt at the right instance.

Media being one of the important means to reach out masses

and influence their thinking and decision making, only to the positive media cannot attract attention of the masses, and to gain viewer ship, negative media has to be incorporated to balance out and attract the masses, but a line has to be drawn between the positive and the negative media in the interest of the younger generation.

Unfortunately, it is very rare for research to tell a story. Researchers frequently disagree about fundamental issues to do with focus, method and theory about how the key questions are to be framed, what might be able to count as an answer and what the implications of these answers might be in terms of what should be done. Such disagreements are common in many areas, but they are particularly acute in research on media efforts. Historically, there has been a clear distinction between researchers in the psychological effects tradition and those in the fields of media and cultural studies, which are broadly sociological orientation. To some extent, this maps on to a distinction between US researchers and European researchers. However, the situation is a little more complex than this.

It is important to recognize that much of the psychological effects research is based on a particular form of psychology. It generally espouses variants of behaviourism and rarely engages with what is termed cultural psychology. Psychologists in the UK and in the Europe are generally much more circumspect about media effects than psychologists in the US and some are strongly critical of the US approach. There are also several leading cultural studies academics in the US who are equally forthright in their criticisms. There are fundamental differences between these two broad traditions, which are not just a question of different areas of interest or simply to do with methodology. On the contrary, they reflect very basic theoretical and indeed political differences. As a result, the debates in this are have been highly polarized and often somewhat less than constructive. At the risk of merely contributing to this polarization, it is important to sum up some of the differences at this point.

Research Effects

Essentially, researcher in the psychological effects tradition are seeking evidence of more or less direct causal relationship between exposure to media and particular consequences in terms of audiences behaviour or attitudes. A classic behaviourist perspective conceives of this process in terms of stimulus and response of which the most obvious example would be imitation. More sophisticated exponents of this approach posit the existence of intervening variables that come between the stimulus and the response and thereby mediate any potential effects; and there is also some recognition here of individual differences in response. Even the basic cause-and-effect model continues to apply.

This research tends to work with a broadly positivist approach. It generates hypotheses about the social world that are then tested empirically through the application of scientific or mathematical methods and thereby verified or falsified. It is assumed that we can measure aspects of media content quantitatively that we can do the same with audience responses and that we can then correlate these in order to gain some measure of media effects. Potential variables in the process can be isolated and controlled or accounted for statistically and any potential influence of the scientist on the design or interpretation of the study can be eliminated or minimized. These approaches claim to provide predictability, objectivity and a basis for generalization and findings of such research can be statistically aggregated by a technique known as meta-analysis.

With the history of communications research in the United States, the use of such methods has served as a form of what Thomas Kuhn calls 'normal science' i.e., they permit a business as usual approach in which established rules and procedures are followed by all and fundamental theoretically challenges are simply ignored. Thus, most media effects researchers tend to display a considerable degree of certainty about their findings. The effects of media violence e.g., are seen as incontrovertibly proven. There is no room for dispute on the matter. Unfortunately, many other researchers from different research traditions have persistently disputed such claim, although effects researchers have attempted to deal with this largely by refusing to engage in debate.

Criticisms of Effects Research

So what criticisms have been made of such research? Again, at the risk of oversimplification it is possible to sum these up as follows:

1. *The evidence of effects is actually equivocal and contradictory, even on its own terms:* Criticisms effects research point out that journals tend only to publish studies that show positive results. The sizes of effects in such studies are frequently small and the level of statistical significance is often marginal, although far-reaching claims are often made on the basis of what amounts to quite flimsy evidence. Critics argue that studies often contradict each other and hence cannot be meaningfully aggregated e.g., in the case of media violence, proof of desensitization would contradict an argument about arousal and so studies in these two domains cannot be seen to reinforce each other. The most telling criticisms of this kind are often made by fellow psychologists.
2. *There are significant problems with the methods used in effects research:* The two key methods that have been used in this work, laboratory experiments and surveys, have significant and well-known limitations when it comes to proving causal relationships between phenomena in real life. The key problem with laboratory experiments is to do with their artificially or lack of what is termed ecological validity. Critics argue that what happens in the context of a laboratory, where one is seeking to maximize potential effects in order to make them observable, cannot be generalized to the real world. Where a whole range of other factors may be in play. The stimulus material used in such experiments is often unrepresentative of media that would be encountered in real life as are the measures of response. Administrating a fake electric shock to an unknown individual in the context of a laboratory following exposure to a random collection of violent incidents on film and without any of the usual constraints that tend to inhibit aggressive behaviour cannot be seen to prove that media cause violence. At best, laboratory experiments can be seen as an indication of

what might possibly happen, rather than as evidence of what actually does happen in real life.

3. *The notion of 'effect' is itself simplistic and theoretically inadequate:* The term 'effect' clearly implies a cause and effect relationship and beyond that it is frequently associated with an essentially behaviourist account of human action. This is a theoretical approach that some effects research continues to employ, although much of it also seeks to specify 'intervening variables' that mediate between the stimulus and the response. However, critics of effects research seek to challenge the basic theoretical assumptions of this approach.

The criticisms here are partly about how we understand the nature of the stimulus in other words, what we assume about the meaning of media. Effects research typically presumes that media texts have singular meanings that will be the same for all who encounter them and that those meanings can be straightforwardly quantified. But Barker has argued that false to assume as effects researchers typically do that violence has a fixed meaning irrespective of the ways in which it is represented, who commits it and who is victimized, the motivations for their actions and so on. Research suggests that there are many different types of media violence and that different people perceive different things to be violent in the first place, not least as a result of their different experiences of violence in real life. The broader argument here is that meaning involves interpretation; it cannot be fixed or defined statistically in the ways that positivist approaches tend to assume.

Critics of effects research also challenge assumptions about the nature of the response. They argue that effects researchers implicitly conceive of media audiences as passive and ignorant victims of media influence. Specific sections of the audience are effectively stigmatized as helpless dupes e.g., in the pathological category of the heavy viewer. This approach to children is particular, where the use of some versions of developmental psychology tends to define children primarily in terms of what they lack i.e., the rationality that is presumed to characterize nature adulthood. Children are thereby defined in terms of what they cannot do, rather than what they can and in the process researchers typically fail to see the issues from children's own perspectives.

4. *Effects research tends to sustain a conservative political agenda:* Behind many of these objections and to some extent motivating them is a broader political argument. Effects research is frequently informed by a conservative moral or political agenda and indeed some of it had been funded by organizations with very clearly defined motivations of this kind. This is most self-evidently the case in research about the effects of sexual content, where researchers moral beliefs are apparent in taken for granted assumptions about promiscuity or healthy sexual behaviour. As I have noted that arguments about media effects have often served to distract attention away from broader social problems and one could argue that as in the case of violence the media are frequently used by politicians as a scapegoat.

The concern here is partly that research helps to sustain a moral consensus in which deviant or marginal tastes and views are suppressed. However, it is also argued that effects research sanctions simplistic and misleading responses to complex social problems rather than looking at a particular social phenomenon such as violence and then seeking to explain it, effects research starts with media and then seeks to trace evidence of their effects on individuals. In this respect, it appears to be asking the questions in the wrong way round.

The debate about media effects can also be of use to politicians who seek to appear tough, blaming the media can help deflect attention away from more deep-seated causes of social problems, which may be more difficult to address at a policy level. The debate about media violence is perhaps the classic instance of this process. This issue has a particularly high profile in the US. There has been a constant succession of governmental inquiries and government-funded research efforts although arguably these have had very little impact on policy. For commentators in other countries, it seems quite obvious that the simplest way of reducing the high incidence of violence in the US would be to restrict the availability of lethal weapons although this is an issue that governments have largely been unwilling or unable to address. In this context, talking tough about media violence provides an easy way of being seen to act.

Role of Media in Indian Democracy

Selection of personal to man the organization is one of the most important managerial responsibilities. The ability of organization to achieve its goal, survive and growth in a dynamic environment significantly and substantially depends upon the effectiveness of its selection process. This is particularly shown in India, as industrial enterprises here are opening in highly dynamic environment conditions. Selection is the next step after recruitment. The selection process involves a series of steps which help in evaluating the candidates. The selection process in an organization has to be in accordance with the organizational requirements. Job analysis and job specifications, along with human resource planning provide the basic requirements, based on which the selection process has to be designed. The process of choosing the most suitable candidate for the job from among the available applicants is called selection.

A manager is a person tasked with overseeing one or more employees or departments to ensure these employees and departments carry out assigned duties as required. Depending on the size of the company there might be a single, dual or triple management layer involved. In large companies management is basically divided into three tires: upper, middle and lower management. Lower management includes managers who operate at basic levels of organization functions. Middle level management overseas lower-management and generates reports for senior management. Upper management commonly consist of a board of directors or shareholders who own and are responsible for making key decisions that affect the organization. In commercial franchises like restaurants, a retail manager ensures the daily business functions smoothly. The office manager might be responsible for a variety of duties commonly divided into individual departments in large organizations. These duties might include accounting, shipping and customer service, where additional employees who act under the office manager carry out most of these tasks.

1. India is federal democratic republic. In a democratic set-up as large as this, the state along with the process of development. Access to information is essential to the health of democracy for at least two reasons: first, it ensures that citizens make responsible and informed choices rather than acting out ignorance or misinformation. Second, information serves 'checking function' by ensuring that elected representatives uphold their oaths of office and carry out wishes of those who elected them.
2. In multi-religious, multi-lingual, multi-cultural and multi-ethnic democratic policy like India, it is not easy for the people like India; it is not easy for the people to identify themselves with the process of change. In this context, the media plays a two way role: on the one hand, of keeping the people informed of the state's policies, development programs and actions on ground and on the other hand, getting the feedback to the planners decision makers and administrators on the reactions and responses of the people. The media is supposed to the mirror in which the state and the people find their reflection.
3. The media in India has also functioned as an instrument of exchange of message between different sections of the people or society between the rural and the urban sectors, industrial and agricultural sector between the majority of the population and the minority groups etc.
4. The relationship between Indian media and the government has seen many ups and downs the lowest point being the emergency. The balance between national interest and media freedom has always shaped this relationship. The dynamics of Indian democracy has thrown challenges raised issues which the media needs to respond to.

Challenges and Issues

1. *Technique of Production and management vis-à-vis content and*

thinking: Indian media has made considerable progress in updating technique of production and management. However there seem to be little change in their contents and thinking. Naipaul comments 'Indian media have a limited vision and there is an absence of inquiry, the absence of what may be called human interest. Indian media is out-of-touch with Indian reality. In fact it has become a part of Indian anarchy. It reported speeches and more speeches, it reduced India to its various legislative chambers, and it turned into national figures those politicians who were least predictable'.

2. *Growing commercialization of all dimensions of media in this era of globalization, privatization and liberalization:* This has created a dichotomy between media ethics and revenue generation. TRP and advertisement revenue vs. quality programs. Media is treated as a commercial enterprise and hence the romance and passion of journalism is gradually vanishing. Even the press commission observed 'it appears to us that a very significant part of the press and media is controlled by persons having strong links with other business and industries. When media is controlled by other big business they become vehicles of expressions of the ideology of their owners and the selection, presentation and display of news would be dictated by that ideology. The media industry in their hands becomes cultural and financial arm of other business and industries. Consequently they take a vested interest in maintaining the socio-economic interest.

3. *Declining Professionalism:* Arun Shourie observes that 'many of us have incestuous relation with other subjects – in particular with government authorities. Many have cavalier attitude towards facts, many are too lazy to inform them of the laws that image on their work- so many are too lazy to examine the allegations they purvey.'

4. *Accuracy is no more the most elementary component in journalism:* No journalist regards in accuracy either inadvertent or deliberate as good thing but never the less, many journalists condone it as a necessary evil in the attainment of speed and the maximum of news interest.

5. *Events get more coverage than the process:* News must include not only the events but also the process. Flood could be an event but 'flood control' is a process. There is tendency to sensationalize the event overlooking the process which is an important. Media in India needs to serve as a social analyst and educator, thus playing a vital role in the national and international struggle to promote human progress. This is what we call 'Development Journalism', which has not been very popular with Indian media, however development journalism can bring a qualitative change in the attitude of Indian media.
6. *I know, what is good for the country syndrome:* This syndrome is not peculiar to the politician and high official only. The media in India suffer from it too except that politician in power can suppress a paper or channel while an editor at best can only work at overthrowing a minister.
7. *Is Indian media making peace with violence:* too much exposure to violence in media has systematically desensitized the people to violence? They are becoming too casual about brutality. We need a rethinking on this issue.

Impact of media in indian society:

Media' impact on indian society can be judged from three perspectives i.e., social, economic and political.

Social impact: Generating awareness of the people on various social evils like dowry, female foeticide and infanticide etc had led to the decline in the incidence of them. Bringing into focus on atrocities faced by weaker sections of the society. This has bought in a sense of security to the weaker sections. Majority groups fear to do any harm to them in the long run this will bring peace and tranquility among communities. Generating awreness on good practices like health, hygiene, nutrition etc there by improving the living standards. Media is responsible for the success of green revolution in India during 1960s by popularising the usage of high yielding varieties, fertilisers, pesticides and other farm management techniques. Green revolution has improved the living standard of poor by enabling their incomes. Many new enterpreneurs from weaker sections of the society emerged. This has enabled them to rise in the social ladder and stay on par with the so called upper castes. Media also responsible for generating pan India identity and enabling people to loosen their parochial and narrower identities. It must be showing in new employment opportunities that are available in the market, this has enabled a common man with requist skills to grab them. In addition to the above, the media is not only responsible for sensiting our administrators on various issues but also responsible for spreading in latest fashion vis-à-vis dressing style, cosmetics, hair style etc.

Economic impact: media is directly responsible for providing employment opportunities and thereby increasing the living standard of the people as well as spread awareness of a new product launched by a company through advertisements and product reviews, this will increase the demand of industrial goods and services thereby promoting industrialisation and increasing the Goss Domestic Production.

Political impact: media has been bringing out corrupt practices practised by our political leaders. This has enabled people to make more rational choices when electing their representatives and it has also been a major force in mobilising people during elections.

Indian journalism is today more than two centuries old. It has come a long way from the two page scandal sheet of James August Hicky which passed for a news paper in 1780 and which introduced an essentially western media into India. Media in India is the rich inheritors of glorious traditions of dedicated journalism commitment and patriotism. While concluding it will be relevant to quote N. Ram 'journalism in India has major strengths and resources, physical and intellectual at its command needs an internal accountability to higher intellectual and ethical standards, a more precise and less breathless style of work, and public advocacy of its role as a vital part of striving for a democratic, just society. It is very much in need of a coherent theoretical framework to justify or checkout its high moral ground claim, some kind of critical theory of an independent and pluralistic media in relation to the struggle for society'.

3

Media Technology and Learning

The rapid advances of technology in literally every field, including communication, medicine, transportation, agriculture, aerospace and energy have tremendously increased the amount of data and information at our fingertips. As we strive to make sense of unimaginably large volumes of data, visualization has become increasingly important. All these only possible with bless of media technology and learning methodology. Students using well-designed combinations of visuals and text learn more than students who only use text which is the perfect benefit of media learning.

Media technologies have affected every aspect of human activity and have a potential role to play in the field of education and training, specially, in distance education to transform it into an innovative form of experience. Contribution of communication technology has become within a very short time one of the basic building blocks of modern society. Many countries now regard understanding communication technology and mastering the basic skills and concepts of information transmission as part of the core of education, alongside reading, writing and numeracy. The mass media are fundamental to development. They enable people to learn about issues and make their voices heard. They can exert a powerful influence, for good or for bad. Free independent media are important to ensure freedom of speech. Promote democracy, good governance, peace and human rights.

Media technologies are the result of knowledge explosion. These include hardware and software technologies and facilitate teaching learning process. Using media technologies learners are now able to participate in learning communities throughout the world. They are independent and free in choice of their programmers of study and access to the resources. They may learn collaboratively, share information, exchange their learning experiences and work through cooperative activities in virtual learning communities.

By media technology we mean advancement of information technology like internet, broadband, hotline and convergence of technology. Development of the technology undoubtedly expedites communication process and activates media machinery in 21st century. IT advancement has proved that communication has no boundary across the globe. It has also given a boost to learning about happenings and changes in and around us.

Information is power. Digitalization is the only way to access easily access information and communication. With improvement of digital technology, information dissemination is getting wider space to reach its audience. In addition, emergence of satellite technology and digital evaluation have impacted media content and given ample opportunity not only for entertainment programme but in diverse field. More young communities are inclining towards entertainment and glamorous opportunity.

In the era of new information age, our economy reflects growth because of technological advances primarily the technologies of the information or communications technologies. These are like, computers, satellites, video cassette recorders, cable systems, digital audio recorders, compact disks, laser disks etc these devices have had a revolutionary impact on the media. Through all these communication technologies, media gives shapes to the society. However, the technical and social convergence brought about as a result of developments in technology is already creating interaction problems in particular in the younger users.

One of the key issues that have arisen from youth culture and new technologies is the growing dependency of such technologies as the internet among the youth of society. Arguments have arisen over the addiction and over reliance some youths have towards new technologies especially the internet and the various online communities it provides, particularly online chatting and online gaming programs. Among the issues that have been addressed are the adverse impacts of cyberspace addiction, and the displacement between reality and virtual reality and its impacts on real world social relationship, health and communication skills.

New media technologies are set to replace demands of traditional Medias. These are increasingly becoming more than just a simple way to pass the time. In fact, some academics suggest that technology is at the very cultural heart of the current generation of young people. Technology, such as the internet, mobile phones, PDA's and iPods to name a bare few, provide young people with unlimited access to opportunity. It has revolutionized the way we communicate and interact with each other. Technology generates opportunities new things to explain, new ways of expression, and new media of communications and create new forms of destruction.

New technologies have over time branched into the various spheres in society and have been implicated within the educational systems of many nations. The development of technologies and the innovation of communication tools have enhanced various learning aspects. Advancements in particular ICT's have improved the standards of vocational education and distance education for youth within various sections of the globe. This advancement of technology facilitates the pace of development.

Constructivist Theory of Learning

Now-a-days constructivist learning theory is gradually gaining the same respect and attention long accorded to behavioural learning theory. Constructivism concerns the process of how students create meaning and knowledge in the world as well as the results of the constructive process. How students construct knowledge depends upon what they already know, their previous experiences, how they have organized those experiences into knowledge structures such as schema and mental models and the beliefs they use to interpret the objects and events they encounter in the world. Cognitive tools help learners organize, restructure and represent what they know. For constructivists, the ultimate nature of reality does not matter as much as its local nature, i.e., learners' unique and shared constructions of reality. According to constructivism, a teacher cannot map his/her own interpretations of the world onto learners because they do not share a set of common experiences and interpretations.

Learners are able to comprehend a verity of interpretations

and to use them in arriving at their own unique interpretations of the world. The mind filters input from the world in making its interpretations and therefore each learner conceives of the external world somewhat differently. Whereas instructor emphasize the transmission of standardized interpretations of the world by teachers and the educational media and technology they use as well as standardized assessments to test the degree to which students' understandings match accepted interpretations constructivists seek to create learning environments wherein learners use cognitive tools to help themselves construct their own knowledge representations. Cognitive tools and the goals, tasks, pedagogies, resources and human collaboration integral to their use enable learners to engage inactive, mindful and purposeful interpretation and reflection.

Learners themselves as Designers

The process of designing instructional materials enables instructional designers to understand content much more deeply than the students whose thinking will be constrained and controlled by the very materials they are developing. It follows that empowering learners to design and produce their own knowledge representations and educational communications can be a powerful learning experience. Langer reminded us of the important of mindfulness in learning. Students learn and retain the most from thinking in meaningful ways. Representing knowledge is a mindfully task that can be enabled by cognitive tools such as multimedia construction software or electronic spreadsheets. Cognitive tools require students to think in meaningful ways about how to use an application's capabilities and features to represent what they know. Students not only learn deeply and mindfully with cognitive tools, their opportunities for reflection are also enhanced. There is considerable evidence that reflective thinking is under-utilized in education by teachers and their students, a problem that cognitive told may help to ameliorate.

Effective learning through Technology

Salomon et al. describe the distinction between the effects of learning with and of technology as'first, we distinguish between two kinds of cognitive effects: effects with technology obtained during intellectual partnership with it, and the effects of it in terms of the transferable cognitive residue that this partnership leaves behind in the form of better mastery of skills and strategies'. Cognitive tools are important in both respects. Salomon et al. maintain that 'cognitive effects with computer tools greatly depend on the mindfully engagement of learner in the tasks afforded by these tools', and that educators should empower learners with cognitive tools and assess their abilities in conjunction with the use of these tools. Such a development will entail a new conception of ability as an intellectual partnership between learners and the tools they use. Although some worry that this partnership makes learners too dependent upon the technology, many performances are meaningless without the technologies which enable them. Allowing students to demonstrate learning in collaboration with cognitive tools may be attacked by parties invested in existing assessment systems. However, who would assess the ability of an artist without allowing the use of brushes, paint and other media.

Intelligent technologies become as ubiquitous as pencil and paper and we are not there yet by a long shot how a person functions away from intelligent technologies must be considered. Moreover, even if computer technology became as ubiquitous as the pencil, students will still face an infinite number of problems to solve new kinds of knowledge to mentally construct and decisions to make for which no intelligent technology would be available or accessible. Cognitive tools are learner-controlled, not teacher-controlled or technology-driven. For example, when students build databases, they are also constructing their own conceptualization of the organization of a domain of knowledge. Cognitive tools are intended to be used by students to represent knowledge and solve problems while pursuing investigations that are relevant to their own lives. These investigations are ideally situated within a constructivist learning environment. Cognitive tools won't be effective when used to support teacher-controlled tasks alone.

Design of Media Technology for Education

Depending upon the talent, resources and timelines availability for the development effort media technology is designed. There are numerous scientific principles to guide design but every instructional development effort involves large amounts of creativity and hard work. There are no comprehensive or infallible instructional design formulas. In fact, the design of media and technology for education retains as many aspects of a craft as it does a science. Evaluation has an especially important role in the instructional design process, but it is often underutilized. Implementation at the local level is as important as instructional design. In most instances, the conditions under which students actually experience and use media and technology in schools are decided within the confines of single classrooms by individual teachers. While some educational technologists have recommended that media and technology innovations should be 'teacher-proof' to ensure fidelity in implementation, teacher empowerment is more likely to have positive effects than attempts to limit the prerogatives of teachers to implement media and technology as they wish.

Teachers had to make significant changes in their classroom management styles, giving up more control to technology and students. This also changed slowly. Initially, media and technology were primarily used within the context of traditional pedagogical methods and most teachers required years of experience before they adopted more innovative strategies such as project-based learning. Finally, teachers struggled with fundamental incongruities between traditional assessment measures and the kinds of learning occurring in their classrooms. In fact, assessment problems proved to be the most resistant to solutions and many remained unresolved.

The bottom line of the project is that pedagogical innovations and positive learning results do eventually emerge from the infusion of media and technology into schools, but the process takes longer than most people imagine. Educational administrators who imagine that a summer workshop or after school seminars by consultants will enable teachers to implement media and technology in their classrooms are mistaken. Huge investments in time and support for teachers will be especially critical if the adoption of constructivist pedagogies accompany the infusion of media and technology.

Research on Media and their Application

Communication research plays a pivotal role during the pre and post policy formulation period. It connects the idea of development from the government to the people. Communication research on media inputs and programme warrants research and public opinion whenever any programme becomes a subject of controversy or debatable. Many a time people have objected media contents and special programme like Rahul Dilhania i.e., Jayega, Rakhi Sawant's swayambar, screened in NDTV imagine as well as Rodish programme of MTV channel. These women centric reality shows have become objectionable and debated by many feminists and activists. Visuals shown on FTV are often highlights nudity of women and portray unfair parts of women body. Women are used as objects of showing sensuous appeal. In reply to National Commission for Women's interference, the programme makers of NDTV replied women are voluntarily participating in Rahul Dulhhania Lejayage. They never force women or group up girls to play roles in making of the programme.

According to media survey reports, demand for the programme is on increase especially attracts youth and influences their life style. Youth viewers have never criticized the programme. Market research on different youth based programme like employment opportunity, career programme, serials, reality shows and fashion shows etc are conducted after each episode. Commercialization of programme and special issues on youth attracts much and continues depending on market research and communication research scholars. Many debate on depiction of nudity of women have become a regular practice in media in special issues and special stories from local to metro media. The trend is visibly more in metro media in regular basis and colourfully. Circulation is high among youth viewers and readers, according to media houses. It is not media which highlights, but voluntary offer of bolly-wood actors and actress for publication in largest daily matters a lot. Though media's commercial interests are there but self regulation is beyond control.

Ministry of Information & Broadcasting and NCW observed

in many cases be it proactive or sex appeal publications or programme should be screened keeping in mind on social decency. Awareness, self regulation and Law are required to check objectionable scenes and photos before final release. In the wake of controversy and resistance movement, research on media inputs is conducted. As MTV shows on youth culture was restricted after showing for many days. Subsequently media personnel introduced reality shows with participation of popular actors who are crowd pullers and media pullers in western countries and later influenced east audience.

Communication experts and media professionals always stress on one key point 'media literacy for the youth', which has become a necessary amid diversions in changing times. In order to transform social and economic institutions, media literacy is a must. Absence of media literacy one cannot efficiently make out media highlights and research outcomes. Since media now affects and motivates public opinion and life style, so relevance and importance of media literacy be given on priority basis.

After research, the New Indian Express had to change Youth Express magazines and came out with alternative colourful magazine like E-dex for development of youth potential. Similarly the Asian age had to change its exclusive page on women what was shown 12 years ago. In E-Dex the New Indian Express has given more coverage on promotion of educational and employability skills youth which deserves appreciation. Undoubtedly these are reader's choice especially youth oriented and sharing concern for educated youth.

Media and Human Resource Development

Media has significant contribution to human resource development. Its contribution is as important as other disciplines of knowledge. It is to be noted that media facilitates development of human resources in different sectors. It means, it promotes understanding about social, economic and media literacy to their readers in changing times. Most specifically, different organization has their policy and strategy to development employability skills and look after future career of educated and semi-educated youth in our country. For instance, national largest English daily, Times of India brings out Education Times and the New Indian Express Edex, which gives coverage on promotion of knowledge, skill and attitude. On the other hand, other dailies and channels also provide entertainment exclusively for the youth audience. Similarly, TV channels also broadcast career programme.

For best human resource management and shooting crisis, media gives special coverage and discovers conflict management in companies and organization along with solution. For example, national English Daily the Hindu brings out a special supplement in 'Opportunities' on human resource management in different jobs, crisis in jobs and care and concern for the youth. Apart from these, the fourth pillar of democracy provides a lot of employment opportunities for the young budding journalists and spreads its wings in different sectors excluding media sector. Though the opportunities for journalists in journalism are endless, simultaneously media jobs have become more challenging. Journalists have to compete with the each other for the good coverage, fast and quick coverage for the news or any other event.

As the journalists working in national and international fields are especially knowledge broker in society, there is need of training to increase the investigation as well as analysis capacity. Keeping in mind to develop the standard of professionalism national and international bodies like IPDC and IIMC conducting many training programmes. Even UNESCO's new communication strategy gives high priority to free flow of information at national and international level. In order to increase participation of developing countries in the process of communication, the strategy has given significance to promotion of better balanced dissemination of information through capacity building in community.

Media and Social Networking

Social networking is considered as the development of social values through networking. Here networks are created through internet and called as twitter, face book, linked in also. The uses of social networks in media have doubled pace of dissemination. This is perhaps the boldest campaign ever to have broken on Indian Television screens. Sites like Face book even have the options of social games which are gaining in popularity. Their target audience are young because they understand quickly and edgy instead of straight talk. As the youngsters are most tech savvy generation, public participation in media has increased. Media subsequently is getting feedback through this social network. It gives instant space to send feed back to the sender. It helps media to update its specific issues with the increasing demand. According to communication experts, social media governance is a boon for enriching communication among the media company and the e-readers.

Through social networks, the websites of different news paper and channels build awareness for their valuable contents. It helps to increase the company's visibility in the right areas and trying to stick in the minds of the readers through active interaction on different issues. Journalists are getting space to make strengthen their personal cum professional profile. It helps to get connect with high minded persons with the aim of extracting future benefits such as testimonials, links or recommendations. Networking is a way to build relationships that can be mutually beneficial.

Recently an internet and mobile product company ibibo.com has launched its latest ad campaign like voiceover intones in social gaming. The company is likely to join the bandwagon which will help a brand connect better with its audience barring language borders. To promote this kind of ad, these websites are working with television and radio channels allowing their video jockeys and radio jockeys to use the system to build their own benefits also. These ads are being showcased on youth channels like MTV channel V, UTV, Bindass and on certain shows on star one and Sony.

To sum up the whole issue, I would like to say that youths are stepping stone for nation building from the aspect of technological advancement. According to former president of India Dr. APJ Abdul Kalam, 'youth are ignited minds who must not dream a little'. Youth are playing major role in the changing the social landscape of the nation. They are contributing in transformation of economic, social, cultural, scientific as well as political. To accommodate the spirit of social and economic transformation in the nation, media education should be given utmost priority. Media literacy is yet to get place in the syllabus of higher education studies. Youth must know the history and contemporary impact of the fourth pillar of democracy in nation. Students should know that how government and business sector have utilized the mass media and other policies and practices to create a similar vision for the youth.

Active rules and regulation to safeguard the public against excessive collusive coverage of media need to be formulated. Similarly economic and political leaders must not confine the media movement for the urban development. Unless youth put effort through media to address the social problems like poverty, violence, drug abuse, gender inequality, our nation can not reach at the edge of development by 2010.

There is need of a movement to encourage students to examine additional segments of media culture, such as professional wrestling, Disney, rap music, clothing and cartoons, and come to a rich understanding of how kinds are often pushed by corporate executives to enter the adult world at a younger age. Young children are often forced to confront adult or teenage concerns inmost aspects of today's mass media such as sexuality, violence, explicit language and drug use. For instance, large-scale corporations are marketing images and products to very young children, which force to grapple with issues related to their appearance, weight and significantly with pleasing members of the opposite sex. It is very clear that commercial and material forms of entertainment take precedence over getting involved in spending their time 'working for the public good' or interacting with their peers through creative forms of play, activities that 'develop intellectual freedom and divergent thinking'.

Different scholarship programmes and project work based on contemporary issues in journalism are to be introduced whereby prospective youngsters can be trained. It will boost them to know the mechanism behind development plans and policies and the role of media subsequently. Students should be nudged to take a step back and reflect upon how youths are represented in various mass media outlets, such as on newscasts, in magazines, through advertisements, and in popular culture. It will be helpful to make them known about representations of youths in the corporate media and how corporate executives and politicians use mass media outlets to make consumers and voters view youth as inherently 'violent, dangerous and pathological', and frame them as the 'source of most of society's problems'.

It is imperative that students would understand why there has been such a backlash against youths, and similarly would recognize who ultimately benefits from these jaded characterizations. Simultaneously, promotion of citizen journalism can fill the gap between spirit of professionalism in society. In fact, 3R – Read, Report and Research can make the profession successful. It will definitely invite the hands to come together for an inclusive growth of the nation.

Types of median Education Tools

The tools of media education in the modern ear include Radio, Television, Film, Press, publication and advertising. The new outlook and innovative touch to this system has been created new hopes and aspirations among the youth society which has been integrated through electronics media to make it more lively and in-depth love to give a glaring message to this globalization world. The important mass media tools in our country are as follows:

1. Radio
2. Television
3. C.C.T.V
4. Video cassettes
5. Satellite Instructional Television Experiment Programmes
6. INSAT
7. Multimedia Packages
8. Tap slide presentations
9. Radio vision

10. Telecast
11. Teleconference

Radio

Through in 1927 Radio Broadcast started in India at Bombay and Calcutta, the government of India took them over in 1930 and operated under the name of Indian Broadcasting service. The name of the service changed into All India Radio and in 1957 it was made a separate department which is known as Akashvani. This All India Radio is now under the Ministry of Information and Broadcasting with its cut objectives to create a climate of opinion in which social change can take place with a motive to educate the people and to provide them health entertainment along with education in respects of various things to be involved in this process. In Indian context, efforts are made to use the simpler and more economical technology to meet our country's economic, social, linguistic and geographical requirements. This has tended for the effective utilization of radio for broadcasting educational programmes through out the country. In comparison to Television, Radio is inexpensive. The technology used in Radio is much simpler and prone to flexibility. Radio sets are available to the people in the remote villages and tribal areas in our country to provide more localized and need-based entertainment programmes to mingle them in the streamline of the progress.

Television

Television in India was launched in Delhi 1959 and a number of TV channels like Bombay, Srinagar, Jalandhar, Calcutta, Madras and Lucknow came into existence from 1975. Now Television covers more than 95 per cent of total population of this country where the urban population coverage is more than the rural one. Television was delinked from All India Radio with a new name Doordarshan on 1st April 1976 and started to function as the directorate of the ministry of Information and Broadcasting. By and by the growth of educational television brought a new dimension in the field of education for effective utilization and quality programming. The significant functions of education TV are:

- Training of personnel to design, develop and promote and utilization of education Television.
- Production of prototype programmes.
- Carrying out research and experimentation to taste and improve systems method and materials.
- Providing in information, resource and consultancy services for enhancing efficiency of educational Television system.
- Working as a coordinating agency with other organisations and institutions working in the field.

Video cassettes

Video is a luxury in our country so is colour TV also. However, video has come to a common picture and we shall have to accept it gladly to get the best use of it. The educational learners have accepted the introduction of the video recorders which offer new possibilities for language teaching and learning. The youth mass has appreciated its use to form video clubs, video library and video cassettes-learning societies. The most important reasons for using a Television video are mentioned below:

- Source of information
- Stimulates for discussion
- Instruments of provocation
- Illustrations of specific language items
- Pure entertainment.

These is a common features between video, radio and television as well as there are important differences. As with audio recorders, a video-cassette player in a school gives more flexibility to the teachers in their use of broadcast materials. However, there are far fewer video-cassette machines in schools, although the numbers are rapidly increasing. While the proportion of primary schools with video-cassette machines in Britain doubled from 1980 to 1981, this brought the number up to only 25 per cent and few schools had more than one, which meant that they could not play back and record at the same time. Nearly every secondary school had a video recorder in 1981, but the average number per school was only two, not really enough to give the ease of access and flexibility required in secondary schools. Hayter concluded that an increase in video recording and playback equipment would do more than anything to increase the effectiveness of schools television.

There is a significant increase in using the equipment alŏng with the television, particularly in secondary schools. Nevertheless, there is still not enough equipment yet in schools to justify the transfer of schools television to night-time transmission although, technically, it is easier to record television than radio off-air because of the inbuilt clock on most video. The Inner London Education Authority used to distribute its own programmes and those of the broadcasting organizations, via a cable system at all the schools in its areas. Because of the high cost of renting the lines from the Post Office it closed down its cable service in 1979, since when it has distributed its programmes on video.

There are several reasons for the rapid growth. Machines can be rented for as little as 10 per month, and there are many high street shops and back-street dealers from which video programmes, including feature films, can be hired at little cost. Because many of the broadcast programmes are still of high quality, it is also worth while recording these at home, especially since the range of choice at any one time is limited to four channels in the current absence of widespread cable TV system.

In 1981 eleven per cent of Open University students had access to video recorders in their homes and another eight per cent had easy access to recorders elsewhere. By the end of 1982, twenty per cent of Open University students had access to machines in their home and another 22 per cent convenient accede elsewhere. Video progarammes require different production formats from broadcasts, the design features of audio-cassettes will not always be appropriate for video production. The production requirements of a video programme are much more demanding technically and in terms of manpower. This means that recording of material and its editing is separate from the preparation of the texts to which it relates and makes it more difficult at the design stage to develop the very close integration between text and programme that is possible with audio-cassettes, although careful advance planning and editing of both programme and text can go some way towards this.

Whereas students can easily integrated video programmes and text simultaneously, because they cannot watch video and read the text at the same time taking notes during a video sequence is much more difficult than during an audio sequence and tends to lead to concentration on detail rather than on principles or general points. In practice, this means that video sequences will tend to run for longer without interruption, with interrogation of material taking place segments, with some replay to assist. Particularly where students are having to share equipment – either a machine at a study centre, with other students waiting to use it, or at home, with the television set wanted by the rest of the family. It will be more difficult for students to spend a great deal of time working repeatedly through the cassette. This is less of a problem with audio-cassettes. It is clear that in the next few years there will be scope for a great deal of experiment and innovation to identify suitable video formats for education.

The most important aspect to audio and video is the control over the medium that they offer the learner compared with broadcasts. It is worth looking more carefully at this comparison since it highlights some of the unique characteristics of television, as well as certain weakness of broadcasting as an instructional medium. With either a broadcast programme or a cassette, each individual member of the target audience is sending the same material. No matter how specialised the target audience, each individual will vary in ability to learn from the programs.

Ways of using video

- To exhibit a film.
- To record of air programme from the domestic television channel and play it for the class.
- To record our own programme and play it for the class.

- To record a lecturer given by an export to audience and play it to the class.
- To out the sound off and show short sequences as silent sequences.
- To buy video cassettes available in the market and play them.

When youth workers work with video, they are intended to discover new tricks and new possibilities all the time. Working with video also enhances the potentialities of the worker in term of the content, techniques and flexibilities. The use of video recording has tremendous utilities for the youth mass to develop ideas and materials to support the work they do with it. Some of the important areas are mentioned below:

- Intervenes
- Domestic scenes
- Business scenes
- Social scenes
- Banking, shopping procedures
- Scenes involving high drama
- Usually of a tragic nature
- Crime stories
- Comic situation
- Documentaries
- Fantasy production based on popular myths.
- Recording that demonstrate specific linguistic structures.
- Demonstration, cookery, playing musical instrument discussions.
- Ambiguous situation designated to provoke questioning language.
- Mime to which students watching the recording can add the appropriate language.
- Stories (narrated and acted out).
- News items (read out by students, playing new readers).

- Recording involving toys, objects, sound effects.
- Social fiction programmes.

Satellite Instructional Television Experiment Programmes

For national development and for educating Indian masses living in remote areas, Satellite Instructional Television Experiment was geared up, on July 21st, 1976. Satellites are one of many technologies of current or potential interest to educational technologists and planners. The extent to which satellites will be used depends upon the extent to which educational and communications technology proves responsive to educational needs, the extent to which 'cost-effectiveness' can be demonstrated and the extent to which technology in general finds future use in education. Especially, satellites have the potential for providing relatively low cost educational services. Computer-aided instruction, radio, one-way and talk-back television, library and computer resource sharing etc to large number of people and institutions, provided that economies of scale can be achieved. Such services may prove to be responsive to calls for greater access, individualization and productivity in United States education, as well as the need to extend education and literacy to greater numbers of individuals in developing countries. However, to active this potential suitable organizational arrangements and structures must be devised which respond to the particular educational setting of the country or regions.

Custom of the satellites for communication was first step by radio engineer and science fiction in 1945. With two decades from the radio satellite a series of experiments with low and medium altitude satellites, which required large and complexes earth-stations, the stationary satellite was successfully placed in geo-synchronous orbit. In such an orbit the satellite is some 23,000 miles over the equator and stays in one fixed position relative to points on earth. Three of these satellites in the proper position could bear signals which cover almost the entire surface of the earth. The demonstration of the feasibility of using a stationary satellite in geo-synchronous orbit for communications paved the way for commercial communications satellites.

The satellite technology has reached a point where relatively inexpensive, roof-top type receiving radio and television programs or broadcasts over a wide area from relatively higher-power satellites will be feasible shortly. In recognition of this possibility, in 1971 World administrative Radio Conference was held in Geneva and allocated radio frequencies for a 'broadcasting satellite service' in which signals transmitted or retransmitted by satellites are intended for direct reception by the general public.

Two different classes exist in this service, system allow individual reception by simple receiving units in homes and systems that are designed for community location or through a distribution system covering a limited area. However, it should be pointed out that world Administrative radio conference regulations for broadcasting satellite service do not permit direct reception by non-augmented conventional TV receivers of the type in use today. The applications currently contemplated for communications satellites in education are indeed diverse, reflecting the differences in educational systems and needs of the nations or regions where uses of communications satellites have been proposed. In the United States formal systems of education have been serving large portions of the school-age population and higher education is becoming more widespread with the inception of the community college. The important functions of SITE are:

- To facilitate the approach and conduct of television programme of primary schools.
- To train the teachers for optimum utilization of television programmes in the class room situation.
- To train the resource persons of different states to organize the different training courses for teachers.
- To orient the trainees to do simulation exercises in respect of pre and post telecast and arranging other viewing conditions as the special broadcast are arranged for the training purposes.
- To develop a group of good script writers for young children.

INSAT (Indian National Satellite)

data transmission, nation wide direct television transmission and continuous meteorological earth observation. INSAT television processes two different features: 1. Direct Telecast and 2. National networking using existing terrestrial transmission keeping in mind the objectives of TV services that is to provide support to cover all developmental efforts and their use in the betterment in the life of worker sections of the society particularly in the rural and tribal areas. The role of INSAT in education has assumed greater importance, because of its superior hardware capacities. The INSAT service is insensitive to distance that is remote locations are not cost disadvantage.

Extension like radio and other communication links may be added to ground stations providing flexibilities difficult and terrestrial system. It is recognized that satellite systems are by and large more reliable than terrestrial being reducing remote maintenance problem and operational cost.

Multimedia Packages

Multimedia packages have been developed to initiate an alternative strategy by making use of mass media for in-service teacher education which could cover a large number of teachers simultaneously. In-service teachers training courses in science for primary school teachers by using a multimedia package developed by the centre for educational technology of the National Council of Educational Research and Training represents a major attempt in this direction.

Tap Slide Presentations

Tap slide material are very popular now-a-days. It is useful at all level and suitable for all types of education. It is most suited to introductory type of courses where visuals play a dominant role. It can be used extensively in non-formal education.

Radio Vision

Radio vision is an instruction system in which the subject is presented through two-channels, the audio and the visual. The visuals are presented in the form of charts, slides, projected film strips or models while the explanation is given through recorded narrations. Though mass media is obtained held as producing miracle, it is also though of by meaning in terms of its advantage. The mass media can only modify and guide people but they can not make them interact. The communication is from the communicator to the audience where the audience remains passive. The different problems which create challenges in the field of education for the youth generation are realized as follows:

- Universalisation of primary education.
- Eradication of adult illiteracy.
- Unbalanced distribution of educational opportunities.
- Negligible opportunities of continuing education.
- Substandard formal schooling system.

All the above problems can be solved if mass media are integrated into the total educational system, but in this context state government should provide adequate financial support for organizing audio visual programmes in the school level. Besides RIE, Directorate of TE & SCERT, state universities, teacher training colleges should take initiative for improvisation of media materials. The co-operation of trained personnel's should be available to direct the programme constitute for effective cataloguing, circulation and utilization of the materials in the field of teaching and social environment. However, the revolution in the area of mass media is not probing question rather a burning message for the youth mass, who can improve man's achievements in different fields in a considerable and constructive way, where man is moving rapidly from print media to the machines and software.

4

Impact of Median on Children

Children nowadays have wide choices: many local, national and international programs television channels, thousands of video games and films, radio programs, different newspapers, magazines and even computer games, world-wide web and entertainment on the internet. We need to accept the media, especially television, are a powerful force in children's lives. Children need to feel that the world is a safe place and that people can be trusted. This allows them the freedom to explore their world and approach new experience with curiosity and openness. Children's have to develop a sense that they can affect their world and feelings of inner strength and belief in themselves as competent and capable people. To do this, children have to learn what kind of effects in different situations.

On many children programs the characters display empowerment and efficacy only by using weapons and violence. Using words and wit to solve problems is not often shown. Much of current children's television programs undermine development by failing to provide content that help children develop a sense of empowerment. There are very few characters that serve as role models for achieving positive effects in non-violent ways. The more broadly children approach the question of what it means to be a 'boy' or a 'girl' the more they are likely to develop to their full potential. Children need to be shown that boys and girls can do a wide range of things, many of which are common to both sexes. TV can give children a restricted picture of what it means to be a boy or girl, exaggerating a tendency for stereotyping naturally occurring in young children. The term 'early childhood' generally refers to the years of a child's life from birth to about seven. The central developmental needs in the early childhood years are:

- Playing in a meaning and purposeful manner

- A sense of empowerment and usefulness.
- Developing a sexual characteristics identity.
- Developing a sense of trust and protection.
- The need for autonomy and relationship.
- Understanding how people are alike and different.
- Developing a sense of principles, social systems and responsibility.

Play is a basic to the healthy development and learning of children. Through the process of play, children can master experiences that may have been scary or difficult for them, they can learn to think creatively, take risks and solve problems. Children need to be in charge of their own play–they need time, space and props to encourage them. Children's are developing idea about morality, justice and how people should treat each other. Children's tendency to divide things up into categories–all good or all bad, all right or all wrong–makes those particularly susceptible to material presented in simple black-and-white terms. Most commercial television programs present one-dimensional characters that are either all good or all bad, which lack the complexity of real human character. Questions of social responsibility and morality are not raised when good characters attack and maim bad ones.

Role of Media on Child Growth

Media can never replacement for children's direct experiences in interacting with the world. It can be providing with the kind of content they need to play. Many themes on commercial television programs are removed from children's experience and understanding. Play becomes merely imitative rather than creative. Single purpose toys marketed along with these shows further the tendency to imitation. Children's television does not help children meet their developmental needs through play. Not only does television cut deeply into play time, it also provides a narrow range of content for children to use in play. One of the most important role of parent can play is that of a 'media educator'. You don't have to be trained teacher to do that. Your comments on programs, your discussions with a child about what they have seen, your expression of your values, your identification of the unrealities of programs and commercials are vital to a child's understanding of what he or she has seen and the development of critical viewing skills. When the television or computer is in the family room, rather than the bedroom you can make the most of the 'teachable moment'.

The contemporary researches shows that children's apprehension's levels have been steadily increasing since the 1950s, and that children's level of anxieties and their frequency of sleep disturbances are significantly related to the amount of television they watch. Children who have been scared by something they have seen on TV right up to bedtime are not a good idea. Children watch TV or a video have been through an emotional experience, and may need time to 'work' it off. Time for a bath, reading a story, or a chat with father or mother, will more effectively prepare children for a good night's sleep.

Children's lack grown-ups experience of the world and so are unable to distinguish between what they see and the likelihood of these events occurring in their own lives may think that when they see the same event over and over again that the event is actually happening over and over again can be made anxious because they think that the events that they see are likely to happen to them. At a young age, they are unable to understand the concept of probability so are not necessarily reassured if you tell them 'it is not likely to happen to us' may become quite fearful if violence in shown in settings with which they are familiar, such as home and families or children and animals.

Terrifying stuff is important for parents and caregivers to remember that television and movies, by their nature, can expose children to frightening images, events and ideas, many of which they would never experience in their whole lives, without such exposure. Children see and interpret film and TV content differently from adults and the impact of scary content can have a quite powerful and lasting impact on children. Exposure to terrifying content can result in short term effects such as intense fear and crying and longer term effects such as sleep disturbance, refusal to be alone concern about being hurt or killed and dependence on unusual bedtime rituals. Long term disabling fears can emerge.

Children may have been exposed to terrifying or violent material on television, film or video. However, the events of September 11 have brought to many people's attention that children can also be traumatized by being exposed to reports and images from frightening world events. For each age group below there are tips for dealing with both kinds of media trauma. Some children will exhibit fear through behaviour not words. Behaviors that could alert you to the fact that they may have been exposed to terrifying material are crying, abnormal fussiness or agitation, sleep disturbance, bed wetting, unusually clingy behaviours and greater than normal sensitivity. At the extreme end, there are documented cases of children being so traumatized by viewing violent material that they have had to receive inpatient psychiatric treatment. If you are with your child at the time that they are exposed to terrifying or violent material, the more immediate your response the better, in the first instance calmly removing them from the situation. Following this or if you become aware that your child is reacting to something they saw while you were not with them, the best overall strategy is to acknowledge their fear and reassure them.

Violence in the media is easily accessible to children. It occurs in cartoons, in news updates in family programs, and in blockbuster movies screened on TV. Many computer games feature violent themes. Trailers for forthcoming programs on TV often contain a collection of the most violent scenes. Parents often feel ambushed by these as they cannot be anticipated. There have been few content analyses done on TV or media for levels of violence. Overseas content analyses, which have some relevance as much of our programming, particularly on commercial TV is from the US, show that children's cartoons carry the most acts of violence. Violence in the media is all pervasive and difficult to avoid. Frequently the violence is glamorized and violent solutions offer the way to be powerful. Mostly the heroes are male and the victims are female, showing who does the violence and to whom it's done. Violence media and products are actively marketed to children and young people. The products themselves are frequently in a classification not recommended for children. There is much cross promotion of violent products, e.g, by fast food chains and cinema links, toys and TV series; toys and cinema films.

The patents arte taken the precautions towards their children is: minimize exposure to programs and products which feature glamorized violence. Minimize exposure to news programs for children less than ten to twelve years. These children are unlikely to understand that it is not likely to happen to you as they don't understand probability. Be a media educator express your views and discuss program content for example talk to children about what would happen if they did those violent things at home.

While there may be many entertaining experiences for children to be had on TV, with video and with computers, it is important to keep in mind what children of different ages need for healthy development. It is important that children have time to be in the real world, and to build strong bonds with real caring people. Media can be a thief of children's time that they really need for other experiences–active physical play and 'ads on activities of all kinds. Children need experiences that enhance their development, and all too frequently media content can reduce the impact of programs and games where harmful messages are constantly repeated.

Advertising directed to children includes paid advertisements or commercials that appear in TV programs specifically made for children or in other programs for children and where the product is principally of interest to children under the age of ten years. The amount of advertising can be high as 15 minutes per hour. Sometimes, the descriptions of prizes for a competition or the demonstration of a product in a cartoon program can be construed as advertising. Such practices should occur in discrete segments within the program. Pay TV also carries advertising directed to children, but at a lower level of minutes per hour. Advertising directed to children also occurs on the Internet e.g., in banner ads. Advertising to children is an unfair practice. Hit works by making you unhappy with lives, anxious and unsatisfied. It sells to them by damaging their mental health. The messages for food ads on

TV are encouraging children to the view that what's good to eat is 'good for them'. I fact, television food ads during children's viewing times disproportionately promote foods of low nutritional value-foods high in fat, sugar or salt. The largest categories of foods advertised tend to be chocolate and confectionery, fast food restaurants and sweetened breakfast cereals.

Toys are promoted very heavily to children through a wide range of media. They are presented in such a way as to make them look very attractive and great fun to play with. The children shown playing with them is cute, petty or cool. Toys are promoted on television, by promotional segments within television programs, spin-offs from movies, and links with fast food chains. Other methods include 'virus marketing'. The parents must minimize young children's exposure to commercial media, build a selection of non-toy related videos and choose age specific toys that meet children's real play needs.

The impact of using screen media on children's physical health has a number of aspects. These aspects include direct impacts of prolonged use such as: eyestrain, repetitive strain injury and postural problems. There may also for some children be risks relating to: epilepsy and electromagnetic radiation. There are also displacement effects, that is, that computer use can displace involvement in physical activity. In addition, daily hours of commercial TV will include a high level of advertisements for fatty, salty, sugary and fast foods. These can influence children's attitudes in the direction of 'what's good to eat' rather than 'what's good for them'. Children also tend to snack while watching TV. The impact of hours at the TV set and eating frequently advertised foods is contributing to a rising problem of obesity in children.

Computers and video games were first developed in the 1970s. As technology and programming improved games became more accessible to individuals in their own homes and video games are programmes that are designed for recreational use. They can be used on a variety of platforms that is on many different types of machines, systems or devices. Games can be brought or downloaded from the internet. Keep an eye on your child's overall health and wellbeing and take note of your child's reactions after they have been playing computer games. Watch out for sign that your child is becoming addicted to playing computer games. Changes in eating habits, moods, school performance, interaction with friends and involvement in non-computer activities might indicate that a problem is developing.

Media impact on Children Education

Now-a-day's media and technology have been introduced into schools because it is believed that they can have positive effects on teaching and learning. With respect to education, media are the symbol systems that teachers and students use to represent knowledge. Technologies are the tools that allow them to share their knowledge representations with others. Unfortunately, it is common for practitioners and experts alike to confound the meanings of media and technology in education, and they are often used synonymously. The confounding of media with technology is unlikely to go away in popular discourse about education any time soon, but the distinction between media and technology must be clarified as unambiguously as possible if their impact is to be understood.

The important doubt about the impact of media and technology in terms of increasing access to education and reducing the costs of education are especially high on the agendas of politicians and government agencies around the world. In the USA, the Panel of Educational Technology of the President's Committee of Advisors on Science and Technology included as one of its six major tragic recommendations that technology be used to 'ensure equitable, universal accesses. Another part of the same report called for realistic budgeting for technology-related expenditures within schools, nothing that the much-touted return-on-investment for educational technology was a long-term prospect. Another reason for the attention being paid to media and technology in education reflects commercial or corporate interests. Although printed material continues to be 'the dominant medium format in schools', a recent presidential report in the USA recommended that 'at least five percent of all public K-12 educational spending in the United States should earmarked for tech.ology-related expenditures'.

Another reason for focus on media and education stems from sharp disagreements about the value of media and technology in education. Enthusiastic endorsements of new media and technologies in education are easy to find in news reports, political speeches, and other sources. Many of these proclamations seem overly-optimistic if not hyperbolic. Because of the pervasive and potent impact of hyper learning technology, we now are experiencing the turbulent advent of an economic and social transformation more profound than the industrial revolution. The same technology that is transforming work offers new learning systems to solve the problems it creates. In the wake of the hyper learning revolution, the technology called 'school' and the social institution commonly though of as 'education' will be as obsolete and ultimately extinct as the dinosaurs.

There is no good evidence that most uses of computers significantly improve teaching and learning, yet school districts are cutting programs – music, art, physical education that enrich children's lives to make room for this dubious nostrum and the Obama Administration has embraced the goal of 'computers in every classroom' with credulous and costly enthusiasm.

There are two major approached to using media and technology in schools, students can learn from media and technology and they can learn with media and technology. Learning from media and technology is often referred to in terms such as instructional television computer-based instruction, or integrated learning systems. Learning with technology, less widespread than the from approach, is referred to in terms such as cognitive tools and constructivist learning environments. Regardless of the approach, media and technology have been introduced into schools because it is believed that they can have positive effects on teaching and learning.

Since the educational television broadcasts began in Iowa in 1933, there have been decades of research focused on the educational effects of television in schools and society as a whole persist. A review of the television research literature however, indicates that such claims are largely based upon subjective observations rather than theory-guided investigations, and there is no conclusive evidence that television stultifies the mind. There is also no consistent evidence that television increases either hyperactivity or passivity in children. Another popular belief is that television viewing is detrimental to the academic achievement of school-age children and teens. While some studies have reported a negative correlation between the amount of television viewing and scholastic performance, such statistic are susceptible to misinterpretations because of intervening variables such as intelligence and socioeconomic status.

The most positive research news about learning from television can be found in the classroom where 40 years of research show positive effects on learning from television programs that are explicitly produced and used for instructional purposes. In addition, most studies show that there are no significant differences in effectiveness between live teacher presentations and video of teacher presentation. There is strong evidence that television is used most effectively when it is intentionally designed for education and when teachers are involved in its selection, utilization and integration into the curriculum. In the past, the biggest barrier to the integration of television programs into the classroom was the fixed limitation of instructional broadcasts, but the wide-spread availability of video cassette recorders has provided teachers with the ease-of-use and flexibility they require. Unfortunately, there is a paucity of developmental research focused on how teachers might best use television in the classroom to enhance academic achievement. We know that motivation is an important factor in gaining the most from any educational experience, but we don't know how teachers can effectively motivate students to attend to educational television. We know that feedback concerning the message received from television is important but we lack clear directions as to when and how teacher should provide that feedback and even when recommendations for using television in the classroom do exist, there is little evidence that these guidance's are integral parts of the curriculum in most teacher preparation programs.

The personal computer is the most common interactive technology used as a 'tutor' today. Interactive instruction via personal computer is known by many names and acronyms such as computer-based instruction, integrated learning systems and intelligent tutoring system. The personal computer as a tutor or surrogate instructor has been the subject for much research and evaluation since its development in the late 1970s. Critics of computers as tutors have been around since their inception and there are vocal opponents of computers in classrooms today. The earliest forms of computer-based instruction were heavily influenced by the behavioural psychology of Skinner. These programs were essentially automated forms of programmed instruction. They present information to the students in small segments, required the student to make overt responses to the information as stimulus and provided feedback to the student along with differential branching to other segments of instruction or to drill-and-practice routines. Although this basic behavioural model continues to dominate mainstream educational applications of computers such as integrated learning systems, interactivity in some of today's most innovative applications, such as constructivist learning environments, is based upon advances in cognitive psychology and constructivist pedagogy.

Cognitive tools have around for thousands of years, ever since primitive humans used piles of stones, marks on trees and knots in vines to calculate sums or record events. In the broadest sense, cognitive tools refer to technologies, tangible or intangible that enhance the cognitive powers of human being during thinking, problem-solving and learning. Something as complex as a mathematical formula or as simple as a grocery list can be regarded as a cognitive tool in the sense that each allows humans to 'off-load' memorization or other mental tasks onto an external resource. Today, computer software programs are example of exceptionally powerful cognitive tools also referred to as mind tools. They will be referred to as 'cognitive tools' here. As computers have become more and more common in education, researchers have begun to explore the impact of software as cognitive tools in schools. Computers as cognitive tools represent quite a different approach from media and technology as vehicles for educational communications. Compuer-based cognitive tools have been intentionally adapted or developed to function as intellectual partners to enable and facilitate critical thinking and higher order learning.

In recent years, learning theory has gone through what can be called a 'paradigm shift'. Constructivist learning theory is gradually gaining the same respect and attention long accorded to behavioural learning theory. Constructivism concerns the process of how students create meaning and knowledge in the world as well as the results of the constructive process. How students construct knowledge depends upon what they already know, their previous experiences, how they have organized those experiences into knowledge structures such as schema and mental models, and the beliefs they use to interpret the objects and events they encounter in the world. Cognitive tools help learners organize, restructure and represent what they know.

Following the maxim that the surest way to learn something is to teach it to others, the process of designing instructional materials enables instructional designers to understand content much more deeply than the students whose thinking will be constrained and controlled by the very materials they are developing. It follows that empowering learners to design and produce their own knowledge representations and educational communications can be powerful learning experience. Langer reminded us of the importance of mindfulness in learning. Students learn and retain the most from thinking in meaningful ways. Representing knowledge is a mindful task that can be enabled by cognitive tools such as multimedia construction software or electronic spreadsheets.

Teachers had to make significant changes in their classroom managements styles, giving up more control to technology and students. This also changed slowly. Initially, media and technology were primarily used within the context of traditional pedagogical methods and most teachers required years of experience before they adopted more innovative strategies such as project-based learning. Finally, teachers struggled with fundamental incongruities between traditional assessment measures and the kinds of learning occurring in their classrooms. In fact, assessment problems proved to be the most resistant to solutions and many remained unresolved.

Children and the Internet

Most children art stage will use the internet. Many parents, on other hand, have had little or no exposure. As a result, parents often find it difficult to understand the issues involved and therefore have problems discussing them with their children. The internet is a massive network of computers from around the world all connected by cable and satellite. When users are connected to the internet, they can receive text, images, video and sound on their computer from computers anywhere in the world. Just as there is a book or magazine on nearly every subject in local libraries, bookshops or newsagents, so is there information on virtually every subject on the internet. The internet is sometimes called the world side web. Being on the internet is called being on-line. Playing on the internet or hunting for information is called 'surfing' the net.

Any individual or organisation can create a 'website' on which they can provide any information they choose to. Information on a website is usually separated in a logical way into 'web pages'. These can provides information about a company and its services, promotional materials, information on any topic, reports facts and figures, links to other relevant websites and so on. Once you have gone to a particular website, you will often find links to other websites. In this way you can jump between many websites to look for the information you want. Searching for information by going from one website to another is known as surfing.

Email is an electronic form of sending a letter to another person. You can attach documents and photos which arrive at their destination in the same format as you send them. Email is a very quick and cheap means of communicating and is very widely used.

Your ISP will set up an email address for you when you join up with them. The internet can provide children and adults alike with a world of exciting opportunities. It offers: educational games and programs, research information for school projects and business, the opportunity to communicate with people from all around the world, the opportunity to share resources and ideas with people that have the same interests and shopping around the world without leaving your computer.

There are no regulations or controls on the material that is placed on the internet. While there are three million perfectly safe children's sites on the net, children can unexpectedly come across material of a sexual or violent nature, language that is rude the advertising of children's products. Quite innocently they can bring up sites that do not relate to the topic they are looking for, or someone can send them images or messages that are not appropriate. Therefore there are many things on-line that are not suitable for children or that is cause for concern. The main dangers to children are that they may : access inappropriate information, inadvertently from 'friendship' with strangers, be subjected to advertising pressures, risk their personal health through excessive use and endanger their privacy by revealing person details about themselves, such as their name and address.

The parents are must taken several things at the time of using internet by the children. Being a parent must do to help counteract the dangers of the internet while allowing your children to use its benefit: learn more about it yourself, be aware of what your children are doing on the internet, establish guidelines about safe internet use, teach your children to be criticall users of the internet, put in place reasonable boundaries, use blocking software or filters and if necessary, lodge complaints. The internet is a useful tool for finding information, for contacting friends by email, and for chatting to others with similar interests. However, the internet is but one means of communication and one source of information among many. This topic outlines a few issues of a general nature that parents and caregivers may like to consider: the child's age and developmental needs, reliability of information accessed, safety

The internet links computers and databases world wide. It provides a most valuable communication system for obtaining information, sending mail and chatting with others with similar interests. However, it is an adult world and as such it can be a dangerous place for children to play because they may: inadvertently access inappropriate information, come into contract with pedophiles, be subjected to invasion of privacy and unsolicited advertising. The internet is a most valuable communication system for obtaining information, sending mail and chatting with other similar interest. However, there are risks with using the internet. Some parents may wish to consider internet filtering software as a method of reducing the risks of their children being exposed to undesirable material on the internet.

There are a number of internet filtering tools that parents can use. However, such tools are not infallible, and must easily achieved when children use a web-connected computer in the family room, and not in their private filtering software are filters, labels and safe zones. Filters are software programs that can be put on your own computer, or can be made available though your internet service provide. They are: block access to web sites, or on keywords or phrases, can stop search engines from searching for unsuitable topics, may block access to newsgroups, chartrooms and email, some can be set ability to shut down creation sites are accessed.

Commenter's also noted several difficulties with employing technology without acceptable use policies to protect children. First, commenter's noted that technology protection measures are not the entire answer. These commenter's emphasized that technology protection measures are most effective when teachers and educational institutions can customize technology and use it in connection with other strategies and tools. As one commenter stated, children need to be trained to think critically and use the internet safely. Technology cannot replace education and judgment. Second, one commenter noted that technology protection measures can give a false sense of protection. This commenter stated that children should be educated to avoid improper content in the same unfiltered environments children experience in their homes, libraries and offices. He argued that filtering provides an inauthentic atmosphere that thwarts teachers' preparing their students to deal with reality. Alternatively, another commenter argued that acceptable use policies that appropriate use policies are a good protection avoid offensive material simply by education. He also contended that time limits imposed by acceptable use policies have not been found to stop the ability of children to access inappropriate material online.

The National Research Council report also discussed several issues relating to acceptable use policies. The Council recommended that these policies should distinguish between adult and children, determine how to measure compliance, avoid overly broad wording and strive to list specific inappropriate behaviour and material, protect against liability, and define a user's rights. The best practices and lessons learned that are set forth above provide valuable information for communities to consider as they develop and implement internet safety policies. Technology protection measures are most effective when teachers and educational institutions can customize technology and use it in connection with other strategies and tools. Educational institutions prefer local decision making that gives leaders the flexibility to select the appropriate technology that fits best with their unique circumstances and to consider non-economic factors that may influence technology selection decisions.

Media violence and children

Now-a-days becoming more and more violent in their day-to-day life. They are becoming so self-centered all are willing to do any illegal activities for their own purpose. James Q. Wilson, who is one of the foremost expert on crime has observed, 'youngsters are shooting at people at a far higher rate than at any time in recent history'. The Centers for Disease Control and Prevention reports that a recent survey showed that some 5.90 per cent of the American high school students surveyed said that they had carried a gun. Equally troubling, that survey also shows that 18 per cent of high school students now carry a knife, razor, firearm or other weapon on a regular basis and nine percent of them take a weapon to school. While recent studies show that the amount of youth violence has started to decline, the Centers for Disease Control warn that 'the prevalence of youth violence and school violence is still unacceptably high'. Countless studies have shown that a steady diet of television, movie, music, video game and internet violence plays a significant acts committed by youth.

American media are exceedingly violent. With television, analysis of programming for 20 years found that over the years, the level of violence in prime-time programming remained at about five violent acts per hour. Like television, the cinemas are full of movies that glamorise bloodshed and violence and one need only listen to popular music radio and stroll down the aisle of almost any computer store to see that the music and video games are similarly afflicted. Not only the media exceedingly violence, they are also ubiquitous. The percentage of households with more than one television set has reached an all-time high of 87 per cent and roughly half per cent of American children have a television set in their room. Forty-six per cent of all homes with children have access to at least one television set, a VCR, home video game equipment and personal computer and 88.70 per cent of such homes have either home video game equipment a personal computer or both.

The majority of the existing social and behavioural science studies, taken together, agree on the following basic points:

- Constant viewing of televised violence has negative effects on human character and attitudes;
- Television violence encourages violent forms of behaviour and influences moral and social values about violence in daily life;
- Children who watch significant amounts o television violence have a greater likelihood of exhibiting later aggressive behaviour;
- Television violence affects viewers of all ages, intellect, socioeconomic levels and both genders; and
- Viewers who watch significant amounts of television violence perceive a meaner world and overestimate the possibility of being a victim of violence.

The young children are also influenced to violence due to

televisions. The researchers have performed longitudinal studies of the impact of television violence on young children as they mature into adults. The researchers describe that boys at age of eight years who had been watching more television violence than other boys grew up to be more aggressive than other boys, and they also grew up to be more aggressive and violent than one would have expected them to be on the basis of how aggressive they were as eight year olds. In respect of girls arrived at a similar conclusion: children who watched more violence behaved more aggressively the next year than those who watched less violence on television and more aggressively than anticipated based on their behaviour the previous year.

Music affects our moods, our attitudes, our emotions and our behaviour. In Plato's Republic, Socrates said that 'musical training is a more potent instrument than any other, because rhythm and harmony find their way into the inward places of the soul, on which they mightily fasten'. We wake to it, dance to it and sometimes cry to it. From infancy it is an integral part of our lives. As virtually any parent with a teenager can attest, music holds an even more special place in the hearts and minds of our young people. Academic studies confirm this wisdom. A Swedish study has found that adolescents who developed an early interest in rock music were more likely to be influenced by their peers and less influenced by their parents than older adolescents. With good reason, then, parents are concerned about the music lyrics their children hear and parents should be concerned. Despite historic, bipartisan remedial legislation by the state and federal governments, it is stunning even to the casual listener how much modern music glorifies acts of violence.

Music video studies are valuable in their own right, but they do not provide information about the effects of exposure to violent lyrics without video. Music videos are much more like other video media in that they can tell a story with graphically violent images, the finding that they produce similar effects is not surprising. Long-term effects accrue via the development of highly accessible knowledge structures and emotional desensitization to violence by well-established social-cognitive leaning and systematic desensitization processes. In brief, each media violence episode constitutes a learning trial in which one rehearses aggressive thoughts and primes aggression-related affects, creating and making chronically accessible hostile attitudes, beliefs, expectations and scripts. Video games often present violence in a glamorized light. Typical games cast players in the role of a shooter, with points scored for each kill. Furthermore, advertising for such games often touts the violent conduct as a selling point – the more graphic and extreme, the better.

5

Role of Media on Transformation of Youth Culture

Youth is the greatest wealth and strength of a nation. The future of a nation lies in the hands of its prosperity. The quality of its youth determines the kind of future, the nation we have. To ensure the bright future for a country there is a need to strengthen and empower the youth. They are the potential energy and considered as powerhouse of a country. It is the youth who brings laurels to their country. The power of youth can be sighted only by mentioning a few names of which every single Indian is proud of such as Sachin Tendulkar, Leander Paes, Mahesh Bhupati, Susmita Sen, Aiswarya Rai, P.T. Usha, Rahul Gandhi, Dillip Tirkey, Abhinav Bindra etc.

Youth in India have their origin in the village based rural environment. For the sake of education, searching for jobs, accompanying empoyed family members, etc migrate to the urban and semi-urban set ups. They are influenced by their peers, seniors, teachers and parents to a great extent both academically, finacially, socially, politically. They are exposed to varieties of information through news papers, books, journals magazines etc in addition to their exposure to electronic mass media, like radio, television, cinema and internet. Since youth is the major force for any country's development, their potential have to be strengthened by applying number of strategies. There is a great need to empower the youth for planning and implementing important activities in industrial, educational and social sectors. The activities of the youth has to be observed and modulated from time to time for building a super structure of the youth culture.

Youth are distinct from adults, more self-aware and subject to peer group rather then parental and adult influences. Looking at their behaviour it can be said that fashions, styles in clothes, music, use of leisure time, travelling, playing in groups, interaction with opposite sex are some of the qualities which they display before children as well as elders. Taking together the above aspects, the general youth look forward and develop habits which ultimately arrive at a new style of living. There is gender variation in youth culture. Boys and girls differ on various aspects of their behaviour for themselves and others. Youth are influence to a great extent by electronic media which are born in advance age of science and technology particularly mass media like radio and television.

History of Youth Culture and Technology

The concept of youth culture and ne technology is a relatively new term, however the rate at which technology has moved into the lives of the young as stated by Seel 'is historically unprecedented'. The growth within this area began in August 1981, when IBM released the IBM personal computers. From here the industry continued to grow with Apple in 1983 releasing 'Lisa' than their latest project. Lisa contained many ground-breaking functions such as mouse, drop down menus, icons, folders, windows and copy and paste abilities among other features. Following the establishment of home PC's the 1980s also bought it the introduction of video games; items which soon to dominate the toy market. Video games were one of the first mediums to combine visuals and active participation for children and youths, as defined by the Wikipedia, they are a form interactive multimedia used as entertainment.

As describe in Steel by 1989 out of 20 of the best selling toys on the market 16 were video games and related things. The next major development following this was the internet, which was established in 1990s. it has been described as the combination of the interactivity of video games, the information of computers and the images. Thus the internet created an entirely new means of social interaction. In countries there are high rates of broadband connectivity many of there are able to play online games together. The players are not physically located in the space, they are often involved in socializing together by connecting domestic spaces and time zones through online gaming communities. These activities can have a large impact on the broader youth culture.

Importance of Youth Culture and Technology

According to Roy Morgan Research all most 80 per cent of Australian aged 14-24 access the internet at least once in a week, more than two-third said they cannot live without a mobile phone and 44 per cent are beloved that the computers and internet have given them more control over their lives. The network generation's trend towards online activities and interactive media has also resulted in a dramatic decline in traditional activities such as newspaper readership. More than half of the Australians aged 18-29 read the newspaper. New media technology is increasingly becoming more than just a simple way to pass the time. In fact, some academics suggest that technology is at the very cultural heart of the current generation of young people. For the new culture, a trip into virtual reality is far more significant than remembering. Technology, such as the internet, mobile phones, PDA's and IPods to name a bare few, provide young people with unlimited access to opportunity. It has revolutionized the way we communicate and interact with each other. Technology generates opportunities, new things to explain, new ways of expression, and new media of communications and creates new forms of destruction.

Young people's access to new technology at home, at school, in the work place even at the local restaurants allows for constant connectivity to the networked world. Youth are plugged into every possible outlet, 100 per cent of the time, partly because they want to be and partly because they need to be competitive and play participatory role in today's world. As youth use the new technologies, they produce the substance of every day and making the meaning of their culture. However, the technical and social convergence brought about us result of developments in technology is already creating interaction problems in particular in the younger users. The implication is that in an arena where the law is largely not applicable, socially agreed upon values and boundaries must be upheld and respected in order for us to make full use of the technology available.

New technology has had an influencing impact within society, affecting the way in which people, largely the young populace, interact, socialize and work. Though since the introduction of new technologies there has been many issues that have arisen by the public and the scholars as to the impact new technology has over youths of society. One of the key issues that have arisen from youth culture and new technology is the growing dependency of such technologies as the internet among the youth of society. Arguments have arisen over the addiction and over reliance some youths have towards new technology especially the internet and the various online communities it provides, particularly online chat and online gaming programs. Among the issues that have been addressed are the adverse impacts of cyberspace addiction and the displacement between reality and virtual reality and its impacts one real world social relationships, health and communication skills. Further more issues have stirred over privacy issues of internet content as well as the unrestricted filtering of information that youths are able to again access to.

New technology has over time branched into the various spheres in society and have been implicated within the educational systems of many nations. The development of technology and the innovation of communication tools have enhanced various learning aspects. Advancements in particular ICT's have improved the standards of vocational education and distance education for youth within various sections of the globe. ICT crept through the side door into education with promises of time saving, efficiency and improvements in learning. Many new technologies can see as a deconstruction of barriers between the physical spaces, as communication technology has enabled users to communicate directly from various sections across the globe. The increase in new technologies has made way for industrial convergence, leading to the deconstruction of local centers of powers, as industries move towards a global market place. This has created several central issues for youths, including the ability to adapt to the emerging technological advancements and the global market place, information can now be obtained from several points and young people must know how to access this information if they are to enter the workplace and communicate effectively. The loss of national identity through youths due to global presence is also another issue raised by academics.

Indian Youth

The period of youth is the most important period of human life. Poets have described it as the spring of life of human being and an important era in the total life span. The proper handling of these stages develops integrated personalities whereas mishandling retards the normal growth. A satisfying completion of each stage enables the individual to deal more successfully with future developmental programs. Youth are supposed to be the most powerful human resources of our country. They constitute a huge magnitude of our population. Again the future world is Indians since India is going to have highest youth population and energetic youth force in the world by 2020. An important segment of the youth population is the adolescents. The adolescents of today are the youths of tomorrow in transition. He is neither treated as a child nor as an adult, he is denied the indulgence accorded to a child or seriousness accorded to an adult. So to understand the young adults or youth, we should know their needs and problems.

Influence of Mass Media

Social gatherings during religious fares, community functions, newspapers, radio, television and internet are important events and elements of the human society which put great impact on persons starting from a primary learner to old and illiterate citizens. Various activities, programmes, reality shows and instructions regarding health and hygiene, discipline etc are some of the components of mass media that influence everybody.

In ancient days there was very little scope for individual to interact with various elements of the environment around him. The effects of seasons particularly summer, spring, winter and rain bring changes in dress, food, sshelther and other lifestyles. More particularly the knowledge about nature of the world, moment of earth, life style of people in different cases, living culture of the people etc. change from time to time. Scientific inventions like radio, television, newspapers etc increase the store house of the individual mind by providing more and more knowledge to the persons concerned. In addition to the general public, the majority of youth in the society are influenced by each of the mass media to a great extent as they are more prone to receive information.

Indian youth from the most dominant ethnic variety of the peer group of the world. They constitute about 34 per cent of the total population of the country. They include a wide spectrum of categories like those in school, out of school, employed, unemployed, married, unmarried, tribal, rural and urban areas. The country can reach untold heights only by harnessing this powerhouse. We need to empower our youth for their better tomorrow. Hence, the foremost way to strengthen our youth is to provide them right kind of education which makes them scientific, logical, open-minded, self-respecting, responsible, honest and patriotic.

Youth psychology and the role of Media

Parenting has often been referred to as life's most difficult job and in recent years it seems as though this job has become increasingly rigorous. Technical development in recent years have given rise to novel opportunities for children and adults to access information. Many of these advancements are aimed specifically at the youth culture. All over the world, the media is extremely influential in shaping the lives of today's youth. Today, given the meteoric rise in the accessibility of new technology, more information is currently available for public consumption than at any other time in history. Children and adolescents are especially impressinable and often creave what Heinz Kohut termed 'Self Objects' in order to help cope with the psychological rigors of youth. This hunger for connection to someone or something that feels bigger than one's self is a normal psychological process. However in tody's media dominated culture, the youth seem especially vulnerable to potentially destructive influences.

A study in 1995 at the University of Maryland Studied the phenomenon of the idealization of celebrities among several cohorts of teen and pre-teen groups including kids ranging from 10-17 years of age. The study produced results indicating that each group evidenced some degree of idolization and modeling behaviour related to the media created celebrities that were included in the study. This psychological phenomenon was termed as 'narcissistic idealism' by Kohut who belived that adolescents engaged in this process in order to compensate for the narcissistic injury of the inevitable failure of one's parents to live up to their child's lofty needs and desires. This widespread infectious nature of the public desire for celebrity seems to be all too acceptable in today's world. Entertainment is a major aspect of the fabric of our culture which was built in the desire to be rich and famous and the need to be entertained. As a culture we devour and consume constant entertainment which seems to be both supplied and created by the media. This hunger for entertainment seems to be most pronounced amongst adolescents who are driven towards the egocentric filling of self object needs.

Thus the media strongly affects youth culture. The media executives are quick to defend their role in youth violence and bullying while selling millions of dollars in ads focused on youth. TV producers, network executives, motion picture companies and others in the media deny any impact of their programs on the attitudes and actions of the youth. Meanwhile they continue to spend millions on special effects and marketing geared to increase appeal to youth markets. While corporations spend millions on market research and advertising to creat products targeted at a youth demographic, the still deny ability to influence youth. If this were true to fact, would NIKE continue to spnd millions every year on product development, marketing and advertising? Would McDonalds still be using cartoon like characters to sell hamburgers? Would music labels be increasing the level of violence and sexual contact in the music geared towards the youth audience? Would liquor companies be using youth oriented activities in their advertising? Of course it works on influencing youth otherwise its ideals advertising would not be a multi billion dollar a year business. If it had no influence MTV wouldon't consultant on spending huge amounts of money to ensure that they are keeping up with the youth culture. Clothing companies are spending millions to get good looking individuals to make plain and boring clothes look appealing to the youth. Youth respond to visual advertising more than other forms. This is due to the fact that the youth want to visualise themselves using the product or service. Even adults are manipulated by these practices.

Positive effects of the Media

Besides the conventional notion that the media that has strayed from its boundaries and is responsible for corrupting the minds of youth, the media still has a host of positive effects on the youth culture. The media has served as a boon to mankind. It has provided us with an exposure to the world outside our cozy homes. It has resulted in an exchange of on a variety of subjects, thereby leading to a global sharing of knowledge. Mass media has given the youth of today, an appropriate platform to voice their opinions on all sorts of social and political issues and share information with one another. The negative influences of media that are the result of an overexposure to it are often talked about. It is true to a certain extent that has affects the society in a negative manner. But, undoubtedly the media has proved as bliss.

A recent psychological research has revealed that the media is responsible for influencing a major part of our daily lives. Media contribute to a transformation in the cultural and social values of the youth. It has a direct impact on the lifestyle of the society because the presuasive nature of the content presented over media influences the thoughts and behaviour of the general public. Media has brought about a major transformation in the way the masses think. It has given them an excellent platform to present themselves before the world and contribute in their own way to the changing world scenario. Thus the media has been responsible in making the world a smaller place to live in.

Mapping Media Effects

The remit of the Byron Review is to address 'the risks to children from the exposure to potentially harmful or inappropriate material on the interest and in video games'. Several general points occur from this. First we need to acknowledge that there might be a range of potential risks here, beyond those that appear most obvious and similarly that harm or what is deemed inappropriate may take many different forms. Secondly, we need to accept that some risks may be unavoidable, and even a valuable part of young people's development. It may be necessary for children to encounter risks if they are to learn ways of dealing with them. Thirdly, we must be recognized that risks and benefits may be difficult to separate and that avoiding risks may also mean avoiding potential benefits. These three issues are considered in turn this media mapping effects.

Defining Negative Effects

Looking across the research literature, one can see that a very wide range of potentially negative effects of media have been identified and disused. These can be including effects relating to:

- Violence including imitation in the form of aggression or antisocial behaviour, desensitization and fear.
- Sexual contents include imitation in the form of promiscuous or unsafe practices, arousal and shock or disgust.
- Advertising in relating to misleading claims as well as consumerist or materialistic attitudes more broadly.
- Inappropriate or unwanted contract with others e.g. in the form of stranger danger or bullying.
- Health i.e., to do with smoking, alcohol and drug-taking.
- Eating behaviour in relation to both obesity and eating disorders
- General personality disorders, such as low self-esteem, identity confusion or alienation.
- Physical effects of excessive use for example RSI type conditions and eyesight problems relating to computers.
- The undermining of children's imagination and free play.
- The physical development of the brain, and disorders such as attention deficit and hyperactivity.
- Sleeping problems and other behavioural difficulties.

- Reduced time for family interaction or relationships with peers.
- Reduced levels of educational achievement or reading more specifically mistaken values, attitudes or benefits for example, in relation to gender or ethnic stereotyping.

This is by no means an exhaustive list and it is worth saying at the outset that some of these claims have been much more systematically investigated in research than others. While some of these effects relating to specific media, other apply more generally and as I have noted many of the same concerns have been carried over from old media into debates around ne media, not always appropriately. The obvious reasons, the amount of research on new media is still quite limited and new media are raising new issues. For example around the targeting children for commercial or sexual exploitation that are very different from those raised by older media. It also important to note that there is quite different types of effects. Some relate to specific areas of media content i.e., sex, violence or advertising, while others seem to be the activity of media use In general i.e., to do with effects on brain development or physical effects. Some relate to what might be called the opportunity costs of media use. That is the notion that media use displaces other, potentially more valuable, activities such as physical exercise, school work or family interaction. Other reflect much broader social concerns or concerns about values e.g., in relation to consumerism or stereotyping. All of these things might be seen as risks to children or indeed as potentially harmful also some of them relate to inappropriate material.

Identity of Youth Culture

Youth has its own identity in every society that disguised it from others. They are not silent spectators of happenings but Endeavour to change events in accordance with their own desires, impulses and aspirations. They watch carefully the cultural contents of society and attempt to interpret them in terms of their impulses and urges. This interpretation leads them to build their own culture and this is precisely what we term as 'Youth Culture'. Generally we accept the age range of 15-35 as youth and perceive themselves as physiologically, psychologically and sociologically different from those who are either younger or older. They are having certain characteristics is as follows:

- Most crucial age between 15 to 35.
- With peak intelligence and stamina.
- Time for achievement and career.
- Period of instability with lack of self-control.
- Parental and peer pressure.
- Misconception due to media exposure.
- Craze for city-life, fashion, style.
- High aspiration for more money with less labour.
- More materialistic than spiritualistic.
- Adult mental and identity development.
- Facing unhealthy cut-throat competition every where.
- Seeking freedom from control of parents.
- Transition from socio-economic dependence to relative independence.
- Entering new world of relationship.
- Emerging sexual feelings and desires.
- Dreams and aspiration of future.
- Curiosity and experimentation due to giant-media.
- Stressful life and living conditions.
- Moving towards westernization and modernization.
- Living with doubts and fears etc.

The total picture of youth culture is not crystal clear and also not obscure. Its consequences are fairly visible through strikes and protest in colleges and universities extremist postures, using unfair means in examination are all about to the culture of protest which has become grained in our youth. The youth of today looks towards the west for their inspiration. They show interest in western music, western fashion and western literature.

But looking at the today's time, we realize that our youth is loosing touch with a sense of right and wrong or good and bad. Perhaps we have failed in our duty of capturing their energy and molding it in the right direction and not helping them in realizing their dreams. Education as a potential and powerful means promote harmonious development of the youth. But the knowledge, information and education received through formal means are not sufficient today for sources like Radio, Television, Newspapers and Computer which contribute for educational development of youth. Those mass-medias are the means through which messages can be communicated to a large section of people and it contribute for their all-round development. During the last three decades, the mass media have undoubtedly played a prodigious role in discovering, debating and supporting the issues related to youth welfare and amelioration.

Impact of Mass Media on Youth Culture

For young people mass media both print and electronic is the most important and powerful medium of instruction, information, education and communication, besides entertainment. With technological revolution in the field of printing and electronics the range of media has grown very rapidly in this generation. Different types of media like the books, newspapers, magazines, films, radio, tapes and television which were familiar to the society of the previous generation, have gone manifold with addition of dozens of cable TV channels, thousands of video and millions of internet sites. In this new incarnation, there has been a new trend in media-media violence.

Culture is what a person cultivates in his living through the process of education and environment given by the society. It is a universal attitude towards life. Culture in literary sense is something ripened and cultivated. Ordinarily, culture implies good conduct, polite behaviour and good taste some consider it a set of social traditions beliefs and customs. Progress in music, dance drama, art, architecture, sculpture etc is considered epitomes of culture. It relates to specific art of living, doing, thinking behaving, talking, using language, readings literature, getting married and the like.

In other words, it refers to the ways of dining, dancing speaking, acting, laughing, behaving, dealing, looking, dressing and decorating, cultivating, growth expansion and development of man from crude life to a graceful and respectable personality is also called culture.

Youth of present day society have no interest in customs, traditions rather they seek to replace it by values derived from other sources like mass media. Hence the youth are changing character, composition and objectives. With the change in role and status of the youth, a change in attitude, values and beliefs is to be admitted and these attitudes generate new forces which will change the social norms. Youth of today have changed their ideas, values and standards which are different from those of older generation. The students of Indian colleges and universities represent their culture and have their significant role to build nation with the changing ideas and value that have brought in modern society.

Due to single family, young children and adolescents have less scope to spend their time with their families. They spend maximum time in watching TV, exploring the internet web sites, using mobiles phones playing video games etc. from these mass media they gain knowledge. But sometimes due to lack of maturity they grasp so many things in an unrealistic manner; which ultimately affect their personality. Due to conflict and frustration young adolescents and youth of today use some mechanisms like negativism, regression, repression, rationalization, fantasy to defend or escape from conflicts and frustration. Sometimes they also commit suicide. Due to mass use of mass media youth are showing less interest to physical activities like outdoor games, social activities, gardening agriculture etc it makes them lethargic and create health problem. Obesity is a common problem found in most of the young adults.

Media strongly affects youth culture. The media executives are quick to defined their role in youth violence and bullying while selling millions of dollars in ads focused on youth. TV producers, network executives, motion picture companies and others in the media deny any impact of their programs on the attitudes and actions of youth. Meanwhile they continue to spend millions on special effects and marketing geared to increase appeal to youth markets. While corporations spend millions on market research and advertising to create products and campaigns targeted at a youth demographic, they still deny their ability to influence youth. If this were true to fact, would NIKE continue spending millions every year on product development, marketing and advertising? Would McDonalds still be using cartoon like charaters to sell hamburgers? Would music lables be increasing the level of violence and sexual content in the music geared towards the youth audience? The liquor companies are using youth oriented activities in their advertising just to influence the youth generation and as profit the companies getting cores of rupees per year. If it had no influence, MTV would not have consultant on staff spending huge amounts of money to ensure keeping up with youth culture. Clothing companies are spending millions to get youth good looking individuals to make plain and boring clothes look appealing to youth. Youth respond to visual advertising more than other forms. This is due to the fact that youth want to visualize themselves using the product or service.

Now without glorifying further the essence of youth like some nostalgic Victorian poet or an old prostitute, I take a direct plunge to the issue of media and the youth. If beauty is instant, intellectuality is slow. Hence, I request my readers an earnest humility to bear my prejudices and endeavourer with a patient and logical conscious. The media has segregated humanity through its representation and stereotyping of characters. Stereotyping the youth has led them to selfish interests with a totally instrumentalist view of achievement. Representation and stereotyping is all due to political, social and economical advantages and discourses of a particular or a personal group. Such stereotypes help the audience in 'effortless gratification' without any self-involvement or debates, the very anti-democratic and capitalistic methodology of communication. Youth, of its inquisitiveness and the mist is moved within the disguises of ideologies. In the advertising world, a fairness cream promises a dark girl a bright career in the airlines. So, is it that Betty lie in complexion? Are the unbeautiful, ugly useless a subject to mere mockery, ridicule and frustration? Is the distribution of wealth and admiring the nature and art only the privilege of the beauty? At least in India, we have the dark idols – Krishna, Draupadi and Ram Whom were worship and lay our faith upon, not of their mere beauty and dark complexion but of their intelligence, self-control and firm ideologies.

The example of another ad, a banking ad (HSBC) shows a boy turning the angle of a telescope pointed at the Saturn to a girl changing her dress and then finally grinning in triumph. The achievement of tuning in to a sensual excitement caused the loss of some new scientific interests. Is this the message of the ad? The carefree action mocked the perseverance one puts in some honest Endeavour. Well, I must pity the media's poor sense of the youth mentality. We are very much concerned regarding the social responsibilities and duties. The unethical representation of the men folk is that they have nothing better to involve in except ideal gossips, cricket fits and girlfriend tensions. We are made to believe that a pimple or an armpit odour, the natural physiological reactions of puberty and job-hunting respectively, can ruin a relationship.

Moving on to the news section and their interpretation of youth. The youth stories are bound within the periphery of sex, crime and Bollywood 'hot newz'. Sensational news captivates our fantasies, giving call to the latent carnal psychological tastes. It is quite a serious issue of how the media includes or excludes views for their political and economical manipulations. Did the news media ever focus on to the pro-reservation OBC's demands and agitations as passionately as the anti-reservation YFE group? The reason being that Arun Shorie, Rajdeep Sardesi, Parnab Roy, Vir Sanghvi and Prabhu Chawla fo not come from the OBC fraternity. Films lead in the rat race of stereotypes. To avoid the shock therapy and a faster box-office turnout, heroes have to be Prince Charming and the girls have to be Cindrellas. Love is monopolized with the bold and the betutiful. Such constructed and fascinated representations are not fair, as they do not portray the reality. Thus, a youth has noting better to do except flirt his girlfriend or ride macho bikes in the streets. A youth cannot have 'jawani' if he cannot dance in the DJ or doesn't sport Jockey underwear. Mardangi in films is all about aggression, howling, bloodshed and Sunny Deol.

Stereotypes in media have limited our range of imagination and the reality. Positive and negative characters are often the result of such unjust representation. Though, they help in cultivating some general views, the media also need to show the responsible youth. Let not the media range our thoughts with their capitalist models stereotypes gulfs social ties. Media must socialize people into beliefs, roles and behaviours. Let every youth live his life fully, give form to every feeling, expression to every thought, and reality to every dream and not get under the influence of the creeping images of stereotypes. Surely, we shall erase out the maladies of confusion and live out our individualities to its fullest potential, pride and liberty.

In order that the youth may grow up in a conducive atmosphere, a lot of preparation and care has to be taken by the government to see that they are guided properly and grow up in a good setting so that they can become better citizens tomorrow. Thus, the government has a definite role to play in this process. The youth are to be brought up well and they have to be provided with every facility available within their means for a healthy and proper growth. The educational system provided to them has a responsibility to see that they groomed well and are well prepared to meet the challenges that may be posed to them in tomorrow's world.

The Government has evolved a National Youth Policy. Its main objectives are to instill in the youth respect for the principles and values enshrined in our constitution, to promote among them an awareness of our historical and cultural heritage, to help develop in them the qualities of discipline, self-reliance, justice and fair play and to provide the youth with maximum access to education in addition to developing their personality. It also aims at making the youth conscious of international issues and involving them in promoting world peace and just international economic order. The Government has set up the Rajiv Gandhi National institute of Youth Development. Its objectives are training, documentation, research and evaluation and extension work for all youth related activities in the country. It also functions as a research agency and think-tank for youth programmes, policies and implementation strategies, to develop multi-faceted programmes for youth, function as an institute for advanced studies in the field of youth, function as a Centre for documentation, information and publication pertaining to youth development and work as a Resource Centre.

The media has a positive role to play in molding children and youth. This role is not given or authorized by anyone but the media is vested with this role by itself. Media moulds the character of citizens by providing information, education and entertainment to them. Media also acts as the forum for public discussion and debate thus providing an opportunity for citizens to express their ideas and vent their feelings. When it comes to youth, media provides to them not only information but also educates them on various aspects of the society pertaining to their higher studies, moral and spiritual growth and entertainment needs among others.

With the increasing involvement of private sector in the media, particularly the electronic media, which has tremendous influencing power, both positive and negative, the media has to play with restraint and foresight so as to channelize the youth and develop in them the spirit of national pride, respect for India's cultural heritage and responsibility for environmental issues besides social cohesiveness and empowerment of the deprived section of population. In a highly commercial competitive atmosphere, government has to evolve minimum regulatory regime to ward off undesirable elements trying to exploit the passions of youth and the impressionable minds of the children.

Electronic Media

Now-a-days electronic media has emerged as a popular and potential means of social interaction and propagation. The birth of electronic media took place with invention of Radio followed by television. The last century witnessed the tremendous strides made in the electronic technology. The simple telephone of long ago has been joined to sophisticated television sets, computers, stereo music, mobile phones and internet. Channels are sprouting up; FM Radio is coming into its own. The internet is showing signs of a revival. Mobile is emerging, newspapers are proliferating, digital developments in media and telecommunications receive the greatest attention and time is the mixed-media-age.

Radio and Television

The Radio and the Television are two very effective channels through which the masses could be reached. Through the television come all types of news, talk-shows, documentaries and the ubiquitous advertisement, clips. Large number of people is reached daily in this way; people with extraordinary talents, new ideals and dreams are exposed and propagated by the television. The modern life style has been changed due to the extensive use of this mode of communication. But today, violence, crimes, murders, turmoil on television and films also do a lot of harm on the young viewers. Guns, knives, bombs and other type of killing tools were increasingly displayed. The youth of today accepted a hero or heroine as his icon of life. They dress like a movie star, color their hair, drive like them and living a life of unrestrained imitation of what they see on television. It is harmful when they are carried out to extremes that they lose touch with themselves and so live in a fantasy world, reality has little to do with such shows. The educational values of some programmes are unquestionable. Most of the programmes gave us a better perspective of the world we live in the dangers, our heritage and the responsibilities we have etc the various channels keep the youth vigilant and updated. It keeps the inquisitive mind busy and satisfies every intellectual query of a probing mind.

Youth of today with a FM radio in ear and spending hours together before the so-called, idiot-box and become victims of the little 'devil'. Their bodies duffer from physical and mental laziness. No one wants to engage in other more creative activities like conversing, reading or simply sharing together. On the whole, the usefulness of TV as a source of entertainment and recreation is undoubted. But the danger lies in the possibility of addictions to TV. So the use of TV with care will be a boon for youth along with TV. There are other means of electronic media like cinema, internet, which are fast growing and are extremely popular day-by-day.

Films and Advertisements

Enjoying a movie is the most popular means of entertainment for a youth. They watch cinema not only as a means of entertainment but also as an escape from the monotony boredom, anxiety and troubles of life. For them it is a restful, pleasurable and entertaining means of rewarding and relaxing after a long days work. As the most effective means of mass communication cinema has been educative value and it is a very effective reformative instrument. Films on issues like dowry, women education, female feticide, youth unrest, corruption, unemployment, poverty, illiteracy can create social awareness among the youth. But the youth of today are mostly interested on the commercial film than the art films. Film is a great unifying force for the youth. They should not only enjoy the music, dancing but also the script, direction also. Unfortunately, films of today has distracted the youth from the right direction. The culture of crime, violence, murder, terrorism is reflected so powerfully thought this media; the youth face difficulty to keep him aloof from this. They are forgetting to realize the sensible and relevant themes of the films. The average song of the commercial films is replete with vulgar thrusts. Women are depicted through physical attributes on excruciating close up.

Films need not be didactic but they still can pass on constructive messages subtly to the masses. The silver screen spreads and sells not just dreams but captivates the hearts of young boys and girls. Hence, this medium should be used judiciously and wisely and can show right direction to our youth. Used with pure sensibility, this media can help in bringing about positive changes in the youth minds. At present advertisements stare and scream at us from every street corner, every newspaper, every magazine, every hoarding, every stall or shop or showrooms to walls of every public building, vehicle, radio, TV and internet. It has invaded every aspect of our day to day life dealing our conversations, our thoughts, behaviours etc. One has to rely upon advertisements from education to career building, from buying soap to a mobile. Particularly the youth are more biased by those advertisements. They feel that as if nothing can be achieved without advertisements. Advertisements have touched all the aspects of modern complexities and have complicated man's life more. People became more confused than finding any solution to their problems. The ad-medias are playing and encash upon the psychology of youth in order to achieve their ends. It is being seen, these day's advertisements are capturing the minds of youth and then create a whole new tantalizing world of fantasy, glamour and unreality among them. Psychologically, they became confused, restless, dependent etc.

Print-Media

Along with electronic media, the role of print-media has been augmenting day by day. There has been a world-wide growth and circulation of the print-media around the world through the emergence of electronic media and the internet. As a vigilant watching, it has created awareness among the people. They can update themselves just by going through the newspaper, getting news from every corner of the world. All magazines and newspapers have special columns for youth. The youth of today going through the current events can intelligently participate in the political, social and economic affaires of the country. Print-media provides great incentive to every section of people by advertisements on sale, shops, electronic goods, matrimonial, job opportunities etc. On the other side people associated with robberies, thefts, murders, rapes, drugs, alcoholism, terrorism activities are exposed through this media. Sometimes, young people are biased by that news either positively or negatively. People involved in wrong or unethical business know the power and potential of print-media and suppressed themselves.

Many times, the newspapers, books, journals cater to the transient needs of life and appeal to the emotions of masses. Particularly, the youth are easily motivated by communal propaganda and inclined to particular ideology. Their aspiration for earning more money in less time sometimes put them in loss and it becomes extremely disastrous for the society. Hence, an impartial print-media is the need of the hour and it should try to broaden the outlook of present young masses by generating interest and awareness through constructive ideas.

Cell Phones

With high levels of mobile telephone, penetration a mobile culture has evolved. It is very common that every adult own a mobile phone in his pocket. It has become a fashion object with users decorating, customizing and adding different accessories to their mobile phones to reflect their personality. In stead of necessary now it has become a prestige and status symbol especially for young boys and girls. This has given rise to an increase in criminal and unethical activities so that they can get extra money to satisfy this growing need to snob. The youth mass are using it in prohibited places like libraries, schools, colleges, examination halls, assemblies. More over recent research and scientific evidences support that there is a high health risk for its users. Such mobile phones have mostly connected with road accidents. Specifically it is found that people lose their control of the vehicles while talking on the mobile telephones simultaneously while driving. Mobile has been major distracters on roads and is proving to be as harmful as driving under the influence of alcohol. It is also alleged that during the conversation on a mobile people are ignoring the persons sitting besides them. Users often speak at increased volume in a publication, with little regard for other people nearby. Some how that small screen also depict the erotic and sexual exposure of young boys and girls in negative use. All these informative models have great influential to way-ward youth.

Despite all the abuses of cell phones, one can not deny the uses of mobiles. No doubt, it saves a lot of time, energy and increase one-ton-one relationship. The SMS is also a convenient way to keep in touch with many persons and spending a quick message. But unfortunately it is misused. It is a great source of entertainment for youth. They lisen to songs, play games, get live cricket results etc. Every youth should use it in a proper and beneficent manner. All one has to remember that mobiles are invented for our conveniences not to creat nuisance. If used judiciously, wisely, mobile can be of great use.

Internet

The internet has revolutionized the computer and

communications world like nothing before this internet is at once a worldwide broadcasting capacity, a mechanism and interaction. It has a lot of advantages for the current age. People of all ages, colours, creeds and countries freely share ideas, stories, data, opinions and products. A great deal of information is easily available within a fraction of seconds. In the age of '.com' the internet is a boom for youth providing variety of information on employment, education, research, matrimonial, business, industry etc. It is especially good for students providing a powerful economical way to conduct a real job search. The youth of 21st Century has been governed by cyber-world, syber-space and computer cybernetics. Most of them are miss-utilizing this media for entertainment purpose only. Cyber-crimes, chatting, accessing to web on-line has been made fashion for youth. The cybernetic revolution has changed their lifestyle, made of living etc. For a youth of rural it is still a mirage whereas it acts as a miracle for urban.

Problems of the Youth

- Adjustment in home, school, society and to opposite sex.
- Freedom from home.
- Unemployment or vocational problems.
- Occupational adjustments.
- Financial problems.
- Health adjustment.
- Religious conflicts.
- Conflicts with friends and family members.
- Failures.

The media enacted problems of youth will be there, but their attitudes, values, influences and character to be given due attention. Problem areas like corruption, confrontation, divisiveness, communalism, regionalism and intolerance continue to affect the social life of youth. Due to increasing unemployment, we have been unable to keep our youth busy in constructive works. Unless harnessed and tapped in the right way, this very energetic youth can tip over the other side and become destructive and dangerous for the society. Crime and violence will be his life and living. As an agenda for the new century the media should take up the challenge of depicting real images and preparing the growth for a developed nation. The creative potential coupled with their zeal, enthusiasm, energy and versatility can work wonder for the country. Let us focus on constructively using the youth power for the betterment of the nation. Let us aim at empowering our youth for a better future and a brighter tomorrow where goodness is valued and greatness is respected.

The new media technology is something other than a progressive chain of events. The storm of progress blows so hard as to obscure our vision of what is actually happening. What is hyperbolized as revolutionary train of events can be seen as a far more evolutionary and transforming process. Three decades of societal and cultural alignment of digital machinery yielded a host of innovations, trials, failures and problems, accompanied by hype-hopping popular and academic discourse. Meanwhile new media studies crystallized internationally into an established academic discipline. The new media technologies are changing very frequently. They are changing how news is produced by including story telling process. It has revolutionized the day-to-day work of journalists and they provide new opportunities for the young journalist and information scientists to work more efficiently and more professionally. Media in India has to bear in mind that it has to be socially responsible in order to survive and carry on its course of work naturally. Article 19(1)(a) of the Indian Constitution talks about freedom of expression and speech. This covers the freedom of press too. This theoretically means that the media is free to do anything that pleases it. But it is bound by certain limitations and self-imposed moral obligations.

6

Media Impact on Health

Mass media are inttensively employed in public health. Mass media are tools for the transfer of information, concept and idea to both general and specific audiences. They are important tools in advancing public health goals. Communicating about health through mass media is comples, however, and challenges professionals. One of the key functions of mass media is educating in deverse disciplines. The mass media are capable of facilitating short-term, intermediate-term and long-term effects on audiences.

An issue of great importance of public health today is how to mount programs that change behaviour in order to improve the health of our population. Although theats to the public have come from various domains, health behaviour is a primary concern because of its large contribution to morbidity and premature mortality. Therefore, it is very essential to promote health of the people. Health promotion is the process of enabling people to increase control over, and to improve their health. To reach a complete state of physical, mental and social well being an individual or group must be able to identify and realize aspirations, to satisfy needs, and to change or cope with the environment. Health is therefore, as a resource for every day life, not the objective of living. Health is a positive concept emphasizing personal and social resources as well as physical capacities.

Health promotion is just the responsibility of the health sector, but goes beyond healthy life style to well being. Health promotion activities are strongly linked with the social context, among others with the mass media, who is a powerful companion in health promotion actions. Media is widely used as a tool for health promotion. Beside explicit health communication there is also plenty of implicit health information in the media, message which unintentionally and unconsciously are related to health. Talking about heaalth promotion, i.e., health promotion discourse in the media is influenced by cultural determinants, such as societal values, norms and beliefs.

The aim of mass media in health field is to promote health and well being among individuals, communities and populations, enabling them to address the broad determinants of health in order to reduce the vulnerability and risks to ill health, disability throughout the life cycle, especially among poor and marginalized groups and promote human rights, bring social advancement through the use of creative media.

The appropriateness of mass media as a vehicle for health promotion or as generators of health insight is subject to debate. Since the 1970s it has gained increasing popularity as a strategy for delivering preventive health messages. Mass media programs appear to have a number of advantages over traditional public health strategies. On the other hand, the public health community has long been concerned about the mass media as a source of problems. Various types of advertising and the portrayal of health compromising behaviours and products in the media have been identified as promoting disease rather than health. The potential influence of movies, advertising media and television programming has been considered in regard to alcohol, tobacco, violence, nutritional behaviour, sexual behaviour, traffic safety and various other public health threats.

The advantages of mass media programs include the ability to reach a large propotion of the population. Although it is important to bear in mind that a health promotion 'exhibition' will probably only draw in people who are interested, the people who are motivated and most probably not the people who are aware of any need for health promotion. Perhaps more to the points mass media interventions are relatively inexpensive method of exposing the population to health information. The mass media can make use of 'visually potent images' to invent a hard-hitting and powerful message which is more often than not available to other avenues. However, the role of the media in initiating widespread and long-lasting behaviour change may be overrated. The constant mass media support constitute a valuable help in educating people to properly improve their behaviour health problems.

With television programs and even cable channel designed and marketed specifically for babies, whether kids under two years of age should be watched becomes an important question. While we are learning more all the time about early brain development, we do not have a clear idea how television may affect it. Some studies link early TV viewing with later attention problems, such as ADHD. However, some other the exports disagree with these results. One study found that TV viewing before age three slightly hurt several measures of later cognitive development, but that between ages three and five it slightly helped reading scores.

The earlier years are crucial in a development. The Academy is concerned about the impact of television programming intended for children younger than age two and how it could affect your child's development. Pediatricians strongly oppose targeted programming especially when it used to market toys, games, dolls, unhealthy food and other products to toddlers. Any positive effect of television on infrants and toddlers is still open to question, but the benefits of parent-child interactions are proven. Under age two talking singing, reading, listening to music or playing are for more important to a child's development than any TV show. In addition, TV can discourage and replace reding. Reading requires much more thinking than television and we know that reading fosters young people healthy brain development. Kids from families that have TV on a lot spend less time reading and being read to and are less likely to be read.

Literally thousands of studies since 1950s have asked whether there is a link between exposure to media violence and violent behaviour. All but 18 have answered, 'yes'. The evidence from the research is overwhelming. Extensive research evidence indicates that media violence can contribute to aggressive behaviour, be sensitization to violence, nightmares and fear harmed. Watching violence shows is also linked with having less empathy toward others.

Violence in the media, psychogists help protect children from harmful effects. Decades of psychological research confirms that media violence can increase aggression. Desensitizing effects of violence media on helping others this study by a University of Michigan researcher demonstrates that watching violent media can affect willingness to help others in need. Congressional public health summit a statement of the American Academy of Pediatrics, America. Academy of Children & Adolescent Psychiatry, American Psychological Association, American Medical Association, American Academy of Family Physicians, American Psychiatric Association.

Children can come to view the world as a mean and scary place when they take violence and other discribing them on TV to be accurate in real life.

- Symptoms of being frightened or upset by TV stories can include bad dreams, anxious feelings, being afraid of being alone, withdrawing from friends and missing school.
- Fears caused by TV can cause sleep problems in children.
- Scary-looking things like grotesque monsters espicially frighten children aged two to seven. Telling them that the images are not real does not help because kids under age eitht cannot always tell the difference between fantasy and reality.
- Many children exposed to scary movies regret that they watch because of intensity of their fright reactions.
- Children ages 8-12 years who view violence are frightened that they may be a victim of voilence or a natural disaster.
- Violence threats shown on TV can cause school-aged kids to feel fright and worry. When the threat is shown as news it create stronger fears than when it is shown as fictional.

Watching the Televison impact on Performance in School

- TV viewing may replace activities that we know help with school performance, such as reading, doing homework, pursuing hobbies and getting enough sleep.
- One research study founded that TV's effects on educational

achievement at age of 16. Watching more TV in childhood increased chances of dropping out of school and decreased chances of getting a college degree, even after controlling for confounding factors.

- Watching TV at age four was one factor found to be associated with bullying in grade school.

TV can affect Children Health

TV is a public health issue in several different ways. First of all, kids get lots of information about health from TV, much of it from ads. Ads do not generally give true or balanced information about healthy lifestyles and food choices. The majority of children who watch health-related commercials believe what the ads say. Second, watching lots of television can lead to childhood obesity and overweight. Finally, TV can promote risky behaviour, such as trying dangerous stunts, substance use and abuse and irresponsible sexual behaviour.

Watch more TV are more likely to be overweight

- University of Michigan researchers found that just being awake and in the room with the TV on more than two hours a day was a risk factor for being overweight at ages three and four-and a half.
- The effects can carry on into adult wight problems. Weekend TV viewing in early childhood affects body mass index or overweight in adulthood.
- University of Michigan researchers and their colleagues who investigated whether diet, physical activity, sedentary behaviour or television viewing predicted body mass index among 3 to 7 years old children, found that physical activity and TV viewing are most associated with overweight risk. TV was a bigger factor than diet. Inactivity and TV became stronger predictors as the children aged.
- Children who watch TV are more likely to be inactive and tend to snack while watching TV.

- Many TV ads encourage unhealthy eating habits. Two-third of the 20,000 TV ads an average child sees each year are for food and most are high-sugar foods. After school TV ads taget children with ads for unhealthy foods and beverages, like fast food and sugary drinks.
- All television shows, even educational non-commercial shows, replace physical activity in your children's life.
- While watching TV, the metabolic rate seems to go even lower than during rest this means that a person would burn fewer calories while watching TV than when just sitting quietly, doing nothing.
- The food and beverage industry targets children with their television marketing, which may include commercials, product placement and character licensing. Most of the products pushed on kids are high in total calories, sugars, salt and fat and low in nutrients.
- Children watching Spanish-language TV after school and in the evening see lots of ads for food and drink. Much of it targets kids and most of the ads are for unhealty foods like sugared drinks and fast food. This advertising may play a role in the high risk of overweight among kids.
- Results from recent studies have reported success in reducing excess weight gain in preadolescents by restricting TV viewing.

Watching TV can cause sleep problems

- Television visin is associated with altered sleep patterns and sleep disorders among children and adolescents.
- Regular sleep schedules are an important part of healthy sleep. A recent study found that infants and toddlers who watch TV have more irregular sleep schedules. More research is needed to find out whether the TV viewing is the cause.
- Those sleep disturbances may persist. Teens who watched three or more hours of TV per day had higher risk of sleep problems by early adulthood.

Attempt to mimic stunts

- Injuries are the leading cause of death in children and watching unsafe behaviour on TV may increase children's risk-taking behaviour.
- Kids have been injured trying to repeat dangerous stunts they have seen on television shows.
- Many kids watch TV sporting news events. Researcher surveyed TV sports event ads to assess what kids might be seeing. Almost half of all commercial breaks during sporting events containing at least on ad that showed unsafe behaviour or violence.

TV viewing may promote alcohol use

- The presence of alcohal on TV runs the gamut from drinking or talking about drinking on prim-time shows, to beer ads, to logos displayed at sporting events.
- Many studies have shown that alcohol drinks are the most common beverage portrayed on TV and that they are almost never shown in a negative light.
- Alcohol has damaging effects on young people's developing brains and the damage can be permanent. TV ads are a major factor in normalising alcohol use in the minds of children, adolescents and college students.
- Ads for alcohol portray people as being happier, sexier and more successful when they drink. Alcohol advertising including TV ads, contrinutes to an increase in drinking among youth.
- Television ads for alcohol such as alcopop which combine that sweet taste of soda pop in a liquor branded malt beverage may target youth especially girls and hispanic and African American kids.
- The center on alcohol marketing and youth at Georgetown University found that in 2003 the top 15 prime time programs most popular with teens all had alcohol ads.
- Alcohol is increasingly advertised during programs that young people are more likely to watch than people of legal drinking age.

Even though tobacco ads are banned on TV, young people still see people smoking on programs and movies shown on television. The tobacco industry uses product placement in films. Smoking in movies increased throughout the 1990s. Internal tobacco industry documents show that the tobacco industry purposefully markets their product to youth. The industry uses subtle strategies like logos at sporting events, product placement and celebrities smoking to get around the ban on TV advertising for their products. Kids who watch more TV start smoking at an earlier age. The relationship between television viewing and age of starting smoking was stronger than that of peer smoking parental smoking and gender. Now the Center for Media Literacy believes in empowerment through education that kids need to learn how to think critically about TV and other media. Media Awareness Network is a Canadian group with a wealth of information for parents. The Center for Screentime Awareness sponsors National TV turn-off week each year. Future TV turn-off weeks are spring and fall: 19-25th April 2010 and September 19-25, 2010. TV turn-off week is supported by over 70 national organisations including the American Medical Association, American Acamdey of Pediatrics, National Education Association and President's Council on Physical Fitness and Sports.

7

Role of Electronic Media

The role of the electronic media in India is promoting the formation of democratic regimes. With the dramatic expansion of various forms of electronic interchange, including electronic mail and the internet opportunities for communication across national boundaries and cross fertilization of ideas are greater than ever before. An attempt here that access to electronic information can have positive impact in promoting democracy by providing civil society with greater leverage vis-à-vis the state and political elites and pros and consequences of electronic media (other than internet, because discussed separate).

The general belief holds that representative government is the form of democracy that is feasible in today's sprawling, heterogeneous nation-sates. However, interactive telecommunications now make it possible for tens of millions of widely dispersed citizens to receive the information they need to carry out the business of government themselves, gain admission to the political realm and retrieve at least some of the power over their own lives and goods that many believe their elected leaders are squandering.

Since the earliest conceptualization and discussion of the political, communication has held an equally prominent position both in terms of its necessary for political ideas to be transmitted and replicated and as a tool by which political actors seek to ensures the predominance of their ideas through improved methods of communication. In the polls, as conceived by Aristotle, direct communication among and between all the political actors in the system was an attainable ideal. The growth of large and more geographically diverse states necessitated the development of alternative modes of interaction as societies moved from direct political interaction to representative political action. Those chosen to represent the interests of others in the political system have historically used a variety of methods to obtain information about their constituents' preferences, including physically touring their districts periodically, reading letters from constituents and polling their constituents about key issues. All these methods can be time consuming and costly to employ, limiting the frequency with which they can be used and by extension the quality of information which can be regularly obtained. However, the changing nature of communication ushered in by the drawing of the age of electronic communications and the concomitant decline in the costs of communication on a global scale has profound implications for political interaction among representatives and their constituents and for economic and political development throughout the world. In this chapter focuses explicitly on the impact these changes have on communication and potentially on the formation and maintenance of democratic system in India.

Media Scenario

As India concluded its celebration of 63 years of independence this year, having initiated a process of economic reform in the early part of the decade, the forces of privatization and globalization have unleashed dramatic changes in the country's media. Admidst a deluge of film-based entertainment, news and current affairs provided by private channels. All India radio and Doordarshan once the country's officially anointed public service broadcasters have become undecided incarnations of their former selves. This time the history of Indian media is critical: it's overwhelming in the quick and dramatic changes over the last few years and frustrating in the current impasse thanks to the imbroglio over the newly instituted Broadcasting Authority of India.

For those in the business of renting eyeballs, the delinking of radio and television from direct state control has given endless joy. But media analysts and NGOs have varied responses. Some of the deregulation of broadcast media is potentially aiding the emergence of community radio and other forms of more democratic, participatory communication. Others despair that Indian audiences have been, to borrow a phrase, amused to death. They observe that market imperatives have already forced the once state-owned AIR and Doordarshan to abdicate their responsibilities, ringing the death knell on the state's role in public service broadcasting. The role has been one of mixed successes. Over the last four decades, the state's forays into development communication, the ruling communication paradigm at that time, have been significant. But then the successes of Satellite Instructional Television Experiment or the Kheda Communications Project are offset by the phenomenal failures of other projects such as PREAL and in the long run, undermined by the vacillating fortunes and commitments of rapidly-changing governments.

Today vastly changed media scenario calls for a recasting of the role of media in promoting pro-social change. This paper discusses the prevailing media tends in India in a historical context, highlights the issues being debated and describes the responses of NGOs and development agencies to the changes and the new opportunities they present. An underlying premise is the need for some of the key stakeholders for social change communication-donor agencies and NGOs to strengthen the linkages between the discourse on media trends and their own investments in communication, whether to promote child rights, HIV/AIDS education, sign fly, women's empowerment or the environment.

BROADCAST MEDIA

Radio

The number of radio stations has increased from 100 in 1990 to 209 in 1997 and the land area covered from 84 per cent to 91 per cent in addition to it many FM radio are established from 2004 to 2009 to cover the maximum area. However, despite its tremendous reach and the fact that it presents the best option for low-cost programming, radio has been treated as a poor relative for over two decades. Listenership has either dropped or reached a plateau. In some cases listenership has raised, although very negligible, in some urban area allotment to private companies on five FM stations. Film and other popular music constitute the main fare of such stations, contributing to an increase in commercial time and revenues from Rs. 527 million in 1991-92 to Rs. 809 million in 1995-96.

Some efforts have been made to use radio for social change, as in the case of the state-support radio rural forums for agricultural communication in the 1960s to promote adult literacy in 1980s. More recently NGOs have helped broadcast programmes on women and legal rights, emergency contraception and tele-serials advocating girls education. But it is clearly a medium waiting for a short-in the arm. A key need in India is for local broadcasting that reflects issues of concern to the community. In this regard, some communication experts believe that an increased and accelerated commercialization of radio will eventually drive down the costs of FM radio sets, thus facilitating local radio. The increasing devolution of political power initiated through the 73rd and 74th amendment to the constitution in 1988-89 has also set a climate conductive for the empowerment of communities and local governance. A key area requiring attention is advocacy for community radio and the provision of training to NGOs and communities to use this medium for articulating their concerns as one Bangalore-based NGO is currently doing.

Television

The number of private television channels has increased from none in 1990 to more than 80 channels in these recent years. Entertainment constitutes about 51 per cent of the total programme content, even though some channels such as Star Plus follow CNN's example in delivering news on the hour, every hour. Certain channels are established exclusively 24 hours news. Some other channels 24 hours for comedy as well as 24 hours songs and other entertainment channels also established.

However, in a bid to give themselves a halo of social responsibility, some channels broadcast programmes with a veneer of public interest, soap that incorporate socially relevant themes such as women's education and empowerment, interactive talk shows on whether smoking should be banned and open forums with government representatives responding to audience queries.

on human rights abuses or consumer rights. These programmes combine varying degrees of social value with commercial appeal in a competitive market. The open forums, in particular have played an important role in familiarizing the public to the political and legal system and in building a demand for political transparency and accountability.

Another genre, that of the edutainment pro-social soap continues with serials such as Tara with dealt with the life of a strong-willed woman. However, while the first Indian edutainment soap Hum Log (1985) transfixed much of the nation the audiences for subsequent edutainment serials have been comparatively smaller. There is no longer the captive audience of the mid-80s and there are several competing channels and soaps to choose from. These include reruns of long running teleserials of the late 1980s such as Ramayana and the Mahabharata which enjoy cult-like status. An emerging trend and one that also reflects the current programme focus of development agencies is the targeting of specific segments of the audience in particular young adults. Urban middle to upper class youth especially, constitutes a key target group for private channels. Music channels such as MTV and V channel which rank among the top ten favourite channels are popular role models for a young generation.

Cashing in this trend, UNAIDS, India initiated in 1996 collaboration with V channel for an on-air and on-ground campaign for HIV/AIDS. In another effort, the Ford Foundation, India funded BBC training for radio and television producers on reproductive and sexual health. The six project proposals shortlisted for additional funding, all of which target children and youth are in entertainment formats of musicals talk shows and animation.

The usefulness of TV as a source of entertainment, recreation and knowledge is undoubted. But the danger lies in possibility of addiction of our youth to it. In this context Josephson reported that the adolescents those who continue to believe in the reality of TV and to identify with its violent heroes are the ones likely to be more aggressive than their counterparts. Hence the use of TV with proper care can be of immense beneficial for our youth.

Encouraging adolescents and youth to express their opinion and to analyze and question TV contents is a parental strategy that can be adopted to reduce adolescents fear and aggressiveness as well as to improve their critical approach to the medium. One highly influential action parents can take for toddlers in this direction is to examine and regulate their own viewing behaviour since toddlers highly influenced by their parents viewing habits.

It would be a long debate to get into the positivity and negativity of the women characters. Almost all serials are women-documented, and if one leaves the family drama and moves to the more modern soaps, there have been some great one, that have taken up bold themes, uncommon themes and worked on them. Soaps like 'Astitva-Ek Prem Kahani' dealing with a young man falling in love with a much older woman or 'Jassi Jaisi Koi Nahin' where a common ordinary looking girl makes it to the top on basis of her merit, have been some milestones in influencing the youth. 'Jassi Jaisi Koi Nahin' has inspired common looking girls, with no glamour to back them, to stand for themselves and crate their own niche in society definitely a very positive play of psychological interpretation of the human mind.

The fact remain that much ever critics cry themselves hoarse over the portrayal of women and the one sided views presented. The serials will go on. A dedicated audience sits glued to the sets and in order to reward this, star channel (India) came up with the 'Star Parivaar Awards' where viewers are given a choice to create their own family choice, so much of that there was a best 'Star Atithi', who shared the limelight with the hallowed star cast. The awards bring forward the view that soaps are not just limited to the women who stay at home, but also women who are working and who unwind with their daily boost of late night serials. Serials in India, claim to have pulse of their viewers, Balaji Telefilms mainstay Ekta Kapoor is of the idea that her serials are the essence of Indian sense and sensibility and her characters and plots are normal people and normal incidents. Again there is no getting into a debate over this since the majority of viewers swear over the characters and their actions. One thing is for sure, it can be an eyesore for some can hate it, there may be historical debates over them, but soaps are here to stay. They have found their way and embedded themselves into the mindset of millions across the country. If nothing binds to strangers, discussions on soap have brought forth the most animated response. Style statements are being set, progressive or regressive attitudes are being set, and emotions are running wild as characters drip tears or acid. The ball has started rolling.

Research has associated exposure to media violence with a variety of physical and mental health problems for children and adolescents including aggressive behaviour desensitization to violence, fear, depression, nightmares and sleep disturbances. More than 3500 research studies have examined the association between media violence and violent behaviour. But out of which 18 have shown a positive relationship. Consistent and strong association between media exposure and increases in aggression have been found in population-based epidemiologic investigation of violence in American society cross-cultural studies experimental and natural laboratory research and longitudinal studies that show that aggressive behaviour associated with media exposure persists for decades. The strength of the correlation between media violence and aggressive behaviour found on meta-analysis is greater that of calcium intake and bone mass, lead ingestion and lower IQ, condom nonuse and sexually acquired human immunodeficiency virus infection or environmental tobacco smoke and lung cancer association's clinicians accept and on which preventive medicine is based without question.

Parent blaming their young children for excessive and unsuitable TV viewing is a very common syndrome all over the world but at the same time, children appear to be most unhappy about this. Our parents keep on saying, read, read... all the time. They want us to do nothing but study. They don't let us watch TV. We do need some entertainment also. 'Without it studies become dull and uninteresting' said one boy. 'Whenever I watch some programme my mother tells me to go and study. She thinks that I am wasting my time. But while I am reading she may call me to help her in her household work without bothering about my studies. A girl pointed out that 'When I am watching TV she will again tell me to study'. The parents say you will spoiled, if you watch MTV, another boy butted in. These answers are among the few, posted by young boys and girls in the response to a question: Is TV an Idiot Boxes? However, there are always two sides of a coin. If TV has made any bad impact that is due to our misunderstanding of potential of the medium with decide: TV is an Idiot Box or an Intelligent Box?

The concept of youth culture and new technology is relatively new term, however the rate at which technology has moved into the lives of the young is historically unprecedented. Young people today can now communicate to other youths around the world as well as access information from the internet via their mobile phone. At today's historical juncture, media culture has arguably become the most dominant force defining the sense of self, driving our understanding of the 'other and providing symbols, myths and resources' for generating a common culture. Youth culture is poorly understood by the mass media including television and in many cases the lack of connection can lead to disengagement in the educational sector. Media (il)literacy is important for many reasons and a light-hearted treatment of the effect of the mass media in the educational sector can lead to undesirable outcomes. Teacher-educators must use the mass media including Television in their teaching to stimulate reflection and engagement on the part of present and future teachers. We must address various issues pertaining to the use Television by the youth of this generation who has already started listening to radio and the sound television from his/her mother's womb.

Children are influenced by media they learn by observation, imitating and making behaviours their own. Aggressive attitudes and behaviours are learned by imitating observation models. Research has shown that the strongest single correlate with violent behaviour is previous exposure to violence. Because children younger than eight years cannot discriminate between fantasy and reality they are uniquely vulnerable to learning and adopting as reality the circumstances, attitudes and behaviours portrayed by entertainment media. It is not violence itself but the context in which it is portrayed that can make the difference between learning about violence and learning to be violent. Serious explorations of violence in plays like Macbeth and films like saving Private Ryan treat violence as what it is a human behaviour that cause suffering, loss and sadness to victims and perpetrators. In this context, viewers learn the danger and harm of violence by vicariously experiencing its outcomes. Unfortunately, most entertainment violence is used for immediate visceral thrills without portraying any human cost. Sophisticated special effects, with increasingly graphic depictions of mayhem, make virtual violence more believable and appealing. Studies show that the more realistically violence is portrayed, the greater the likelihood that it will be tolerated and learned. Titillating violence in sexual contexts and comic violence are particularly dangerous because they associate positive feelings with hurting others.

In addition to modeling violent behaviour, entertainment media inflate the prevalence of violence in the world, cultivating in viewers the mean world syndrome, a perception of the world as a dangerous place. Fear of being the victim of violence is a strong motivation for some young people to carry a weapon, to be more aggressive to 'get them before they get me'. For some children exposure to media violence leads to anxiety, depression and posttraumatic stress disorder or to sleep disturbances and nightmares. Some defend media violence as an outlet for vicariously releasing hostility in the safety of virtual reality. However, research testing this catharsis hypothesis found that after experiencing media violence, children displayed increased overt aggression because of lowered inhibitions. Numerous studies have shown that the most insidious and potent effect of media violence is to desensitize all of us to real life violence.

Interactive media, such as video games and the internet are so new that there has been little time to assess their influence on children's physical and mental health. Early studies of these rapidly growing and ever more sophisticated types of media indicate that the effects of child-initiated virtual violence may be even more profound than those of passive media, such as television. Experimental studies have shown that after playing video games, young people exhibit measurable decreases in pro-social and helping behaviours and increases in aggressive thoughts and violent retaliation to provocation. Playing violent games has been found to account for a 13 per cent to 22 per cent increase in adolescents' violent behaviour, by comparison, smoking tobacco accounts for 14 per cent of the increase in lung cancer.

Children learn by observing and trying out behavioural scripts. Repeated exposure to violent behavioural scripts can lead to increased feelings of hostility, expectations that others will behave aggressively, desensitization to the pain of others and increased likelihood of interacting and responding to others with violence. Active participation increases effective learning, video games are an ideal environment in which to learn violence. They place the player in the role of the aggressor and reward him or her for successful violent behaviour. Rather than observing part of a violent interaction, video games allow the player to rehearse an entire behavioural script, from provocation to choosing to respond violently to resolution of the conflict. Moreover, video games have been found to be addictive, children and adolescents want to play them for long periods of time to improve their scores and advance to higher levels. Repetition increases their effect. Interpersonal violence, as victim or as perpetrator is now a more prevalent health risk than infections disease, cancer or congenital disorders for children adolescents and young adults.

Recommendations

Given the current scenario and the needs of the development, the following recommendations can be made:

- Develop a regulatory framework that defines public service broadcasting to include not only state-owned media but all non-commercial broadcasting. This would empower non-profit institutions such as universities, community organizations, local bodies and NGOs to participate in development communication. This was suggested in a privately drafted, more holistic, alternative to the current Broadcasting Bill, the Prasar Sewa Bill, which was drawn up by a group of communication and media experts. This draft bill suggests that there should be three streams of broadcasting public service broadcasting funded by the state, market-driven satellite broadcasting including cable, terrestrial and satellite services and community service broadcasting by autonomous citizens groups, universities, trusts and NGOs to make more programmes reflecting local realities. However, the draft bill has not been taken into consideration.

- Media education and literacy to create demand for better need based media stories and programmes.
- Decentralization and provision of training for communities to enable local broadcasting and community media. Putting communication resources in the hands of the community is a sine qua non for participatory communication.
- Sensitization and training of media professionals from print, radio and television in social development issues.
- Strengthening linkages between media trends and communication investments of development organizations.

In the absence of a concerted effort by media analysts, NGOs, Donor agencies and the public to support need-based, socially relevant media, the current waves of, and I borrow a phrase here; the LPG mantra will drown the impulse for a media with a conscience. The oft-cited cliché then of the dichotomy between India and Bharat between the cyber-savvy India elite and the monsoon dependents farmer, will unfortunately ring true.

8

Role of Print Media

Mail is the most democratic form distributions of information. It does not discriminate based on income level, demographics status, geographic position or technology use. It provides something tangible convenient, colourful and occasionally persuasive. Print is a medium that must be physically delivered form the originator to consumer in other words, printing in the age of the web and beyond. From its invention 550 years age, though a renaissance and a reformation, though the industrial and information ages, though competitors such as radio, cinema, television, and even computer networks, paper-based communication has dominated our society and our culture. Print is not one thing – it is many different products and each one has different dynamics in relation to distribution methods.

Print media can be a highly effective tool in marketing your business. Using various types of print media, you can build awareness about your business. Print media, such as articles can build your professional credibility and credit worthy of your business e.g., if you are the author of an article about a topic that is related to your industry, the position you will as expert in your field. When a reader of that print publication reads it, it help to form an opinion on your standing in your industry. 45.23 per cent of the printed products are distributed by mail. Major categories are including periodicals, catalogues, direct mail and transaction materials, whereas 26.15 per cent of print products are distributed through retail locations. Majority of this category are periodicals, books, packaged products and greetings cards. 22.38 per cent of all print is distributed by other methods, such as home delivery and direct-to-business private services and 6.20 per cent of the print products are distributed through non-store newsstands, primarily newspapers, periodicals and some books.

Over the last two decades most of the benefits of print media productivity have been passed back to the print buyer. Commercial printers are selling full-colour print at prices below those for the same product twenty years ago. This has been the result of automated presses, computer-to-plate, and on-or-off-press and advanced digital workflows. Over that same period, even with significant investments in automation, postal costs have increased. Print is a bargain and its record of relentless cost reduction mitigates some of these increases.

Based on the above information, the print media is very close to the public and the people are in a position to afford to utilization of those services. The circulation of the print media by day by day increase even thought there is increasing in the electronic media. The print and electronic media are the direct competitors or supplementary? For convey the news point of view those are the competitors, but for circulation point of view there is no relationship. Suppose even though a common man is having a television and the person who have television, also purchasing the newspaper regularly, so both of them also supplementary.

Given national literacy rate is very low, limited reach of newspapers and magazines and the distinctly urban educated readership profile, the role of print media has been defined more in terms of information dissemination and advocacy. The picture is a lopsided: circulation figures are rapidly increasing advertising revenue, but this is especially true of English publications, which account for 71 per cent of the total and revenue of members of the Indian Newspaper Society. A key feature of these publications, unfortunately, is increasing preponderance of glossy, ad friendly films and TV based reporting. That the sole trendsetter in this increasing corporation of the fourth estate, the Times of India, also ranks 10th among the top selling newspapers in the world, is no coincidence. Given the increasing costs of newsprint production and the pressure of market imperatives, newspaper houses have followed the piper in carrying ad friendly fluff at the cost of more serious development and health reporting. Leading dailies have over the last few years dropped their special sections devoted to development and health. The low literacy rate and production costs have also stymied the possibilities of smaller alternative publications that could potentially reflect the concerns of the development sector.

A newspaper is a regular scheduled publication containing news, information and advertising. By 2008 there were 6580 daily newspapers in the world, selling 395 million copies a day. The worldwide recession of 20008, combined with the rapid growth of web-based alternatives, caused a serious decline in advertising and circulation as many papers closed or sharply cut back operations. General-interest newspapers typically publish stories on local and national political events and personalities, crime, business, entertainment, society and sports. Most traditional papers also feature an editorial page containing editorials written by an editor and columns that express the individual opinions of writers. Other facial appearance includes display and classified advertising, comics and inserts from local merchants.

Print media is anything that is offline that promotes your business. The most common types of print media include newspapers, magazines, newsletters, brochures, pamphlets, advertisements, billboards and signs. Print media is any vehicle that is tangible and can spread the word about your business by gaining the attention of your target audience. The newspaper is typically funded by paid subscriptions and advertising. A wide variety of material has been published in newspapers including editorial opinions, criticism, persuasion and obituaries, entertainment features such as crosswords, Sudoku and horoscopes, weather news, advice, food, education news, job opportunities and other columns, reviews of movies, plays and restaurants, classified ads, display ads, editorial cartoons and comic strips.

Print media in marketing can present itself in several different formats. Two of the more population forms of print media include newspapers and magazines. Essentially, through print media is any type of tangible printed material that contains information of some sort about your business. Print media provides tangible information about your business that a prospect can walk away with items in print help to add credibility to you and your business and seeing your business name in print provides affirmation to existing customers that their decision to be business with you is the right one. For prospects, print media provides your business with a way to communicate with them and get in front of them in an effort to win their business.

History of Print Media

Before invention of newspapers in the early 17th century, official government bulletins were circulated at times in some centralized empires. In ancient Rome, Acta Diurna or government bulletins were made public by Julius Caesar. They were carved in metal or stone and posted in public places. In China, early government prepared news sheets called tipao circulated among count officials during the late Han dynasty i.e., second and third centuries AD. Between 713 and 734, the Kaiyuan Za Bao (Bulletin of the Court) of the Chinese Tang Dynasty published government news, it was handwritten on silk and read by government officials. In 1582 these was the first reference to privately published newssheets in Beijing during late Ming Dynasty.

In early modern Europe was increased cross-border interaction created a rising need for information, which was met by concise handwritten news sheets. In 1556, the government of Venice first published the monthly Notizie scritte, which cost one gazetta. These avvisi were handwritten newsletters and used to convey political, military and economic news quickly and efficiently to Italian cities (1500-1700) sharing some characteristics of news papers though usually not considered true newspapers. However, none of these publications fully met classical criteria for proper newspapers as they were typically not intended for the general public and restricted to a certain range of topics.

The emergence of the new media branch in the 17th century has to be seen in close connection with the spread of the printing press from publishing press derives it name. The German language Relation aller Furnemmen and gendenckwurdigen Historien printed from 1605 onwards by Johann Carolus in Strasbourg is often recognized as the first newspaper. At that time, Strasbourg was a free imperial city in the Holy Roman Empire of the German Nation, the first newspaper of modern Germany was the Avisa, published in 1609 in Wolfenbuttel. Other earlier papers includes: the Dutch Courante Uyt Italien, Duytslandt & Company of 1618 was first to appear in folio-rather than quarto-sie. Amsterdam a center of world trade quickly became home to newspapers in many languages, often before they were published in their own country.

The first English-language newspaper Corrant out of Italy, Germany etc, was published in Amsterdam in 1960. A year and a half later, Corante weekly news from Italy, Germany, Hungary, Poland, Bohemia, France and the Low Country's was published in England by a Nathaniel Butter and Thomas Archer. The first newspaper in France was published in 1631, La Gazette. The first newspaper in Portugal, A Gazeta was published in 1654 in Lisbon. The first Spanish newspaper Gaceta de Madrid was published in 1661.

Post-och Inrikes Tidningar was first published in Sweden in 1645 and is the oldest newspaper still in existence though it now publishes solely online. Opregte Haarlemsche Courant from Haarlem was first published in 1656 is the oldest paper still printed. It was forced to merge with the newspaper Haarlems Dagblad in 1942 when Germany occupied the Netherlands. Since 1942 the Haarlems Dagblad when Germany occupied the Netherlands. Since then the Haarlems Dagblad appears with the subtitle Oprechte Haerlemse Courant 1656 and considers itself to be the oldest newspaper still publishing. Merkuriusz Polski Ordynaryjny was published in Krakow, Poland in 1661. The first successful English daily 'The Daily Courant' was published from 1702 to 1735.

1960 in Boston, Benjamin Harris published Publick Occurrences both Foreign and Domestic. This is considered the first newspaper in the American colonies even though only one edition was published before the paper was suppressed by the government. In 1704 the governor allowed the Boston News Letter to be published and it becomes the first continuously published newspaper in the colonies. Soon after, weekly paper publishing in

New York an Philadelphia began. These early newspapers followed by the British format and were contain four pages. The most news carried from Britain and content depended on the editor's interests. In 1783, the Pennsylvania Evening Post became the first American daily. John Bushell published the Halifax Gazette in 1751 was the first Canadian newspaper.

By the early 19th century many cities in Europe, as well as North and South America published newspaper-type publications through not all them developed in the same way, content was vastly shaped by regional and cultural preferences Advances in printing technology related to the Industrial Revolution enable newspapers to become an even more widely circulated means of communication. The Times acquired a printing press in 1814 capable of making 1,100 impressions per minute. Soon, it was adapted to print on both sides of a page at a time. This innovation made newspapers cheaper and thus available to a large part of the population. In 1830, the first penny press newspaper came into the market Lynde M. Walter's Boston Transcript. Penny press papers cot about one sixth price of the other newspapers and appealed to a wider audience. In France, Emile de Girardin started La Presse in 1836 introducing cheap advertising supported dailies to France. In 1848 August ang an Austrian who knew Girardin in Paris returned to Vienna to introduce the same methods with Die Presse.

Impact of Television and Internet

By the late 1990s the availability of news via television channels 24-hours and the internet posed an ongoing challenge to the business model of most newspapers in developed countries. Paid circulation has declined, while advertising revenue – which makes up the bulk of most newspapers income has been shifting from print media to new media, resulting in a general decline in profits. Many newspapers are around the launched online editions in an attempt to follow or stay ahead of their audience.

However, in the rest of the world, cheaper printing and distribution increased literacy, the growing middle class and other factors have more than compensated for the emergence of electronic media and newspapers continue to grow. On April 10, 1995 the American Reporter became the first daily newspaper, with its own paid reporters around the world and all-original content to start on the internet. The Editor-in-chief and founder is Joe Shea. The site is owned by 400 journalists.

Newspaper Categories

While most newspapers are aimed at a broad spectrum of readers, usually geographically defined some focus on groups of readers defined more by their interests than their location e.g., there are daily and weekly business newspapers and sports newspapers. Moreover specialist still are some weekly newspapers usually free and distributed within limited areas, these may serve communities as specific as certain settler populations or the local community.

Daily

A daily newspaper is issued every day, sometimes with the exception of Sundays and some national holidays. Saturday and Sunday editions of daily newspapers tend to be larger include more specialized sections and advertising inserts and cost more. Typically the majority of these newspapers staff work Monday to Friday so the Sunday and Monday editions largely depend on content done in advance or content that is syndicated. Most daily newspapers are published in the morning. Afternoon or evening papers are aimed more at commuters and office workers.

Weekly

The weekly newspapers are common and tend to be smaller than daily papers. In some cases, there are also newspapers that are published twice or three times a week. In the United States, such newspapers are generally still classified as weeklies.

National

Most of the nations have at least one newspaper that circulates throughout the country. A national newspaper was contrasted with a local newspaper serving a city or region. In the United Kingdom there are numerous national newspapers including the Independent, the Times, The Daily Telegraph, the Guardian, the Observer, the

Daily Mail, the Sun, the Daily Mirror and the Daily Express. In the United States and Canada, there are few national newspapers. Almost every market has one or two newspapers that dominate the area. Certain newspapers, notably The New York Times, the Wall Street Journal and USA Today in the US and the Globe and Mail and the National Post in Canada are available throughout the country. In India newspapers like the Times of India, the Hindu and the Hindustan Times are extremely popular and have large reader bases. Large metropolitan newspapers have also expanded distribution networks and with effort can be found outside their normal area.

International

There is also a small group of newspapers which may be characterized as International newspapers such as the International Herald Tribune have always had that focus, while others are repackaged national newspapers or international editions of national scale or large metropolitan newspapers. Often these international editions are scaled down to remove articles that might not interest the wider range of readers. As English became the international language of business and technology, many newspapers formerly published only in non-English languages have also developed English-language editions. In places as varied as Jerusalem and Mumbai newspapers are printed to a local and international English-speaking public. The advent of the internet has also allowed the non-English newspapers to put out a scaled down English version to give their newspaper a global outreach.

Online

Virtually all printed newspapers have online editions, which depending on the country may be regulated by journalism organizations such as the Press Complaints Commission in the UK. But as some publishers find their print-based models increasingly unsustainable, web-based newspapers have also started to appear such as the Southport Reporter in the UK and the Seattle Post-Intelligencer, which stopped publishing in print after 149 years in March 2009 and went online only.

Customized

A new trend in newspaper publishing is the introduction of individualization through on demand printing technology. Customized newspapers allow the reader to create their individual newspaper through the selection of individual pages from multiple publications. This 'best of' approach allows reviving the print-based model and opens up a new distribution channel to increase coverage beneath the usual boundaries of distribution.

Organization and personnel

In USA, the overall manager or chief executive of the newspaper is publisher in small newspapers, the owner of the publication is usually the publisher. Although he or she rarely or perhaps never writes stories, the publisher is legally responsible for the contents of the entire newspaper and also runs the business, including hiring editors, reporters and other staff members. This title is less common outside the US. The equivalent position in the film industry and television news shows is the executive producer.

Most newspapers have four main departments devoted to publishing the newspaper itself editorial, production/printing, circulation and advertising although they are frequently referred to by a variety of other names as well as non-newspaper specific departments also found in other businesses of comparable size, such as accounting, marketing, human resources and information technology. The English speaking world, the person who selects the content for the newspaper is usually referred to as the editor. Variations on this title such as editor-in-chief, executive editor and so on are common. For small newspapers, a single editor may be responsible for all content areas. At large newspapers, the most senior editor is overall in-charge of the publication, while next senior editors many focus on one subject area, such as local news or sports, these divisions are called news bureaus or desks and each is supervised by a designated editor.

Newspaper editors' copy edits the stories for their part of the newspaper, but they may share their workload with proofreaders and fact-checkers. Reporters are journalists, who primarily report facts that they have gathered. Reporters writing longer, less news-oriented articles may be called feature writers. Photographers and graphic artists provide images and illustrations to support articles. Journalists often specialize in a subject area called a beat, such as sport, religion or science. Columnists are journalists who write regular articles recounting their personal opinions and experiences.

Printers and press operators physically print the newspaper. Printing is outsourced by many newspapers, partly because of the cost of an offset web press and also a small newspapers' print run might be require less than an hour of operation, means if newspaper had its own press it would sit idle most of the time. If the newspaper offers information online, web masters and web designers may be employed to upload stories to the newspapers website. The staff of the circulation department communicates with retailers who sell the newspapers, subscriptions and supervise distribution of the printed newspapers through the mail by newspaper carriers, at retailers and through vending machines. Free newspapers do not sell subscriptions, but they still have a circulation department responsible for distributing the newspapers. Sales staff in the advertising department not only sells space to clients but also help advertisers design and plan their advertising campaigns. Other members of the advertising department may include graphic designers, who design ads according to the customers' specifications and the departments' policies. In an advertising free newspaper, there is no advertising department.

Zonal and other Editions

Newspapers often refine distribution of ads through zoning edition. Zoning occurs when advertising and editorial content change to replicate the location to which the product is delivered. The editorial content often may change merely to reflect alter in advertising – the quality and layout of which affects the space available for editorial or may contain region-specific news. In rare case, the advertising may not change from one zone to another, but there will be diverse region-specific editorial content. As the content can vary widely, zoned editions are often produced in parallel.

Editioning occurs in the main sections as news is updated throughout the night. The advertising is usually the same in each edition. Each edition represents the latest news available for the next press run, these editions are produced linearly, with one completed edition being copied and updated for the next edition. The previous edition is always copied to maintain a Newspaper of Record and to fall back on if a quick correction is needed for the press e.g., both the New York Times and Wall Street Journal offer a regional edition, printed through a local contractor and featuring local specific content. The journals' global advertising rate card provides a good example of editioning.

Newspaper circulation and readership

The number of copies distributed on an average day or on particular days is called the newspapers' circulation and is one of the principle factor used to set advertising rates. Circulation is not necessarily the same as copies sold, since some copies or newspapers are distributed without cost. Readership figure may be higher than circulation figures because many copies are read by more than one person, although this is offset by the number of copies distributed but not read.

According to the Guinness Book of World Records, the daily circulation of the Soviet newspaper 'Trud' exceeded 21,500,000 in 1990, while the Soviet weekly Argumenty I Fakty boasted the circulation of 33,500,000 in 1991. According to the United Nations information in 1995 Japan has three daily papers the Yomiuri Shimbun, Asahi Shimbun and Mainichi Shimbun with circulation was more than 5.5 million. Germany's Bild with a circulation of 3.8 million was the only other paper in that category. In the United Kingdom the Sun is the top seller, with around 3.24 copies distributed daily.

In India the Times of India is the largest circulation English newspaper with 3.14 million copies daily. According to 2009 Indian readership survey, the Dainik Jagran is the most read, local language (Hindi) newspaper with 55.70 million readers. In the US the Wall Street Journal has a circulation of approximately 2.01 million, making it the most widely distributed paper in the country. American newspaper was vending machine featuring news of the 1984 Summer Olympics.

A common measure of a newspaper's health is market penetration, expressed as a percentage of households that receive a copy of the newspaper against the total number of households in the paper's market area. In the 1920s on a national basis in the US daily newspapers achieved market penetration of 123 per cent. As other media began to compete with newspapers and printing became easier and less expensive giving rise to a greater diversity of publications, market penetration began to decline. It wasn't until the early 1970s. However the market penetration vaulted in below 100 per cent by 2000, it was 53 per cent.

Many paid-for newspapers offer a variety of subscription plans e.g, someone might want only a Sunday paper or perhaps only Sunday and Saturday may be only a work week subscription or perhaps a daily subscription. Most of the newspapers provide some or all of their content on the internet, either at no cost or for a fee. In some cases free access is available only for a matter of days or weeks after which readers must register and provide personal data. In other cases, free archives are provided.

Advertisement

Newspaper typically generates 70-80 per cent of its revenue from advertising and the remaining from sales and subscription. The major portion of the newspaper income is advertising is called editorial content, editorial matter or simply editorial, although the last term is also used to refer specifically to those articles in which the newspaper and its guest writers express their opinions. Newspapers have been hurt by the decline of many traditional advertisers. Department stores and supermarkets could be relied upon in the past to buy pages of newspaper advertisements, but due to industry consolidation are much less likely to do so now. Additionally, newspapers seeing traditional advertisers shift to new platforms. The classified category is shifting tc sites including craigslist, employment websites and auto sites.

National advertisers are shifting to many types of digital content including websites, rich media platforms and mobile. In recent years, the advertorial emerged. Advertorials are most commonly recognized as an opposite-editorial which third parties pay the fee. Advertorials commonly advertise new products or techniques such as a new design for golf equipment a new form of laser surgery or weight loss drugs. The tone is usually closer to that of a press release than of an objective news story.

Print vs. Online

Newspapers, since the dawn of internet have to contend with online media. These did not bring about the demise of printed newspapers. Reading newspaper print has a lower impact on global warming than reading online according to one of the world's leading papermakers. Reading a newspaper has a lower impact on global warming than reading the news online for 30 minutes. According to Torraspapel's paper the alternative to climate report change.

Role of Media in Modern Society

There are many different ways in which people communicate i.e., through phone, through personal encounters and by attending work place, school, seminars etc. Through media is not only communication medium used to dispense the flow of information, it also importance in developments of countries is worth mentioning as main source to inform people on political issues or current affairs as well as source of entertainment. The flow of information from one geographical location to another has increased in speed considerably with the advent in digitally enabled communication devices. Different network channels over cable or satellite TV, newspapers and radio channels are emerging at rapid pace providing the people with a medium to connect themselves with the outside world. Print media has always been a dominant medium throughout the decades in the western civilization, but it is the emergence of the television which has become the backbone of the global commercial development. Television contains the ability to produce multimedia content and thus has the immense power to change an individual's perception of reality. It is not a wonder that in order to believe in something, one has to have complete faith in the source of information. This source of information could be ranging from one person to any academic institution. However in today's connected society it is the media, which has become the main source of information. The role of media is playing a main source of information is a controversial issue. It is being debated what are the media functions in a society and what are its impact on individual. The term media is a general term is not restrict to a particular entity but in order to understand the term commercial media, the US provides the best platform for critically analyzing the role of media in a society. Regardless of what type of sources of media are analyzed from newspapers to network channels.

Media and our Society

Throughout the year it has been a proven fact that media has a lasting effect on our society. The rising question through, is how is this media affecting our society? It is affecting us in good ways, bad ways or both? There's no question that media has changed over the years and there more media now then ever before. The biggest hope of all is how people think media influences and changes what a person does or thinks. The people who say this may be right, but in certain extent. With that I have found the three major sources of media today are: the news, advertising and music.

For most American families used to be normal to go home and turn on the news to find out what's going on out there in the big world, but lately that doesn't seem to be the case. If I asked you to name fifteen positive things that you can remember seeing on the news this past six months, do you think could? My best bet would be no. The news stations know what draws people's attention in most, and in human nature, that's negativity. Sure, there are positive things that are shown too, but very few. Society has found that the news is no longer enjoyable to watch and find they turning the channel before done. Why is this though? Is the news becoming too much for people to handle? In complaint, some would even go as far as saying that events portrayed on the news leads to more of those same crimes being repeated later on. Is this all in theory, or the truth? Many studies over the past few decades have reported that viewing this violence encourages aggressive behaviour and teaches violent resolution to conflicts. Although I think that the point of news was supposed to be just the opposite. In this day and age, what the news may not fully understand is that it sells what it sells what it shows. But if you look back to when television news was first aired you will realize that it was started to inform the world, not sell.

Social Responsibility of the Press Media

1. *Educate the public:* People can explore at firsthand but a tiny fraction of the world of which he is a part. To know and understand the world, man must depend largely on the printed word. Not only can the press furnish man with the information he needs to formulate his own ideas but it can also stimulate him by offering him the ideas of others. For centuries, the press has been regarded as an important carrier of information and ideas. Running through John Milton's Areopagitica of 1644 is the the them that a free press is indispensable in the quest for truth. As Milton put it, where there is much desire to learn, there of necessity will be much arguing much writing, many opinions, for opinion in good men is but knowledge in the making. Although Thomas Jefferson wrote no unified work on the press, his scatttered wrings time and again touch upon the importance of a free press to public enlightenment. In a letter to M. Coray in 1823, he remarked: 'the Press is the best instrument for enlightening the mind of man and improving him as a rational, normal and social being.
2. *Help to the political system:* Closely allied with the public enlightenment function of the press is the second function of servicing the political system. The nature of democratic government imposes a heavy responsibility on the press, which is granted a privileged position under the constitution. As Carl Becker once remarked, 'Democratic government rests on the assumption that the people are capable of governing themselves better than any one or a few can do it for them. If the citizens are to rule themselves wisely, they must be aware of the issues and problems at stake and must have access to views and

information on which to base sound decisions. Therefore, the press must serve as an engine of democracy, as a transmission belt between the people and their elected representatives. The very success of government may depend in large measure on the extent to which the press services the political system and the extent to which the people make wise use of the press.

3. *Profitable manner*: The traditional concept of media is freedom provide cogent justification to a fourth function of the press – making profitable manner through proper use of its freedom. The theory holds that that only a free press operating under a system of private enterprise, can fulfil the tasks of enlightening the public servicing the political system and safeguarding personal liberties. The syllogism behind that assumption runs somewhat as follows: only a free press can serve the cause of truth. A press beholden to the government or to any special interest group cannot be free, because it will inevitably be subjected to environmental and financial pressures. Therefore, to be free to present news and views without fear of favour, the press must be a self sufficient business enterprise. Carried a step further, this line of reasoning has been used to justify large communications enterprises. The argument is that a large prosperous medium is better able to withstand pressures than a small, marginal one. The entry of the government into the communications field, according to traditional theory, is bad. For one thing, governmental media would no doubt be more interesting in perpetuating the party in power than in truth. For another thing, a subsidised governmental press would threaten the economic sufficiency of a private enterprise press. With no need to show a profit, such a press would have an unfair economic advantage over the regular commercial press.

4. *Assist the economic system*: Related to the profit-making function is a fifth task of the press, one which emerged with the development of modern advertising, that of servicing the economic system. Long before advertising assumed the importance it has today, the press fulfilled this task to some extent. In Colonial America, newpapers filled their columns

with information about commerce and shipping, material important to an economy in which foreign trade and commerce continued to flourish, even after the penny press of the 1830s made its pitch for the masses with human-interest copy. But it was the rise of a compiled system of mass production and mass distribution that the contribution of the press to the national economy became of major importance. Today a task of the press is to bring together through advertising, the buyers and sellers of goods and services. In performing that seemingly simple task, the press according to some scholars has helped to promote a dynamic, expanding economy.

5. *Providing entertainment*: almost from the time that Caxton introduced printing to England, the press has devoted a part of its output to entertainment. However moralizing may have been their tone, the broadside ballads which flourished in Britain for more than three centuries,were intended less for edification than for amusement. Other offerings pamphlcts and books were also intended to amuse the reader. Early newspapers in England and America were primarily informational, but they too can human-interest copy from time to time. As the press tapped mass audiences, there seems to have been an increase in the proportion of material frankly designed to afford amusement, entertainment or escape. Today, serving up entertainment seems to be one of the main functions of the press.

6. *Evaluating the services of the press*: Historicaly, some of them are of longer standing than others. Public enlightenment is one of the oldest functions, servicing the economic system is a relatively recent addition. As has been shown, some of the functions are inherent in the theory of political freedom. The responsibilities of the press for enlightening the public, for servicing the political system and for safeguarding personal liberties are intimately identified with the Anglo-American concept of freedom of the pree. At least one of the functions, however, is not inherent in the theory. The role of the press in servicing the economic system was recognised only after the development of modern advertising.

7. *Problem involved in publishing*: What hinders the press in carrying out its functions? There are many things. There are limitations imposed by the communication process itself – by way in which we send and receive spoken and written messages. There are limitations imposed by the nature of the media. But two major problems concentration of ownership of the media and the commercial basis of the press system.
8. *Concentration of ownership of the press*: The concentration of ownership of the press which has resulted from among other things, technological advances and the demands by readers for improved service has alarmed many observes. In the daily newspapers field, the number of papers has gone steadily downward as circulations have steadily mounted. As the number of dailies has diminished, more and more cities have been left without competing newspapers. Nixon has throughly documented this situation.

9

Role of Internet

Despite the negative effects of the internet, intelligent use of it provides a verity of information relating to business, education, examination results, employment, matrimonial, research etc. It is particularly very much useful for students, teachers and researchers as an economic way of collecting desired information in course of preparing reports and conducting researches. Again it provides facilities for e-mailing. The youth should therefore, take the advantage of positive use of this modern medium. It is pertinent here to state that while recommending to build a knowledge network interconnecting our knowledge institutions and infrastructure with access speeds of 100Mbps and more with a view to give a major push to collaborations and sharing needed to enhance the quality of our education, research and applications and at the same time to empower our people to be competitive in global economy the National Knowledge Commission (2007) rightly stressed the utility of internet in this knowledge era.

The internet has provided an ideal solution by presenting many articles in multiple languages and permitting the viewer to select the language of his choice. It also elimination of printing and postage costs makes publishing such electronic journals far more economically practical. Another advantage of the internet is the simplicity of making corrections, additions and updates to an article when necessary, a virtual impossibility with conventional printed journals. In addition, with such increased international cooperation, a multi disciplinary panel of experts could eventually be established to serve as a peer review broad for future papers submitted for publication.

The internet is a massive network of computers from around the world all connected by cable and satellite. When users are connected to the internet they can receive text, images, video and sound on their computer from computers anywhere in the world. Just as there is a book or magazine on nearly every subject in local libraries, bookshops or newsagents, so is there information on virtually every subject on the internet. The internet is also called the world wide wed. With the use of internet, it is possible to receive/ transmit information containing images, graphics sound and videos. ISP industry can offer services as:

- Linking consumers and businesses via internet.
- Monitoring/maintaining customer's web sites.
- Network management/systems integration.
- Backbone access services for other ISP's.
- Managing online purchase and payment systems.

The internet is designed to be indefinitely extendible and the reliability of internet primarily depends on the quality of the service providers' equipments. The limitation of the internet is security and privacy and threats are hackers, viruses etc whereas the benefits of internet are:

- Doing fast business.
- Trying out new ideas.
- Gathering opinions.
- Allowing the business to appear alongside other established businesses.
- Improving the standards of customer service/support resource.
- Supporting managerial functions.

There are several characteristics of the internet that may be seen to increase its potential for harmful to children. These would includes: the easy access for users, abundance of material available, its ubiquity and affordability, interactivity of the medium and the potential for individual users to share material, degree of anonymity that users can enjoy and the lack of gate-keepers or authorities that might restrict access. However, these are also the characteristics that are often seen as crucial to the benefits of the medium in terms of facilitating learning, communication, civic participation etc.

Several of the concern that arise in relation to the internet have been carried over from older media and strength be seen to affect in other everyday contexts, although the internet does provide framework in which people may say and do things that they would not face-to-face.

We need to be wary of overstatement it is clear there are some new dangers here for children as well as indeed for adults also. In particular, while giving out personal information is necessary for a whole range of commercial and non-commercial transactions. It also places the individual at risk in generally unprecedented ways. There is a growing body of research on children's and young people use of the internet. Here again, it is potential to identify different research ethnicity, although the situation is by no means as polarized as it is in the case of games. Mainstream communications research has generally avoided the experimental approaches employed in relation to games, tending instead to use large-scale questionnaire surveys to map patterns in access and use.

Given the rapid change of technological and cultural change such studies often have a fairly limited self-life and need to be frequently updated. Further, a great deal of this work is essentially expressive e.g., when it comes to potentially harmful or offensive material, we do know a fair amount at least from self-report data-about whether children is likely to have encountered such material and in very broad terms how they feel about it. However, we know relatively little from this research about how they interpret this material and almost nothing about its effects. Differently, researchers in media and cultural studies have tended to rely on smaller-scale qualitative research. The focus here has been on how families or specific groups of children interact online and make sense of what they encounter. The questions here focus on issues such as identity construction, peer culture and play and on the social or domestic contexts in which the internet is used. While these issues might be considered in terms of effects: is peer group online interaction more positive than offline? How does the internet affect the quality of family life?

The researchers tend to avoid addressing such issues in this way. Again, the emphasis is on taking a holistic view rather than thinking in terms of cause and effect, it is argued that we need to situate children's uses of the internet within a broader social and cultural context in which multiple factors are in play. This approach tends to emphasize children's agency and autonomy and at the same time can come close to celebratory account. Even the two approaches have identified and there is no means of mutually exclusive and some of the best research in the field manages to combine them.

Over the past three years, in cooperation with the collegamento pro-Sindone a number of articles previously available only in one language have been translated into multiple languages and reprinted on the respective websites. In addition, though the efforts of the Cento Espanola do Sindonologia, a Spanish language website has been online for over a year. Non-received articles have also been reprinted for the benefit of researchers and the lay public alike. The Scientific papers and Articles page of the website already includes many of these. One of the greatest challengers to modern shroud research is finding and accessing previously published work. Even with access to a sophisticated research library, many references are very hard to find. Through the cooperation of all of the world's largest shroud collections, a massive bibliography of books and articles has been compiled and is found on the Shroud Booklist page of the shroud of Turin website and the scientific articles page of the collegamento pro-Sindone website. Finally, easily accessible centrally locted bibliographies are available to everyone.

Along these lines, even when a reference is determined, it is often impossible to find the actual paper or journal, many important references are out of print and more than twenty years old. Over the last three years, rights have been obtained to reprint a number of these on the website and more are being added constantly. This will be continued and in time, the network of shroud websites will become the central repositories and primary resources of shroud data for sindonologists worldwide. These often take the form of responses to articles and personal correspondence between individual researchers. The website has already been host to a number of such debates though the good graces of all the participants who have made their materials available for publication. This feature will be expanded and grow to provide a true open international forum for continued discussion that allows other interested parties to enter the debate.

Conferences such as this one have also benefited from using the internet. I regularly checked the Richmond Center website for the up-to-date schedule of the speakers planned for this event and to see the amount of available seating that remained and of course, the final papers presented here will eventually be published on the internet to supplement the production of a written acts or printed proceedings. Already in place on the shroud of Turin website is the 'research registry page' where many researchers have already advertised for material they needed. These have included blood and linen samples, rare books or articles and access to special facilities. In some cases, organizations or individuals with resources to offer for shroud research have posted them on the site to make them available to those who might need them.

With the continued worldwide interest in the shroud, many researchers are often called upon by lay and professional groups to make presentations and give lectures. An international shroud Speakers Directory has recently been added to the website. This provides organizations looking for such speakers a central source of qualified experts to select from. Listings include biographies, topics and geographic availability of each speaker. Another useful function of the website is the gathering of statistical information and data. Some researchers have designed a questionnaire that website viewers fill out and send in. The researchers will receive the information via e-mail and can integrate the responses directly into their analysis.

The increased use of the internet for research by students and scientists necessitated the development of a standardized notation for citing references taken from the web. This has been researched and a number of suggested formats are now included on key pages of the website. Also the growth in other, specialized shroud websites, particularly those geared towards students has provided added resources for the next generation of shroud researchers. The efficient manner of reprinting technical scientific papers was needed that kept the resident symbols, scientific notation, graphs, charts, illustrations and photographs intact over the last three years. New technologies for viewing images on the internet are rapidly becoming available and several are destined to become standards. These are being carefully tracked to determine their future value for website viewers. One such format, live picture, allows viewers to zoom in and out or pan across large, high resolution images using a plug-in to their internet browser software. We hope to add this powerful feature soon and allow viewers to examine the subtlest details of the shroud of Turin at their leisure. Finally, a search capability will be added in the near future that will allow website viewers to enter key words and quickly search through the entire website to find information specific to their needs. This will be particularly useful as the quantity of materials on the site increases.

Recent developments in communication technology have provided us with powerful new tools for instant global communications. With the advent of these new technologies, the obstacles to creating an international shroud center have been eliminated and the center is already open for business. But in this case, the center resides in cyberspace rather than in a physical location and instead of a single website, the center is actually a growing network of shroud related websites around the world, linked together and cooperating to create an exciting and fertile environment for sharing shroud information and presenting ideas from every point of view. The role of the internet in shroud research is no longer a thing of the future. It is today's reality.

Unwanted contact

It leads to a further are of risk, which is that of unwanted contract. The main focus of concern here is on so-called stranger danger i.e., the possibility of threatening contract from unknown adults, particularly pedophiles. Such apprehension about the internet needs to be situated in the broader context of growing apprehension about risks to children offline. Parents' fears of the likelihood of their children being abducted and abused by unknown strangers have risen significantly in recent years, perhaps partly swollen by the high-profile reporting of rare but nevertheless disturbing cases. While the actual incidence of attacks and abductions has not significantly increased, parents are now much more keen to confine their children to the home and to provide them with media and technology that will make the child's bedroom a more smart alternative to the evident dangers of the outside world. Paradoxically in doing they have created the possibility that stranger danger will now be imported into the obvious safety of the family home.

The past study reports that many children have contract online with people whom they do not know, although there has been little research looking in any details at the nature of such contact or at how children respond. Of course, it is possibility of such online contract may be a very positive thing, e.g., it allows children to discuss concerns that cannot be shared with people offline or if it brings them into contract with others from very different cultural backgrounds. In certain cases, online contracts lead to face-to-face meetings, although most of this contract is with people of a similar age and it would be quite wrong to imply that much of it is any more dangerous than contracts that young people might make in any other setting. Of course, it would be negative to deny that the internet has provided pedophiles with new opportunities for contract with children and these risks may have increased with the advent of mobile platforms.

The present all Medias, changes in technology go hand to hand with changes in social use. Only a few years ago, anxiety about online encounters with strangers focused on children's use of chartrooms. Recent research suggested that chartroom use is declining, while use of instant messaging is widespread and suggesting that children prefer to communicate with friends rather than strangers. At the same time, new opportunities to meet strangers online have appeared, such as via online games, though these encounters are less likely to lead to actual meetings and more likely to be confined to the context of play in a fictional world.

Some researchers suggested that the teaching through online is risky. That means the children's are less likely to become victims. However, other researchers suggested that the majority of children are already very well aware of potential risks here and yet this does not tend to prevent them from making such contracts. This would suggest that some young people may actively seek out risk in this context e.g., various forms of flirting and this may be particularly the case for children who are less satisfied with their offline lives. At the same time, there is also a danger that the figure of the predatory pedophile has become a kind of contemporary bogeyman and such warnings are somehow seen as irrelevant to children's own lives. As this implies, there is a need for education about such risks that goes well beyond one dimensional warning of the just say no variety and as we shall see in the following section notions of risk and privacy are becoming increasingly complex in the online environment.

Another different kind of unwanted contract is that of bullying. Again, there is evidence that a significant number of children have experienced online bullying. The internet clearly permits bullying to occur more secretly and yet to be distributed more widely e.g., through the copying and forwarding of images. However, the fact remains that many more children are bullied offline than online and there is no evidence that the internet has led to an increase in bullying to distressing it may be. How online bullying might support offline bullying and the new combinations of techniques that might emerge remain an issue for further research.

Online Violence

There is a little doubt that the internet has made it significantly easier to distribute material that provokes violence of various kinds. Such material would comprise hate sites as well as material that appear to support or celebrate forms of self-harm. Surveys suggest that a significant minority of children have been seen such material and while they generally few of them is dislike. Particularly it can find disturbing. There is again relatively detailed evidence about how children interpret such material and even less about its potential effects. In case of hate sites, much of the research has tended to focus on the analysis of content. Violence among individuals might not otherwise be disposed to accept it. Some have argued that such sites may be relatively ineffective as recruitment tools among adults.

The other studies suggested that depends on the directness and narrative content of the messages. One French study suggested that such material may have the reverse effect of encouraging critical attitudes towards racism among young people. The legal implications of this situation are complex and some of the sites could be prosecuted in the UK under laws on incitement to ethnic hatred, although in the first amendment is likely to offer protection. Meanwhile, there are several educational projects that attempt to children to biases and distortions in such material.

A related phenomenon is that extreme self-help sites related to topics such as eating disorders and suicide. Sites that positively celebrate forms of self-harm or provide advice on how to carry it out more effectively are certainly disturbing and in the past has been deleted or blocked by service providers. Some research suggests that such sites may normalize self harming behaviour. Others have argued that they can support the useful offer that might not be elsewhere and giving voice to such issues is preferable to silencing them. Again the question is raised by such sites, whether they result in an increase in harmful behaviour or simply shift it in a different direction and this is a question on which there is no definitive evidence.

The benefits of the Internet

The potential risks of the internet needs to be balanced against an understanding of its potential benefits. The positive effects of the internet is claims to tent to focus on the value of instant access to information and its role in creating new forms of communication and community. This can be seen particular consequences e.g., in building or renewing civic participation in generating tolerance and global understanding in providing new opportunities for creative expression and overcome social isolation. Popular accounts make much of the new skills and knowledge that are being developed by the so-called digital generation and of the liberating potential of the medium for young people. Such accounts tend to present the internet as an enormous power for social wellbeing. It is seen to offer great possibilities for self-expression, creativity and learning and to bring about great openness, tolerance and trust.

Academic commentary has frequently sought to puncture some of the inflated claims that are made about the benefits of the internet and the forms of technological determinism that tend to characterize them. Ultimately, while the technologically empowered cyber kids of the popular imagination may indeed exist, they are certainly in a minority and are untypical of young people as a whole. Researchers suggested that the majority of young people are not interested in technology in its own right, but simply in what they can do with it. There is relatively little evidence of young people using the internet to develop global connections. In most of the cases it appears to be used primarily as a means of reinforcing local networks among peers. Warschauer pointed out that the potential for multimedia production which requires the latest computers and software and high bandwidth is actually quite inaccessible to all but the wealthy middle classes. Researchers also suggests that young people may be less fluent or technologically literate in their use of the internet than is often assumed. Observational studies suggest that the young people often encounter considerable difficulties in using search engines.

Regarding to the games, the benefit of the internet for young people are predominantly framed in terms of education. It is evidence of the educational value of the internet is somewhere ambiguous. Arguments about the value of instant access to a wealth of information are typically countered with evidence about the proliferation of plagiarism and cut and paste approaches to academic work. The evidence is that technology in itself will serve as a means of raising educational achievements in schools or indeed that it is worthy of the money that is spent on it is far persuasive. As in the case of games, it is clear that the educational benefits of the internet are not automatic or guaranteed rather then they derive from the ways in which it is used. In relation to schools, the educational value of the medium depends very much on the classroom strategies that teachers employ, while in the home, the role of parental support is crucial. As this implies, the benefits of the medium do not follow automatically from simply gaining access rather than they depend very much on the skills and competencies that are developed by users.

Despite these necessary qualifications, it would be quite wrong to underestimate the significance benefits that the internet can offer young people, in terms of learning, communication, creativity and social relationships. The accessibility of global reach is simplicity and flexibility of the medium and indeed the vast extent of material that it brings together does offer significant opportunities for support in learning, for pursuing entertainment and leisure interests an for creating new democratic forms of communication and cultural expression. While something to remain outside the digital world, those who do access to it tend to regard. It is an enormously positive phenomenon and indeed as a necessity of modern life and they feel that the children who do not use it are at a significant disadvantage in respect of educationally, socially and culturally. While this is predictably less of an issue for younger children by the time they reach the teenage years. The internet comes to equal television and mobile phones as a must have medium for young people.

Research to Policy Creation

There is certain proof of specific kinds of harm and offence that can arise from young people's use of the internet. While the evidence on the harm resulting from mainstream pornography is fairly limited, there is no doubt that many other phenomena considered here can be considered directly harmful or at least offensive. Whether they are more harmful than equivalent phenomena offline e.g., whether online bullying is more dangerous than offline bullying could be a matter for debate. At the same time, there is a great claim about the benefits of the internet. In respect of internet, the educational value of children and young people. Many of these claims are inflated and in several cases the evidence from research is some extent limited. Nevertheless, it would be foolish to deny that the internet has considerable potential to benefit children, even if the realization of that potential depends very much on the circumstances in which the medium is used.

The obvious difficulty that arises when seeking to apply research to policy is that of balancing the potential risks and benefits, while recognizing that both are frequently overstated. Fatherly, particular forms of regulation may be considered desirable; these also raise significant legal and technical issues. In respect of the former, the arguments for free speech cannot be ignored and it could be argued that they need to be considered particularly carefully when one is addressing the activities of minority or fringe groups of any kind. On the other hand some types of material considered here are clearly illegal and covered by existing laws. In respect of technology, the evidence suggests that attempts to filter or block access to particular types of internet content, whether in home or public settings such as schools, have rarely proven effective. As Frechette suggests, the software industry is currently generating significant profits from parental anxieties about inappropriate content. Although such software often defines what is inappropriate in narrow ways.

Evidence suggests that the effectiveness of such devices e.g., in schools is decidedly limited. Filters are typically very crude and unreliable and young people complain about how they block access to sites that are needed for perfectly legitimate educational reasons. Researcher also suggest that the use of filters is frequently resisted. School students will often claim that they can evade filters, through a range of inventive and devious strategies and some even boast of their skill in hacking into teaching staff files. The limitation of filtering or blocking programs appears to be accepted even by researchers who strongly agree with them in principle. There is also a danger that too prohibitive or protective an attitude in schools may lead to young people simply giving up on internet use in schools and reverting to home use. This has particular implications for young people whose access at home is limited and it also means that productive educational use – as well as education about risk become much more difficult.

The implication of such findings is that a more educational

strategy is required. There have been some significant educational interventions focused on internet risk and on related issues such as hate sites. In some cases, such strategies have proven less than effective not least because they tend to be narrowly defined and fail to connect with young people's perceptions of issues such as risk and privacy. However, research does suggest that parental intervention and involvement can enhance children's ability to understand web content, to handle risk and use the medium effectively and there is also evidence of successful programmes being developed in schools. However, it should be emphasized that digital literacy is not simply a matter of being able to use technological tools, but also of critically understanding information. The implications of such an approach will be discussed in more detail in the final section of this report.

New and Emerging Media

The median landscape is rapidly changes and as new media forms emerge, so that new concerns about their possible effects. This section focuses on a range of relatively new phenomena, including social networking sites, user-generated content, online communities and social worlds, online gaming and peer to peer file sharing. The academic research on these developments is still in its infancy and so this discussion draws on more speculative and non-academic accounts, some of which have yet to be published. These phenomena continue to evoke well-established concerns of the kind considered above, albeit sometimes in new forms. Social networking sites e.g., generated new anxieties about stranger danger and bullying while file-sharing and user generated content sites have provided new opportunities for circulating sexually explicit or violent material that some consider inappropriate for children. Familiar concerns about addiction about the demise of healthy family life or about the physical effects of excessive use, have all been expressed once more in respect of these new phenomena.

Equally, enthusiasts for Web 2.0 have proclaimed its potential for promoting creative self-expression, interactive communication and democratic participation in the media. These positive and negative consequences must ultimately be seen as two sides of the same coin. These new phenomena do raise new concerns or lend some hitherto fairly marginal concerns a new intensity. Before taking each of these phenomena in turn, it is worth identifying four broader issues that cut across these different areas, particularly relating to the question of risk:

1. **Privacy:** New media forms a social networking sites and blogs posses a form of intimacy. They are easily accessible in the public domain. Users may reveal highly personal information in the belief that they are doing for an audience consisting only of their friends. They may forget, or fail to fully register, the fact that this information is visible to others and indeed to parents, teachers or employers as much as potentially dangerous strangers. This situation provides important new opportunities for sexual predators and for bullying by peers as well as for various forms of deception and identity theft. However, it also raises more far-reaching questions about the changing ways in which young people understand the boundaries between the public and the private issue that has also emerged in relation to phenomena such as reality television and the continuing rise of celebrity culture.
2. **Trust and Credibility:** The new occurrences emphasize existing concerns about how users evaluate online information e.g., Wikipedia is an online user-generated encyclopedia that is very widely cited by students as an authoritative source, although there have been significant critics of the quality of its content. Meanwhile, the rise of blogging has further facilitated the rapid circulation of hate speech, deceptive rumours and conspiracy theories of all kinds. New media offer the benefit of a much wider range of information, but the motivations, identity and quality of those sources are often difficult to ascertain. Communities of users may develop their own standards for judging and maintaining credibility, although this process can be fraught with disputes but very often it is down to individual users to decide what and whom they should trust. In this respect, the media pose significant educational challenges: 'wiring up' schools or homes and assuming that

the social good of information will flow through the screen is at best naïve and at worst positively dangerous.

3. **Commercialism:** Web 2.0 appears to be area in which ordinary users rather than large commercial companies are the authors and owners of content. However, key Web 2.0 site are owned by large global media corporations and offer extensive opportunities for high targeted advertising which is why they are changing hands for billions of dollars. Auxiliary, users of such sites are often required to provide significant amounts of personal information, which can be used by companies as a basis for further promotional activities, is called as 'data-mining'. In other situations, commercial messages may be deeply embedded in the form of branding or promotions in content that outwardly appears to be a harmless form of play. Unlike television or print advertising the commercial dimensions of these activities may be effectively invisible to children and in deed to adults.
4. **Intellectual Property:** The potential of digital technology in terms of copying and circulating content has significantly implications for the notion of copyright and intellectual property. This is most evident case with file-sharing, where copyright material is exchanged illegally by users, and in the rising incidence of academic plagiarism. However, it also applies to the way in which content can be quoted or 'cut and pasted' into very different contexts from that in which it was originally presented. As the intellectual ownership of content is undermined, there is a danger that any ethical responsibility for the consequences of one's communicative actions tends to be dissipated. In this respect, a situation does not only affect the profits of large corporations, but also the communication rights of individuals.

All these dimensions could be seen at present risks for young people. To a large extent, these are risks of the routine rather than the spectacular variety, although in some respects they may be more acute because they are relatively subtle, and because they are not necessarily recognized by teachers, parents or caregivers. Here again, these risks can be seen as an inevitable corollary of the apparent freedom and flexibility that is afforded by new media. In this sense, the issue then becomes not so much one of preventing or neutralizing these risks, but of enabling young people to deal with them on their own behalf. In the following pages, we consider the implications of these issues in relation to a series of specific areas.

Social Networking Services

Social networking sites i.e., MySpace, Facebook and Bebo are some of the most popular online destinations for young people today. These sites provides home pages on which the user can display their personal profile including information such as location, interests and tastes as well as photos or videos, music tracks and links to friends pages. Home page may also include facilities for chat; file sharing, blogging and discussion groups. These sites have many attractions and benefits for young people. These include being able to meet people with the same interests and find like-minded communities the ability to discuss sensitive issues anonymously in potentially supportive environment and the opportunities for self-expression which are not possible to the same degree in face-to-face situations. These benefits shoot partly from the anonymity and the global reach afforded by the internet. Anonymity is most obviously important in discussions concerning sensitive issues. Such situations can also overcome the disadvantages of some face-to-face environment in which there are unequal power relationships. The potential reach of social networks has been important to young artists as a way of developing an audience for their productions and this also aids young people who might otherwise be limited to face-to-face interactions in smaller communities or in communities in which they have minority interest.

Many of the general concerns connected with children and young people use the internet discussed in emerge in social networking. Anonymity brings risks as well as benefits particularly around contract. There is concern that online social networking is bringing bullying into the home outside of school hours, a different experience from face-to-face bullying which is more limited in terms of time and place. Some researchers suggested that girls may be risk of being bullied in this way. Issues of trust are connected to bullying when trust is established on a false basis and then intentionally broken in order to cause emotional harm. Trust and anonymity are also key issues in relation to grooming practices in which older men portray themselves as younger for the purpose of seducing under age girls. The extent to which sexual abuse is occurring through social networking services is questionable. However, it is still the case that the vast majority of sexual abuse occurs in the home and between known contacts where the adult is clearly recognizable. The other concern is relevant here about greater access to hate speech or other anti-social content. In this concern the young people are finding support for activities that the young people are finding support for activities that they otherwise would not found. However, it is unclear about the behaviour and attitudes change when in contact with social networks or people are simply sharing ideas with a wider community than previously available to them.

There are more subtle issues that relate to social network to do with privacy and trust and these are also tied in with the commercial component of social networking services. As evidenced by the recent high-profile sales of social networking sites, this is a highly commodities enterprise. E-market research estimates that revenue from social networking advertisements will amount of $1.9 billion in total by 2011 and marketers are seeing these advertisements as a key point of access to the pocket books of young people. Online marketing on social network site includes data mining information on users' pages and then 'hypo-targeting' individual users with personalized advertisements based on demographic and psychographic data. New social advertising programs are capable of collating individual users actions across a variety of websites and can also access to individuals list of friends for advertising purposes. In addition to these developments, various companies have established their own pages on social networking sites in attempting to capture a young audience these pages frequently offer incentives for users to engage with them or become a friend or fan.

Finally conversational advertising aims at providing young people with branded materials which they use, share and discuss with friends.

The young people are well aware of the risk of sharing personal information, they see in social networking sites as private or peer defined spaces. Research shows that online social networking is seen as part of youth culture, the point of having a page is to be part of peer network, to define one's identity for a wider social group to negotiate and manage public identity and to build a community of friends. Young people see social networking sites as spaces for play, often submitting false information or jointly constructing a single page with a group of friends. Perhaps because social networking is an important part of many youth cultures and traditionally youth cultures centre on practices that are separate from younger children and from adults, it is possible that young people do not see these online practices as public.

Although social networking pages can be marked as private by the user, policies vary from site to site: some services withhold information marked private from marketers, while others, like Facebook, sell such information for marketing purposes, even after a user has quit a service. The research is showing that the companies' privacy policies are difficult to understand and young people are in need of training in order to make the most of the facilities available to them on social networking sites. They are used at present, the private/public settings do not completely meet the needs of young people socializing online.

The privacy options are geared toward individual interactions which do not provide users with the flexibility they need to handle conflicts within groups of friends. Recent reports suggested that the information about young people post online is sometimes used when they apply for jobs, internships, clubs or schools as well as by organizations. There is a need here to develop young people's critical understanding of the public nature of social networking sites as well as the privacy setting available to them. Although media literacy will help in this regard, the companies themselves can also take action.

User Generated Content

Beyond the more customized facilities offered by social networking sites, there is a range of other participatory sites such as wikis, blogs and image-sharing sites, which are designed specifically for users to upload, share or view content. Also there are more personal forms of user-generated content such as e-mail and instant messaging, which are also discussed here. Many social networking sites involve creating content and vice-versa, sites that are focused on user-generated content have the capacity to build social networks and there are clear connections between this section and the previous one. As with social networking sites, young people's desire to interact with media in social, personal and expressive ways is driving the popularity of user-generated content sites. There may even be some unsetting of traditional relationships between media producers and consumers here. We know of at least one school age student who is a senior editor with Wikipedia – an experience of participation in knowledge creation unthinkable in the era of the print encyclopedia.

It is clear that young people are viewing and contributing to sites which include user-generated content, with a study in 2007 indicating that as many as 57 per cent of online teenagers post their own content to such sites. Sharing and discussing media on user-generated content sites such as YouTube is one way in which young people are socializing, much in the same way other media are used in social relationships. User-generated content sites are also seen to be offering young people spaces in which they can have a voice. The opportunity to create and distribute one's own media is being hailed by some as providing the means to a more democratic media environment.

The ease of sharing media and the global reach of such network is leading to the emergence of new participatory cultures online, which may have particular benefits for young people. Jenkins et.al. assert that these participatory cultures build on traditional skills, but the specific new media literacy are also developing. Rather than being based simply on technological skills, this new media literacy involves a set of cultural competencies and social skills. He also identifies eleven new skills associated with online social environments, including appropriation, multitasking, collective intelligence, judgment, networking and negotiation. Importantly, however, educators also have a role to play here. He also outlines three concerns in relation to participatory media cultures which point to a need for educational intervention: the participation gap, the transparency problem and the ethics challenge. In relation to user-generated content, the ethics challenge and the transparency problem are key risks which are discussed in this section.

The ethics challenge discussed by Jenkins et al. includes questions about representation i.e., how young people are presenting themselves, their peers and other materials for comment e.g., in blogs or through photos and videos. There are also questions here about how young people understand the immediate or long-term impacts of such representations on other individuals or social groups. On a wider level, there are ethical questions concerning intellectual property and copyright. The creative commons movement recognizes the benefit of allowing people to share and build on each other's ideas and work. However, it is not uncommon on user-generated sites for young people to draw or build on copyrighted material that does not operate under a creative commons license. Large companies are increasingly tracking the use of their content in spaces such as personal WebPages, social networking sites or YouTube in seeking to identify and prosecute people for copyright infringements. Recently, the Entertainment Software Association called for the implementation of a piracy curriculum for children aged 5 to 11.

Young people's involvement in participatory culture offers a range of benefits in terms of learning, users are making judgments about content, building collective knowledge for the purpose of assessment, comparing and critiquing representations. All of which are helping to develop their skills in critical evaluation. However, assessing the credibility online content remains a key concern, in relation both to information and to social interaction. Engaging in online communication entails making judgments about whether e-mails or instant messages are from people who can be trusted, about whether comments expressed on a blog or in response to user-generated content are valid, authority and expertise of the participants.

Commercial interest also impinge on the credibility of user-generated content, with special e-mail techniques being used by companies which capitalize on friendship networks, promotional blogs set up by companies which appear to be written by an individual with no commercial interest or connection and content posted on chat sites, forums, image sharing sites or informational web pages for the purpose of promotion. As outlined above, online environments are seen as an important means of capturing the increasingly lucrative youth market. In terms of user-generated content, companies are supplying young people with more ways to interact with their brands, including branded instant messaging sites, contests for contributing video or music to advertisements and branded content for instant messaging, blogging or other personal webpage. Whether young people understand, resist, ignore or manipulate these commercial messages is an area for further research.

Online Communities and Online Worlds

The idea of the online or virtual community is by now well established, and there is a significant body of literature relating to this phenomenon. Studies of text based online communities such as forums, chartrooms and bulletin boards, where participants meet to discuss common interests, have explored both the positive and negative aspects of life within such settings. A number of concerns relating to teenage users of such sites overlap with those that have arisen around social networking. A key area of interest has been the ways in which online communities may support dangerous, harmful or illegal activities. Aside from concerns relating to contract with paedophiles, other dangers have also been identified. Recent discussion of suicide pacts between internet users who meet online has suggested that depressed adolescents may be vulnerable. The suggestion through internet chartrooms and websites encourage anorexia and bulimia amongst teens has also been expressed. Although other researchers have challenged this idea, the internet services company Yahoo has appeared to endorse this position by taking down pro-anorexia groups for violating their terms of service.

Media coverage of these environments includes descriptions of the virtual crime that takes place online and concerns about the content of such environments. One recent case, involving a virtual paedophile ring in second life, illustrates this concern. Journalists revealed a hidden virtual playground within second life in which avatars designed to look like children offered visitors sex. Despite restrictions on membership stating that second life is intended to have an over 18 population, the wonderland case raised concerns that activities within this online environment might encourage harm against children in the real world.

Online Gaming

The internet presents children and teens with a range of online gaming entertainment. One increasingly popular phenomenon involves online multiplayer games which may be joined by paying monthly subscription fees. Like the online worlds described above, the involve avatars and immersive two or three dimensional worlds, but introduce set activities and teamwork. Participants begin by creating an avatar and then make their way though levels, increasing their avatar's strength and experience by successfully completing tasks and/or defeating enemies in combat. One key aspect of these games is the social nature of the game play offered, with participants joining forces in clans and guilds. Game play is often supplemented by chat, and teamwork and social interactions are a significant aspect of the gaming experience.

These games are often referred to as massively multiplayer online games (MMOGs) or massively multiplayer online role-playing games (MMORPGs) a development of earlier paper and pencil role playing games such as Dungeons and Dragons. The most famous MMOG titles include the Sims online, Ultima Online, Everquest and World of Warcraft. The academic literature on online gaming explores a range of issues that have been raised in work on console and PC gaming. However, the social aspect of interacting in these game environments and the repercussions of potentially endless forms of gaming entertainment, introduce new issues and concerns, which have been voiced by the media in different ways. Thus it has been suggested that the potentially open-ended, social and goal-driven nature of online gaming is more likely to lead to gaming addiction.

Here we discusses about the identity of the potential risks and benefits of new and emerging forms of online communication. While some of the risks are clearly familiar from studies of previous cultural forms, others are distinctly new. Some of the positive aspects of these phenomena are only just beginning to appear. In this ever-changing environment, it is important to aware that the consequences of technological developments are by no means guaranteed. Technologies may embody certain constraints and possibilities, but which of these proves to be significant depends to a great extent on how the technologies are used. Here again it is important to recognize that the potentially negative effects of these media may well be inextricable from the positive ones, and that the most significant or pervasive risks may be the ones that are less than immediately obvious.

d by
CK BOOKS
sari Road, Darya Ganj, New Delhi-110002
+91-11-40775252, 40775214, 23273880, 23275880
-11-23285873
w.atlanticbooks.com
rders@atlanticbooks.com

ks is an imprint of
lishers and Distributors (P) Ltd

ed 1925
Design Copyright © Peacock Books, 2026

rved. No part of this publication may be reproduced,
rieval system, transmitted or utilized in any form or
electronic, mechanical, photocopying, recording
vithout the prior permission of the copyright
tion for such permission should be
e publisher.
subject to the jurisdiction of Delhi court only.
d in India by Atlantic Print Services

AF516567

Red Oleander

A Drama in One Ac

Rabindranath Tag

Foreword by
Mohit K. Ra

Introductio
Rama Ku

PEAC

Publish
PEACO
7/22, An
Phones :
Fax : +91
Web : ww
E-mail : c

Peacock Bo
Atlantic Pu

First publish
Editorial an

All rights res
stored in a re
by any means
or otherwise,
owner. Applica
addressed to th
All disputes are

Printed & bou

FOREWORD

We are happy to place in the hands of our scholars and lovers of Tagore, all over the world, a new edition of *Red Oleanders* (1925, Tagore's own translation of his Bengali play *Raktakarabī* (published in 1924), with a comprehensive critical introduction by Professor Rama Kundu, by way of paying our homage to Tagore on the auspicious occasion of the year-long celebrations of the 150th birth anniversary of the poet. (1861-1941).

Raktakarabī belongs to the symbolic phase (1922-1932) of Tagore's experimentations with the dramatic form. The themes—materialism versus humanism, industry versus agriculture, possessive greed versus selfless love, etc.—are all superbly integrated into the symbolic structure of the play, which is a powerful dramatic evocation of the evils of mindless industrialism, and celebrates the perennial values of love, life and nature. In its symbolic suggestions and dramatic situations, luminous diction and lyrical resonance, the play is a literary *tour de force* and is comparable with any great play of the world.

In her brilliant and comprehensive Introduction, Rama Kundu touches on all the major aspects of the play, its genesis and themes, ideas and symbols, images and metaphors, historical, social and political contexts, characters and situations, songs and dances, the meaning and the music, and intertextual parallels, leaving virtually nothing *en route.*

I am sure, that the Introduction, while adding to the understanding and enjoyment of the play, will also be immensely useful to all Tagore scholars.

Mohit K. Ray
(Chief Editor)
Atlantic Publishers and Distributors (P) Ltd.

CONTENTS

INTRODUCTION

If you searched for meanings under the petals of the red oleander that would lead to disaster.
['Preface', Rabindranath Tagore]

Raktakarabī (1924)/*Red Oleanders* (1925) is one of Tagore's best plays; and understandably 'meanings' have been sought 'under the petals', in spite of the author's admonition, by countless readers, theatre-goers, performers/producers, and literary critics.

Anyway, as each of Tagore's works calls back and forth to the other works in his great oeuvre, this play too has to be seen in the total perspective in order to get at the 'meaning'. What indeed Tagore did not turn his myriad mind upon? If we consider just the plays, even that can prove a challenging job, in view of the variety and fecundity involved. The plays have been grouped in various arrangements among which the one made by Pramathanath Bishi—a former resident pupil at the *ashram* of Shantiniketan during Tagore's time, and subsequently an eminent Tagore scholar—has been generally accepted as the standard grouping.

According to Bishi, Tagore's plays may be classified into the following eight categories: (1) musical drama, (2) verse drama, (3) romantic tragedy, (4) play of ideas/symbolic drama, (5) social plays, (6) comedy, (7) seasonal plays, and (8) dance drama. Bishi places *Raktakarabī* (*Red Oleanders*) in the fourth category.

Furthermore, Pramathanath Bishi classifies Rabindranath's 'plays of ideas'/'symbolic drama' into three phases: the first phase is represented by *Prakṛtir Pratiśodh*; the second phase includes *Śāradotsav*, *Acalāyatan*, *Rājā* and *Dākghar*; whereas the third phase comprises *Fālguṇī*, *Muktadhārā*, *Raktakarabī* (*Red Oleanders*), *Rather Raśi*, *Tāser Deś*, and *Kabir Dīkṣā*.

Play of Ideas and Symbols

This genre is Tagore's unique contribution to Bengali drama; this had been his own innovation on the Bengali stage, which has been subsequently pursued by very few Bengali dramatists indeed, as Upendranath Bhattacharya points out.

Red Oleanders is a play more oriented in ideas than action. It belongs to the group of Tagore's plays which elaborately draw upon myths, allegories, signs, symbols, while dealing with some major problems/predicaments of human life and situation. The dominance of ideas marks out this group from his other plays, in which the story element or action takes priority; even when a story is there it is the idea which informs and rules the story.

Genesis

Like all masterpieces the process of the creation of *Raktakarabī* (*Red Oleanders*) had started much earlier, and at various turns various elements had entered into the making, and took shape through long years of silent nurturing.

In course of Tagore's trip to Europe in 1912, and return after a long spell abroad, his initial fascination with modern Europe was got over; the disillusionment was further reinforced by a deep anxiety about an impending 'crisis of civilization', which he thought, would overcome mankind as a consequence of its blind mechanical pursuit of material wealth and power. Again, this was the period that coincided with his winning the Nobel award which was followed by many a trip abroad; the publicity attending the award also brought in its train the imposed/attributed image of the spiritual spokesman and messenger of India for the war-torn world; by this time that the First World War came to a close.

In the meantime, Shantiniketan which had been started in December 1901, had already expanded considerably, thereby thrusting more and more wearying responsibilities upon the poet; lack of money had become chronic botheration, along with various efforts taken to tide over the crises. Alongside the demands made upon him by the institution, there were demands of the country and the world—and all this piled upon one another, had been disturbing and eating into his leisure, time and energy. All the time the urge to write was pressing him inside. There was also no end to hostility within the country and abroad. Friends were few; surrounded by dull devotees who looked up to him as the '*gurudev*', and whom he could neither reject nor accept altogether.

It was around this time that a little girl drifted into his life. Her name was Ranu. She came like a breath of fresh wind amidst the suffocating climate around. Her frequent visits to Shantiniketan coincided with the joining of Elmherst in the work of Sriniketan and his delightful vibrant presence.

These various events of personal life were entering the crucible of imagination, and getting metamorphosed there under the wonderful chemistry of creativity, which ultimately took shape in the play *Raktakarabī*.

In a poem of Tagore, titled 'Vijayee' (The Victorious) published in the journal *Prabāsī* in 1918, and later included in the anthology of poems, *Pūrabī*, one can trace some of the ideas of the play in an embryonic form.

Raktakarabī and *Red Oleanders*

Tagore's translation of the play

It may seem interesting that the English version of the play came out before the original Bengali version was published in book form. *Red Oleanders*, the author's own translation of his *Raktakarabī*, was published in 1925, and the Bengali book was published in 1926, although it had come out in the journal *Prabāsī* in autumn 1924.

Unlike Tagore's other auto-translations, a few departures or transformations can be noted from the original in the translation. Certain passages in some of the dialogues have been omitted or shortened. For instance, Nandini's impassioned interrogation of the system in which the King is kept off behind a net becomes a succinct cool composed sharp query in the English version:

> Then again, you hide your king behind a wall of netting. Is it for fear of people finding out that he's a man? (4)

The dialogue between Fagulal and Chandra about the close proximity of tavern, armory and temples in the Yakshapuri has been omitted. On the other hand, some completely new speeches have been inserted on occasions: for instance, Fagulal tells Chandra in a tone of annoyance which only fails to hide his despair: "Don't worry me, Chandra. A thousand times over have I told you that in these parts there are high roads to the market, to the burning ground, to the scaffold—everywhere except to the homeland" (15).

On one occasion the order of speeches in a dialogue between Nandini and the 'voice' has been reversed.

Raktakarabī, like many a play of Tagore, touches the poetic heights, and perhaps it is only natural that often in the translation we miss the pulsation of the original rhythm, the sweet resonance of music, the sharpness of images; the language too seems to have been shorn of much of the fascinating charm of the original.

When it is closely following the original, we find the author using additional words/phrases in order to come up close behind the source. As a result, the simple sentences too occasionally turn complex in the English rendering.

Also some music has been done away with. For instance, in response to Nandini's query why did Bishu leave her silently in the past, Bishu sings a wonderful, deeply moving song in *Raktakarabī*. In *Red Oleander* that song is not presented; instead some lines of the song have been transferred into Bishu's speech: "My boat was tied to the bank; the rope snapped; the wind drove it into the trackless unknown" (21).

In his song Bishu addresses Nandini as 'O waker of my grief!' (21); the musical effect of *ogo dukha-jāgāniā* in Bengali is altogether missing in the English version; the soft endearing intimate colloquial address, along with its melody, loses its charm and evocation in the literally correct translation.

The choric song recurring through the play *Raktakarabī* with remarkable aesthetic effect has been retained in the

English version. But the author has made a slight change from the source; in the Bengali version it is '*Pauş*', meaning winter (December-January), i.e. the traditional harvesting season of Bengal; but in translation, perhaps in keeping with the empirical/climatological context of the TL (Target Language) the author has made it 'Autumn', which is further specified accurately as 'September', which marks the West's season of harvesting and 'mellow fruitfulness'.

Time and Place

Both the space and time have been used paradigmatically, according to the requirement of the symbolic play, and not in the manner of a realistic play.

(a) *Time*

(i) The Diurnal backdrop

Mention has been made of various segments of time, from morning to sunset; but the spectator, under the spell of the play, tends to forget how many days the action is spread over, and what particular era of human history constitutes the location.

Anyway, what is the exact time-frame of the play? Is it just one day? We come to know early that this is a holiday on the occasion of Flag-worship, and Weapon-worship. Yet Bishu stops Nandini's joyous outpour, saying, "let me go to my work". And Nandini implores: "Run away, Kishor, go back to your work, quick! You'll be late again" (3). On a further consideration it seems that perhaps this is not the event of any particular day; many events of many days have been telescoped into the space of one day,—like Solzhenitsyn's *One Day in the Life of Ivan Denisovich*, or like the one week epitomizing the endless time in Kafka's *Castle*.

The opening of the play gives the impression of some morning hour—as suggested by little touches like gathering flower, or stitching a garland of flowers. The harvest song too, sung in that morning, denotes signs of the hour. The mellow morning light of autumn is, as it were, subsumed in the charming golden hue of the ripe corn. Later, as Nandini reports to Bishu about the song she heard in the 'morning', apparently the day has advanced meanwhile. Towards the end it is already evening coming down: 'the play of the field is ended now, and the field-master is taking the ripe corn home' (253).

(ii) Seasonal backdrop

The immediate seasonal backdrop is autumn (though winter in the Bengali version) that provides the backdrop. In the original version the seasonal backdrop is mid-winter, the time for shearing the corn; with the imminent festival of '*Nabānna*', a popular harvesting ritual of rural India, knocking at the door. Again, the winter is also congenial for digging work. Thus the season itself contains the seed of conflict between the principles of cultivation and mining.

Here one must take note of the fact that winter in Eastern India is not the winter of Europe; the connotations are completely different. However, in the English version the poet changes it to 'Autumn'; possibly because in Europe autumn is the harvesting time and winter is associated with the idea of death and hardship, barren landscape, bleak sky, though in India it is the beautiful season of bright pleasant days, flagged off by the harvesting rituals. Incidentally, autumn also happened to be Tagore's favorite season which signified for him nature's prosperity, benediction and fulfillment.

The season in the play foregrounds the counterpoints—harvesting and digging; the call for the delightful festival of the new crop, and the horrifying drunken carnival of *Dhwajāpujā* or Flag-worship. On occasions the song of shearing the crop in the distant cornfields wafts in through the horrible noise of the town. Unlike Tagore's *Śāradotsav* and *Post-office*, the two plays preceding *Red Oleanders*, which show a harmony between the human mood and the seasonal mood, here the disharmony is apparent. In the distant cornfields the season represents the contrastive light and sound to those of the human world in the town; the season has sprinkled gold in abandon through its golden sunlight upon golden cornears in contrast to the dark innards of the earth's bowel with its dead gold. It sends its joyous sun-burnt music which is in contrast to the hideous roar of the machine.

(b) *Place*

Whereas the Yaksha Town takes the foreground as the dramatic space, at the backdrop—far behind though—there is the cornfield with ripe corn, which is evoked rather than presented.

(i) Yaksha town

Tagore writes: "like Swarnalanka, the locale of my *Pālā*, where the events take place, has a name; to the poet's cognition it is Yakshapuri" (trans. present author). The name of the place suggests a mythical or legendary dimension. Yaksha is another name for Kuber, the deity of wealth in the extended Hindu pantheon; but unlike Lakshmi, who is also a deity of wealth, Kuber does not have either grace, or beauty, or benediction; he is a lesser god in the pantheon, who is most wealthy yet lacking in other godly attributes.

The description/account of Yaksha Town that we find in the play carries resemblance to (1) a mining area, (2) a modern industrial city, and (3) a place under the rule of some autocratic oppressive government.

The author says, "It is possible that there should be controversy among cartographers about the exact location of the place. But everybody knows it is called by the name Yakshapuri. Scholars would say, Oh, the legendary Yakshapuri! Isn't it the place of Kuber, with the golden throne? But this play is neither legend nor allegory". The author explains, "The place referred to, contains the treasure of Yaksha kept entombed under the earth" (*Nāṭyaparicay*; my translation).

Yakshapuri represents such a society where there has been a lack of life, a lack of piety which becomes apparent in its assault upon life, love, *joie de vivre*, beauty. Here life is repressed by the ignominy of forced labour, oppression, exploitation, by the denial of light and pure joy of the sunlit cornfield; here life is besotted by stale vulgar mirth of inebriation; here life is crippled and perverted by fear and the worship of weapons; it is a death-in-life existence.

Yakshapuri has been presented as a 'city of eclipse' where people 'in their drunken fury…tear the earth's veils to pieces'

(6). Even holidays here are not like those back at home; because here it is the holiday of 'caged birds', and 'more of a nuisance than work'.

The place makes one insensitive to beauty. Gokul, who is suspicious by nature, cannot trust Nandini, and is particularly suspicious of her beauty; he would opt for features that are 'plain enough to understand'. Bishu sadly replies: "I know the atmosphere of this place breeds contempt for beauty. There must be beauty even in hell; but nobody there can understand it, that's their cruelest punishment" (12).

Once somebody chances to drift or step into the place there is no exit route. The road to freedom in the lap of nature is closed for ever. It is a strange labyrinth from which none can escape. Bishu had once tried to go home: "And then I found that, as soon as one enters the maw of Yaksha Town, its jaws shut fast, and the one road that remains open leads withinwards" (14); eventually a time comes when even the longing to escape has died. "Your Governor has closed the way as well as the will to return" (14). The vast 'prison' allows 'no open sky, no leisure' for its prisoners; and they have no access to pure joy, but only to the polluted drink of the prison (13). Coming here, the men 'go to the dogs' while the women wither up, as the simple charms of life recede for ever.

In contrast to the distant sunlit cornfields, Yakshapuri is a dark, blind, blinding hell of a place. As Chandra appeals to the Governor for leave to go home, she pleads in vain: "Don't you see that your men here work all day in the dark, and in the evening steep themselves in the denser dark of drunkenness?" (16). Such sharp touches seem to evoke the acute Zolaesque realism depicting the shabby seediness of slum life forced upon the industrial labor. Nandini mentions the place as 'this closed fort' (20) in which only 'a bit of sky' has survived between Bishu and herself. Bishu's reply to Nandini brings out the regimentation enforced by the system of the place: "Ever since coming to Yaksha Town the sky has dropped out of my life. I felt as if they had pounded me in the same mortar with all the fractions of men here, and rolled us into a solid lump" (20). This is like 'one day in the life of Ivan Denisovich' inside the inescapable jaws of the 'Gulag', i.e. Soviet concentration camps, as has been recorded by Alexander Solzhenitsyn in his Nobel-winning play.

Yakshapuri represents more of a system than any actual place, and the system thrives on fear. Nandini tells the King without mincing her words: "The people here trade on frightening others. That's why they have put you behind a network and dressed you fantastically" (26-27). It is the 'stone walls around' her that Nandini seeks to defy when she challenges the king, "Your stone walls will also fall away from around me today…" (25). But the system of the place allows no protest; you can at best just survive,—a kind of death-in-life, 'a dead and alive existence' (34); and that too on the condition of abject servility. No show of heroics would be tolerated for a moment. Gajju's humiliation is a case in point. Gajju, the once fearless wrestler is made to realize, "They only feel safe when they rob the whole world of strength" (35).

Even the sound of this place is anti-music, and horrifying.

Eventually the system breaks down,—not under attack from outside, but from internal disintegration, as an exploitative oppressive society may eventually crumble and collapse with rebellious upsurge from within itself. However, if we try to fit the play tightly into this, or any other, abstract frame, that would be an over-simplification. Rabindranath had said, the Yaksha Town existed across ages and places in the world in various forms, and at various layers. It may be compared, in this regard, to Kafka's 'Castle', which is located in no definite time-frame or spatial geography to particularize the setting, so that it becomes the story of all places in all times. It could indeed stand for any place in the modern times where the individual man/woman has been reduced to helplessness and subjected to indignity, humiliation, annihilation by the power-establishment controlling all. The wrestler, after having been 'altogether hollowed out', knows by his own terrible ordeal "These demons know the magic art of sucking away not only strength but hope" (35).

Thus Yakshapuri can be connected with the literary dystopias that were yet to come out; Koestler's 'Dark Noon', Solzhenitsyn's 'Gulag', George Orwell's 'Oceania', for instance, —the memorable semiotics of the unbearable humiliation that can be thrust upon common men in their everyday life. It is also symptomatic of the same pervasive mistrust generated by the stifling atmosphere of the place. Phagulal, who has always trusted Nandini in spite of the situation, is shaken when Bishu disappears, and sadly admits: "Every person suspects every other person in this cursed place" (45).

The perpetrators of oppression throw up a robot-like posture of mechanical operation. The Governor's assumption of dreadful impersonality behind the affairs of the place stuns Nandini, who exclaims: "Dear me, what an awful place! You are not men, and those you drive are not men, either,—you are winds and they are clouds!" (37). Appropriately, here persons are not recognized as individuals, but identified as abstract numbers.

Some factual details are made quite realistic; for instance the labors' twelve-hour day (just two years prior to the publication of the play the working hours were reduced from twelve to eleven); or the impossibility of leaving the job and go home; not only for the slaves, but also for the contract labor in many colonies, (say in the tea-gardens in our country it was valid till 1925,) there was no scope for leaving the job or place; that would be considered violation of contract and punishable with imprisonment or fine. The system is coming back in the form of SEZ today in parts of Asia and the world. So when Bishu says, 'Alas, the road is closed', this is no poetry but harsh reality. Yaksha Town is again emerging as a most adequate prevision of our own times, when "we have become trapped in an inescapable complicated situation because of our avarice for machine-generated prosperity" (Mitra 35; my translation); since the 1960s it has been apparent that, we have damaged and are doing further damage to the ozone layer; poisoned the water, the fish, the milk, vegetables, meat everything by our application of chemical fertilizer and pesticide; that by rending the earth's bosom we have pulled up with our booty "the curse of its dark demon, blind and hard, cruel and envious" (8).

Action

(i) Structure of action: The three phases

Shambhu Mitra, who had staged the play with spectacular success, traced three *Caraṇ*'s (parts/phases) within the continuous pace of the text. The first phase, as identified by Mitra, seems to be a kind of introduction. The end of the first dialog between Nandini and the King marks the end of the first phase, during which the spectator has been introduced to Yaksha Town, its creator, and its potential destructor; the spectator also gets a feel of some imminent storm gathering somewhere in the invisible horizon. We feel that there is some deep embedded conflict in the realm of its thought, its ideology.

During the second phase we get an even more elaborate picture of the Town society, and get hints that the conflict exists at the social level as well. When Nandini leaves with Bishu, following her second conversation with the 'Voice' behind the net, the second phase comes to its close. The transition from the second phase to the third is made poignant with a 'song of waiting', which quivers with sadness and premonition of the moment.

Then suddenly the third phase starts with a bang, as Governor declares harshly and loudly, "No, we cannot…allow Ranjan to enter this parish" (29). With this the pace of events quickens, rapidly heading towards the catastrophe. The conflicts we have already seen in the previous phases now head for crisis.

(ii) The conflict

It can be said, albeit simplistically, that Tagore here brings out the clash between agriculture-oriented civilization and accumulative industrial civilization, or to use his own words, between the *Karṣaṇjībī* and *Ākarṣaṇjībī* (tillers and diggers). It must be remembered however that the play was not written with the deliberate and exclusive intention to bring out the clash between *Karṣaṇjībī* and *Ākarṣaṇjībī*, and announce victory for any of the sides. That would be a rather simplistic and reductive view of the play. And, though this is a problem of a comparatively modern era, Tagore himself would not subscribe to the view that there was any such thing as a 'modern problem', as all major problems of man were held by him as perennial. In order to highlight the perenniality of the problem he has invited us to look back to the realms of the great Indian epic, *The Rāmāyaṇa.*

The Rāmāyaṇa and *Red Oleander:* Some Common Paradigms

(i) The Rāmāyaṇa: An Allegory

Tagore thought that in the clash between Rama and Ravana, the hero and anti-hero in the *Rāmāyaṇa*, the very same conflict had been envisioned by the poet Valmiki. He further claimed the same problem had been addressed by both the ancient poet and the modern playwright, i.e. Tagore himself.

The Rāmāyaṇa itself, Tagore thought, could be considered an elaborate allegory, especially when considered in the light of the two names: "Rama and Ravana, the two names carry two contrastive suggestions; Rama means comfort, peace; Ravana means noise, disturbance. One denoted the grace and sweetness of the new twig, the murmur of the foliage; the other the horrible grating of the monstrous chariot upon the concrete road." (Preface to *Raktakarabī*; my translation)

In another essay written way back in 1816 (*Bhāratbarṣer Itihāser Dhārā* [The course of India's History]) we find Tagore's discourse on the *Rāmāyaṇa* anticipating the view, expressed so many years later in his preface to the play, i.e. connecting Rama with agricultural civilization. It is from this angle that even the episodes of an earlier phase of Rama's life seem to fall in a pattern to the poet's perception. In his perception Rama emerges as the cult hero of an agrarian civilization. So he is symbolically the husband of 'Sita', a name which also means the furrow opened up before the plough; furthermore, Rama releases Ahalya from the curse of remaining a piece of stone by the roadside. 'Ahalya', again, is a name associated with agriculture; 'ahalya' means not ploughable. Tagore's interpretation is that the land which had been left aside by earlier sages as fallow rocky terrain, was brought under cultivation and thereby rejuvenated to life through the agricultural intervention of Rama.

Tagore thus offered an allegorical reading of the epic in which he seemed to have found a paradigmatic rendering of a historical phenomenon—the Aryans' eventual acceptance of the agricultural ways, and a subsequent battle between the community of growers/tillers of the earth with the community of diggers/plunderers of the earth, in which ultimately the former wins over the latter. Similar views are reiterated later (1930) in his, *Jāvāyātrīr Patra* (Letter of the voyager to Java).

(ii) Precursor and Ephebe

According to Pramathanath Bishi, Tagore had cast *Red Oleanders* as far as possible on the paradigm of the *Rāmāyaṇa*. Rabindranath himself has left an observation in this regard which can be considered almost a page taken from Harold Bloom, albeit a much later arrival in this world. Anticipating a typical Bloom-ian tone of delightful mock-insinuation Tagore, as 'ephebe', argues, towards 'exposing' the 'precursor' poet Valmiki's subtle 'appropriation' of an issue of a much later time in his ancient epic. With the ephebe's anxiety to get over the influence of the 'precursor', he writes:

> I shall give another instance to show how the great poet managed to sneak into the treasury house of the future by using his magic cutter of imaginative vision, and with what fine skill grabbed the property of future.
>
> There is a strong conflict between two categories of civilization,—*Karṣaṇjībī* (growers) and *Ākarṣaṇjībī* (plunderers). I often discuss this with my friends. This *Kaliyug* has been unceasingly ruining the villages by means of drawing people from the work of cultivation and engaging them to the work of plunder. Besides, hunger and thirst, the envy and jealousy, the luxury and illusions/confusions of the exploitative civilization are precisely like those of the highly skilled rakshasas. This observation of mine has been secretly appropriated by the poet into his bag of symbols; it becomes apparent to any attentive reader. Ravana, with the ten faces, the ruler of the golden realm, abducts

> Sita, the beloved darling of Ramachandra, with complexion like the fresh green grass; is it a tale of the ancient times, or of our own time? Is it the experience of a sage of the *Tretāyug*, or rightfully that of a poet of the *Kaliyug*, like me? Or had the proprietors of gold mines already coerced the peasants so long ago, the peasants who used to indulge in the luxury of the fresh green grassy land? (my translation)

Tagore had further applied the idea to the life of Valmiki himself. He wrote in the same context:

> Initially Ratnakar was a bandit. Eventually he had given up the vocation and become a devotee of Rama. The implication is that he overcame the lure of plundering as profession and had his initiation in the expertise of cultivation, and it was only then that he got the blessing of the beautiful, and music resonated through his lyre. This theory had touched the minds of people even in those days. As the former bandit emerged as poet, the message of the triumph of forest-dwellers over the golden Lanka resounded so powerfully through his voice. (my translation)

Indeed, this was an idea which had been stirring in the poet's mind since decades. And he has left quite a few observations in this regard.

In his prologue to the play Tagore referred to the *Rāmāyaṇa* in such words as would seem an anticipation of Harold Bloom—that it was the epic poet who had anticipated and hijacked his story instead of Rabindranath adapting the *Rāmāyaṇa* paradigm. He wrote: "I notice a similarity between the narrative direction of the *Rāmāyaṇa* and the plot outline of the present play. But the reason is not that the story has been gathered from the *Rāmāyaṇa*. The actual cause is that it is *Kaviguru* (the arché-poet) who has stolen my story *a priori* by means of his imaginative foresight. If you ask me what is the proof, I shall tell you, nobody will accept that during his time the golden citadel of Lanka was manifest with such enormous towering heights. That it is a phenomenon essentially of our times, remains evident as they lie scattered in thousands of proofs in thousands of instances." In this context one can just cite Harold Bloom's observation which should be self-explanatory: "But poetic influence need not make poets less original; as often it makes them more original..." (Bloom 7).

(iii) Points of comparison

Indeed there are some interesting points of comparison and contrast between Valmiki's epic and Tagore's play.

(a) The basic plot of the *Rāmāyaṇa* is constituted by the abduction of Sita, and the consequent destruction of Lanka. Tagore's play too seems to reify the epic plot within the compact space of the play—by the arrival of Nandini in the Yakshapuri and the consequent fall of the Yakshapuri.

(b) The similarity between the king of Lanka and the king of Yakshapuri has been underscored by the author himself.

(c) The *Rakshasas* in the epic are averse to agriculture and votaries for accumulation through plundering. The analogy can be legitimately extended to the principles of Yakshapuri which depends for its survival and prosperity upon digging and accumulation of wealth hidden inside the bowels of the earth.

(d) In both the epic and the play the basic conflict can also be envisioned as the conflict between man and machine. Rabindranath envisioned the Rakshasa civilization as a kind of machine-civilization.

These are of course ideas finely suggested by the play rather than explicitly stated. However, in his personal observations outside the text Tagore has repeatedly foregrounded the analogy and parallels.

Themes and Thematics

(i) Machine

Tagore wrote in *Rāśiār Cithi* (Letter from Russia):

> Since the time it became possible to multiply profit enormously with the help of machine, the medieval

> ideal of chivalry or the heroic ideal has been made to give way to the ideal of trade and commerce. The inception of the trading era is marked by plundering. The earth had shrieked at the horrid plundering of slaves and treasure that day. Since then the throne of Kuber has been entrenched in the world. Science announced that the rule of machine was the rule of the world; there was no other eternal truth beyond explicit profit-making. The arrogance of competition became pervasive, robbery acquired the prestige of a respectable vocation. Through visible and secret avenues, in the factories, mines, sprawling farms disguised slavery is being carried on, alongside falsehood and fierce cruelty. In the West those who amass money and those who supply it are now about to confront one another in a violent showdown.

Tagore had indeed felt increasingly concerned by the direction, or better to say 'misdirection' that civilization seemed to be taking in the modern times of industry, as the machine was set for pushing the man out. He writes:

> The pressure of ruthless competition makes the workers subordinate to machine. We get stupefied by seeing the huge arrangement of civilization from outside. The terrible genocide that is going on all the time underneath the structure remains hidden. But it cannot be hidden from God; and some news of the consequence can be heard every now and then through social upheavals....
>
> By magnifying the enterprise of work to any extent, by hugely inflating the works, by throwing them into hostile encounter, the poison of unrest and grievance seethes up. The way men have to live crammed up in a mass inside and around these monstrous factories, emitting black smoke, that they are divested of their natural right to space. One's minimum privacy is lost. There is no scope for the necessary space, or time, or contemplation. Thus man gets unaccustomed to his own company, and consequently at the least break from work they strain to get rid of themselves by indulging in

> drink and other distraction. All lose the capacity of slipping into silence, stillness, joy.... On the other hand the privileged ones are tired out by the ceaseless pursuit of fresh excitements...and fail to see self and the world clearly. Everything is seen hazily.
>
> (*Nababarşa* [The New Year]. *Dharma*; my translation)

The discourse on drink by Fagulal and Bishu in the play can be read alongside this observation. Fagulal first appears on the stage looking for the bottle which his wife has hidden. This is a rare holiday, and he wants his bottle in the very morning hour. Bishu can understand this thirst through his own experience:

> *Bishu.* To that boundless tavern, underneath the blue canopy? Alas, the road is closed.... No open sky, no leisure for us; so we have distilled the essence of all the song and laughter, all the sunlight of the twelve hours' day into one draught of liquid fire. (13)

Anyway, it would be wrong perhaps to assume that the play pleads for total rejection of the machine; rather it seems to highlight the need of some sort of balance,—balance between machine and life, power and love, duty and joy in order to ensure fullness of life. But if, for some reason the machine overpowers a society, then that society is headed for destruction, unless this is stopped by the arrival of some Nandini, i.e. the principle of joy. Yaksha Town is such a society where the machine has become all powerful and thereby set to oppress and dehumanize man.

Again, it will certainly be reductive reading if the play is taken to be exclusively concerned about industrialism. Industrialism of course provides the immediate situation; but, looked deeper it seems to be about the conflict between insensitized heart and the call of life as well. Owing to the excess of domination by machine under industrialism man becomes insensitive to what is good and what is evil/detrimental for man, and thus becomes usable tools in the hands of the powerful. Industrialism serves to underscore this issue in the context of the play. But at bottom it is the clash between the principles of vibrant life and inert matter. Nandini represents this vibrancy of life, whereas the total life of the Yaksha Town has rejected this natural urge for natural life and thereby turned inert. Similar paradigm has been worked out again and again in Tagore's plays in which the action revolves around this basic conflict between life and death, flow and stagnation, vibrancy and inertness. The inordinate desire for power renders man insensitive to the good—this is what has been shown in *Free Water*. And the excess of machine orientation renders man lifeless, dull, mechanical; digging up handfuls of dead gold turns man into a dull lifeless mass—this is shown in *Red Oleanders*.

Tagore wrote in 1933:

> There is no meaning in such words as spiritualising the machine; we can spiritualise our own being which makes use of the machine.... Today the profit that the machine brings to our door is too big and we do not hesitate to scramble for it even at the cost of our humanity. The shrinking of the man in us is concealed by the augmentation of things outside and we lack the time to grieve over the loss.... The means that science has produced through which to gain access into Nature's storehouse is tremendously complex which... makes it not only unavailable to the majority of mankind but also compels us to centralise it in monster factories, uprooting the workers' life from its natural soil creating unhappiness....
>
> ...What is called progress is the progress in the mechanical contrivances; it is in fact an indefinite extension of our physical limbs and organs which, owing to the enormous material advantage that it brings to us has tempted the modern man away from his inner realm of spiritual value and thus the balance is lost....
>
> ('Can Science be Humanized?' *EWT* 7:904)

The runners of the system are of blunt shallow efficiency, "who presume to buy human souls with their money and throw them into their dustbins when they have been sucked dry..." ('Can Science be Humanized?' *EWT* 7:905). Precisely this same idea is hinted by the left-over of the king (*rājār ẽto*), the drained battered men churned out by the monstrous machine of Yakshapuri.

In a way, the play is about the impact of machine upon human mind. However, it is not so much about machine, as about the consequent social crisis generated by a machine-dependent civilization.

(ii) Science

Tagore had felt deep anxiety about man's handling of science, i.e. scientific knowledge and resources. He felt science has given man enormous power; with the help of science man today is metaphorically in possession of ten heads and thousand eyes like the legendary demon. But the problem is that man does not know how to mobilize and engage this power towards activities which should be beneficial for himself. He fails to strike a balance between the forces of life and those of machine. Hence the accumulating fatigue that was about to weigh down civilization. Although Tagore appreciated the West's scientific pursuit, he felt apprehensive as well; because he perceived:

> Their [the West] enterprise and boldness does not want to accept any limit to its own demand. One by one they have been discovering all the hidden mysteries of the world, measuring it, weighing it, and taking possession of it. It is by means of their own strength that they have broken into nature's great storehouse of energy, and greedily plundering that treasure....
>
> It is because the pride of Europe regarding its own power has swelled to an extreme that it has no time to consider where its dearth lies. In a land where external nature is excessively imposing or overpowering, human mind gets overwhelmed by it, and becomes self-oblivious; similarly man gets infatuated by the exorbitantly huge volume of his self-accumulated mass of matter and external façade, and thus starts his own defeat. In course of the continuous erosion of the harmony of the mind under the weight of the external

mass a day comes when man's prosperity crumbles down in a terrible disaster to kiss the dust....

Where science serves to alleviate the misery and need of the common people, science attains nobility. But where it is engaged specially to make some person or race rich or powerful, that is the mark of its terrible fall; because our conscience is clouded then, and putting on the armor of big names like patriotism, nationalism, etc, it launches fight against itself. Consequently all over the world today the relationship between the races is thrown off the balance... The state polity, while disseminating political pestilence, gets corrupted inside under the pollution of cruelty and deceit.

(*Swādhikārapramatta. Kālāntar*; my translation)

That Tagore had this apprehension at the back of his mind, this unease and anxiety, while writing the play becomes evident from his own later comments with reference to the play:

> Science has permeated Western life; it no longer has its own cradle in the secluded cells of the learned. In a similar manner, the hungry purpose, having science for its steed, running about unchecked, trampling our life's harvest, is not an intellectual generalization unfit for imaginative literature. It is intensely real; its hot breath is upon us; its touch is all over our shrinking soul. It is the principal hero to-day in the drama of human history; and I trust I have the right to invoke it in my own play, not in the spirit of a politician, but of a poet, possibly a lyrical poet. (see Appendix ii)

(iii) Woman

Rabindranath writes in *Yātrī* with reference to the idea expressed in *Raktakarabi*: "In Yakshapur(sic) the enormous strength of man wrenches up the golden treasure from under the earth. The greedy enterprise of ruthless accumulation has driven out the sweetness of life from the place. By getting entwined in his own trap of complexity man has alienated himself from the world. So he has forgotten that joy is more precious than gold; he has forgotten that there is no fullness to be offered by power. Love alone can bring fulfillment. The huge arrangement there to keep man enslaved has also led to the self-imprisonment of the slave-runner. At such a turn the woman arrives there; Nandini arrives. The force of life confronted the machine. The surge of love began to assault the imprisoning net of avaricious misadventure. Then, how at the mysterious inspiration of the woman did the man set to overthrow the prison of his own making and thereby release the flow of life—this is described in the play". (my translation)

Rabindranath had a conviction about the mutual complementarity of the male and female principles. Such perfect balance is indeed rare in reality. In Yakshapuri the male energy swells to enormity as he sets for the target of invincibility through irrefutable machine. So, to stop this suicidal venture the woman arrives there, Nandini arrives as the symbol of energy, life, love and joy.

In drawing points of comparison between his own play and Valmiki's epic Tagore highlights the role of a mortal woman in the ultimate defeat of the demonic power. 'Ravana', the great accumulator and possessor in the *Tretāyug*, had kept in chain even the deities with lightning and thunder, and made them work for him. His rule could go on unchallenged for ever. But suddenly a mortal girl appeared amidst his god-defying prosperity and at once justice was stirred. He[Rama] defeated the Rakshasha with ignorant, unarmed monkeys. Not exactly the same has taken place in my play; but here too a mortal girl makes her appearance (trans. Present writer). Tagore makes an unambiguous assertion of his conviction in this regard as he writes with reference to the play: "When the woman's lively energy, in its multiple sweet dimensions, is obstructed against instilling the male ventures, then the machine takes over. Then man only hurts and gets hurt by the blow of the machine of his own creation."

Rabindranath argued: "In the woman of the Western world a certain restlessness is noticed which cannot be the normal aspect of her nature. For women who want something special and violent in their surroundings to keep their interests active only prove that they have lost touch with their own true world" ('Personality: Woman', *EWT:* 7). Tagore expressed his conviction:

> She must restore the lost social balance by putting the full weight of the woman into the creation of the human world...woman must come to the bruised and maimed world of the individual ('Personality: Woman')
>
> Woman can bring her fresh mind and all her power of sympathy to this new task of building up a spiritual civilization, if she will be conscious of her responsibilities. ('Personality: Woman')

Tagore further claimed in this connection that "the masculine creations of intellectual civilization are towers of Babel, they dare to defy their foundations and therefore topple down over and over again" ('Personality: Woman'); and "woman's function is the passive function of the soil, which not only helps the tree grow but keeps its growth within limits". ('Personality: Woman')

However, one cannot overlook the fact that in the play it is only Nandini who stands up to this model, whereas Chandra represents another aspect of the female principle; it is the negative, limited, possessive person. Tagore also throws hint about the former wife of Bishu who had allured him to make for this cursed city. There are the wives of the governors, who apparently enjoy the cream of the system. The author makes no attempt to cover up the greed for gold among these women, which may have further contributed to the pervasive 'gold rush' of their male partners.

> *Chandra.* ...you men have gone to the dogs in Yaksha Town...but we women haven't changed at all.
>
> *Bishu.* Haven't you? Your flowers have faded, and you are all slavering for gold.
>
> *Chandra.* No, never!
>
> *Bishu.* I say, yes. That Phagulal toils over and above the twelve,—why? For a reason unknown to him, unknown even to you. But I know. It's your dream of gold that lashes him on to work, more severely than the foreman's whip. (13-14)

Bishu knows even the will to flee the place has been destroyed; so he tells Chandra:

> If you go there (home) today you will fly back here tomorrow, like a caged bird to its cage, hankering for its drugged food. (14)

Except Nandini no other woman, neither Chandra nor the governors' wives, registers any protest against the system.

(iv) Search

Everybody in Yakshapuri seems to be engaged in some search. The professor is looking for the meaning of dead words in his dry manuscripts; the diggers are desperately looking around amidst the dark bowel of the earth for gold; Nandini has been searching for Ranjan; the king himself, behind the net, is engaged in a self-searching without himself being aware of it.

(v) The polarization

In the polarization presented in both the epic and the play, there is the sweetness of life on one side, whereas on the other there is self-destructive wealth; on one side there is joy, as implied by the names,—'Rama' and 'Ranjan'; Rama is one who gives joy, Ranjan is one who brings color to the mind; on the other side there are Ravana, and the supremo of Yakshapuri.

Again, Rama has made Sita his own through love; Ravana's avaricious possessiveness has led to her abduction. And like Ravana, intent on snapping the deep bond of love between Sita and Rama, the ruler of the machine realm in *Red Oleanders* also is bent upon tearing the lovers apart in his greedy, confused jealousy/envy.

Chandra, Phagulal, Bishu are also unhappy dissenters, but their dissent does not have the firmness; it is not prompted by the clarity of vision that we find in Nandini, or the strength of Ranjan that we hear about. The other oppositional tenor has been provided by the harvesting song floating in from the distant fields.

(vi) Message of hope

In the clash between individual vs. organized power, none emerges winner or defeated at the end. Coming out from behind his net, the first thing the King does is breaking the flagstaff, and then joining the rebel diggers against his own establishment run by the administrative executives: the Governor, Headman, Gosai. When Phagulal seeks to clarify, "we are out to break your own prison", the King says: "Yes, it is my *own* prison. You and I must work together, for you cannot break it alone".

Phagulal. As soon as the Governor hears of it, he will march with all his forces to prevent us.

King. Yes, my fight is against them.

Phagulal. But the soldiers will not obey you.

King. You will be on my side!

Phagulal. Shall we be able to win through?

King. We shall at least be able to die! At last I have found the meaning of death. I am saved! (50)

Tagore wrote elsewhere:

> We must know with absolute certainty that essentially we are spiritual. This we can do by winning mastery over self, by rising above all pride and greed and fear, by knowing that worldly losses and physical death can take nothing away from the truth and greatness of our soul. The chic knows when it breaks through the self-centred isolation of its egg that the hard shell which covered it so long was not really a part of its life. That shell is a dead thing, it has no growth; it affords no glimpse whatever of the vast beyond that lies outside it. However pleasantly perfect and rounded it may be, it must be given a blow to, it must be burst through and thereby the freedom of light and air be won, and the complete purpose of bird life be achieved. (*Sādhanā*)

Shambhu Mitra writes: "Rabindranath had envisioned the humiliation of the individual in the face of organized power. He had hoped man's irrepressible force of life would ultimately save him. Perhaps. But even then he had mentioned the waste of so much harvest as it falls scattered on the dust" (my translation). Mitra draws attention to Tagore's awareness of the waste that is involved in the process.

Ultimately the King succeeds in breaking through his iron net. Freedom is achieved from the gigantic system of machine-ruled materiality. Though this freedom comes at tremendous cost—the death of Ranjan and Kishore—vibrant youth and innocent boyhood, still it signals the message—howsoever confused/overpowered man may get under the rule of machine and materialism, his basic life-force is never destroyed altogether. Sooner or later it will resurface at the inspiration of life; Nandini ushers in that inspiration of life.

One should not, however, miss the fact that Tagore had taken care to point out repeatedly that the book was a vision and not a propaganda.

> I can assure my readers that I never meant to use this book as propaganda. It is a vision that has come to me in the darkest hour of dismay. I have a stronger faith in the simple personality of man than in the prolific brood of machinery that wants to crowd it.

Furthermore, he maintains,

> This personality—the divine essence of the infinite in the vessel of the finite—has its last treasure-house in woman's heart. Her pervading influence will some day restore the human to the desolated world of man. As in the animal world the physically meek has to-day inherited the earth, woman will one day prove that the meek in soul, through the sure power of love, will rescue this world from the dominance of the unholy spirit of rapacity. The joy of this faith has inspired me to pour all my heart into painting against the background of black shadows—the nightmare of a devil's temptation—the portrait of Nandini as the bearer of the message of reality, the saviour through death. (Appendix ii)

Some critics have conjectured about the possibility of the impact on Tagore's imagination of Delacroix's famous painting (1830) of the fall of Bastille during the French Revolution (1789), in which the rebellious crowd is shown as being led by a peasant woman.

Characters

Anonymity, Names, Naming

Roland Barthes in his S/Z mentions the anonymity of the Proustian narrator, "his perilously maintained lack of name", which he thinks, "creates a serious deflation of the realistic illusion" (Barthes 102). Here anonymity largely prevails among the citizens barring just a few proper names. They are not, as it were, fully alive, but only shadowy presences swaying about in the 'death's dream kingdom' of this nightmarish domain. In his talk to Elmherst in 1924 Tagore observed: "This is a world where, with every available means in his power, the Great King exploits the resources of the underworld, of nature, of the mind, of science and of human physique and intelligence, using all the weapons of organization and the elaborate machinery of a highly centralized bureaucracy in order to add to his wealth. This wealth he measures in gold, or in souls or in facts, or in human bodies, so that *men are men no longer but numbers.*" (emphasis added)

The diggers say, once they were persons when they were in their home-village; now they have become numbers. 'We are not men to them, but numbers' (15). Phagulal is No. 47 V, Bishu is 69 Ng. The Governor addresses Bishu as 'Hullo, 69 Ng' (16). Governor and Gosain exchange notes about different slums and people in terms of their respective numbers:

> *Governor.* Parish T-D. No. 71 T is headman there. It ends to the left of where No. 65 of Row M lives.
>
> *Gosain.* My son, though Parish T-D may not yet be quieted, the whole row of M's have lately become steeped in...meekness. (18)

Gosain also addresses Phagulal as 'friend 47 V'. This is obviously much more than funny number game; it points to a grim reality of the situation. The bulk of personae here are not individualized; they represent one or another group/category in the hierarchy of the place. This shows how under the impact of machine human distinctiveness and uniqueness are on the wane. In this society, built up on the basis of avarice, "which is not social in character, but utilitarian" (Tagore), everything seems to have been set in order to fit into some prescribed pattern. This applies not only to the area plan, but also to the humans. The moment they enter the factory, i.e. the system, they get reduced to abstract numbers. The other, prior identities fall redundant. The localities are known and mentioned in terms of abstraction: T-D parish or M parish, and the residents are known as numbers (Huxley: *Brave New World*; Orwell; the politics of naming). With the advent of industrialization the workers were displaced from their village and forced to live by the factory. In the village they were free workers in control of their own schedule. Here they are forced to follow the schedule of the factory; furthermore while in the village the whole family could work together, now they are separated, fragmentized. Hence the nostalgia of the workers for the 'home', when they cannot go home any more.

Those who are not numbers, are mentioned by their vocation instead of a personal name: Professor, Gosain, Physician, etc. It is the epitome of regimented life. Even the 'King' seems to have been cast in the same paradigmatic design of anonymity. In this connection one can recall Tagore's anxiety over the elimination of the 'personal' from institutions.

> To-day another factor has made itself immensely evident in shaping and guiding human destiny. It is the spirit of organization, which is not social in character, but utilitarian. Christian Europe no longer depends upon Christ for her peace, but upon the league of Nations, because her peace is not disturbed by forceful individuals so much as by organised Powers. Naturally, in all organizations, variation of personality is eliminated, and the individual members, in so far as they represent the combination to which they belong, give expression to a common type and very little to their uniqueness of individuality.

Tagore's critique of this regimentation is reflected in a significant aspect of the play which had drawn the attention of Shambhu Mitra's playing troupe: each of those whom the authority does not consider human, and sees only as numbers, has been conferred individual names by the playwright; for instance, Phagulal, Chandra, Bishu, Gokul, *et al.* Thus Bishu, who is just 69 Ng to the establishment gets back his own name among friends, along with the distinction of an additional epithet—'pagal'. On the other hand, the bosses, who do not take cognizance of these commoners as individuals, have been given only the brand-name of their vocation; for instance, Governor, Deputy Governor, Professor, Physician, Moṛol (Headman), etc. Only Gosain is given a first name; and that name is 'Kenaram'; Mitra wonders if the name 'Kenaram' which means 'a purchasable person', a man with a price tag, is a name or an epithet, because 'he takes the name of God, but takes the food from the Governor' (*RO*).

In contrast to the average residents of the place Nandini is individual. So are Ranjan and Kishor. Significantly, the most important person remains a 'Voice' and 'King', without a personal name. The 'personal man' is apparently forced to take the backseat by the 'organised man' in him.

Individuals

Nandini

Nandini is one of those characters who are simultaneously individuals and symbols.

Nandini occupies the centre-stage through the play; in a way it might be considered the story of a woman called 'Nandini'. She gets revealed against the backdrop of pervasive oppression all around. She is like the fountain which bursts up beautifully through the very obstacles, and sends its sprays of laughter, tear, melody all around and high upwards. The very life it registers by the burst is enthralling and liberating with its beauty, splendour, daring. Nandini is the liberating force in Yakshapuri. Nandini arrives in this dead place as the symbol of energy, life, love and joy. Where does she hail from? The author has left it vague.

The semantic meaning of the name is a girl/daughter/giver of joy; because daughter gives joy; this is further related to aesthetics, the principle of beauty; the beauty which has its appeal to all through joy.

Again, Nandini's close connection with the earth has been carefully highlighted. Nandini's costume, the fresh flowers on her hair and neck, her rural way of donning a sari, which is again of the color of ripe paddy; this is also another variation of the color of gold—not flashy or dazzling, but soothing, subdued; the background music of harvesting greeting her ears and making her restive.

Rama and Ravana in the epic come to clash on account of the abduction of Sita. In the play the same event resurfaces as an idea. Here the clash takes place between the votaries of growing plant and the band for plundering underground wealth. Tagore points out, Sita suggests the line of the furrow opening before the plough; and thereby Sita manifests the agricultural ways. The two communities with two opposite cultures clash upon this 'Sita'. Tagore's own play too veers round in course of the action upon the clash between two opposite ways of life; and it is Nandini who sets it snowballing.

The poet has left hints in the play that Nandini does not belong to the dark world underground where people search for hidden treasure. She belongs to the zone of light, upon the earth's surface, where beauty dances, love ripples at ease; Nandini is part of that simple easeful happiness and beauty.

Nandini represents a dynamic life-energy-emotion; and thus lends dynamism to the action. It is because of her that ripples are sent through the stagnant situation. So long things were following the same dull, monotonous, repetitive course; but as Nandini enters the scene people begin to react in various ways. Nandini is an anachronism in the place; so some would try to appropriate her, whereas others would prefer to drive her out of the domain. The play starts at this point. Tagore writes: "sometimes by accident some uneatable aquatic creatures happen to get caught in the fishermen's net; not only do they refuse to fill the stomach or the pocket; in course they tear off the net itself. A girl named Nandini has chanced to step into the web of incidents in this play. The façade shielding Makarraj is about to collapse with her advent" (trans. present writer).

Nandini can connect with different kinds of people with perfect ease, naturally, without inhibition, yet she is never without an innate dignity, although at one point she gets so infuriated that she would tear off Gosain's rosary and wrap, and admonish Governor in unambiguous terms: "Aren't you afraid of me, because I am a woman? God sends His thunderbolt through His messenger, the lightning spark—that bolt I have borne here with me; it will shatter the golden spire of your mastery" (37).

But Tagore would rather not present her as an abstraction: "I am glad to find that my critics readily acknowledge that Nandini, the heroine of the play, has definite features of an individual person. She is not an abstraction, but is pursued by an abstraction, like one tormented by a ghost. And this is the drama. Nandini is a real woman who knows that wealth and power are *māyā*, and that the highest expression of life is in love, which she manifests in her love for Ranjan" (Tagore: Appendix ii).

The other characters can be understood in terms of their respective responses to the event of Nandini's arrival in Yakshapuri; because they have been presented precisely that way.

The King

A 'King' often makes his presence in Tagore's plays. But the King of *Red Oleanders* is unique in his own way, and cannot be reconciled with the images of the 'King' in *Post Office*, or the King in *King of the Dark Chamber* or *Phālgunī*. Tagore himself had said, "Thanks to scientific power the limbs and heads of man have invisibly multiplied. There are hints in the play that the King of my Pala grabs and devours through this excess of power. So he had compared this King to the mythical demon king Ravana. Nandalal Basu, the renowned painter and an Ashramite during Tagore's time, defined the King as 'the scientific intelligence of today's man' (cited in Mitra). Tagore himself, in an interpretation of the play, mentions the King as an 'apparition' or 'abstraction' representing "megalomaniac ambition, while an acquisitive intellect plies its psychological curiosity, probing into the elusive mystery of love through vivisection" (Appendix ii).

The King is the supreme ruler of Yaksha Town which has been built by his strength alone. Though it is run by the governors, they do it for him; the diggers dig for him. People are sucked out until reduced to skin and bones because he would rise big. He stays behind a net, beyond the access of all. Several questions can stir in the reader/spectator's mind while following the play:

(1) Is it of his own accord that he keeps behind the net? Or, is it according to the plan of the governors, who may have found this system advantageous to their interest?

(2) It is the governors who appear the keenest to defend status quo for the system; then is it possible that they enjoy the cream out of the King's enterprises?

(3) Is the change at the end inconsistent with the earlier impression we get about the King? In connection with this issue it may be pointed out that the King is not mean; he is not selfish or heartless. That is why he is the King; he has the regality, the towering dignity, the peerless strength. As the play starts already chinks are showing up, fissures have appeared in the solid structure of his strength. In course of the play he arrives at self-knowledge; but the process has started with the very start of the play; therefore, it seems only natural that when the chance comes he should lose no time in prevarication; he can instantly declare war against the very system he has built up himself day by day.

(4) Shambhu Mitra, whose production of *Raktakarabī* had been a memorable event for the Bengali stage, interprets the King, following Nandalal Basu, as the symbol of science. One wonders, however, if this is an adequate explanation/definition of the person who seems more an enigma than a real human.

(5) Is it possible to relate the symbolic king to the author himself at the time, just as Nandini can be traced back to the lively beautiful little girl Ranu, and Ranjan to the delightful lively young Elmherst? [Incidentally, the play was dedicated to Elmherst.] Nirod C. Chaudhuri hints at the poet being weighed down by the pressure of work, a lonely alien inside, helpless prisoner of his own public image, fatigued

> at meeting demands from all quarters, yet aware of the impossibility of cutting through the prison-bar, metaphorically speaking (*Ātmaghātī Rabīndranāth*); the existentialist angst of the song of Tagore, *Āmi jato bhār jamiye tulechi sakali hayeche bojhā*, and the appeal, *e bojhā āmār nāmāo bandhu nāmāo* can also be recalled in the context. ["Whatever I have amassed has become such a wearisome burden! Oh my friend, help me to put down the burden!"] (my translation)

The King is ambivalent in his response to Nandini; he is simultaneously attracted and repelled by her, drawn towards her and repulsed away. Nandini fascinates him; yet he would also be relieved if he could drive her away. Where the King is the ruler of Yakshapuri, where he is the biggest machine of all the machines in the place, Nandini repels him. The King has a hunch this girl has come to put a stop to his machine-oriented activity.

However, there is also a hidden self within the hidden King; from behind his impenetrable net, the man in the King, his human heart, occasionally stirs and becomes eager for the touch of another human heart; it is in this self that he feels the tremendous pull of Nandini. He is constituted by the opposites of the machine and human, and is torn between the opposite pulls.

The King appears to command limitless strength. This has been further reinforced by intelligence and scientific resources, thereby enhancing his strength to any degree. Yet he is torn by opposite pulls of the right inspiration and wrong motives. Amidst his vast material prosperity a girl steps in. She proves instrumental in stirring up the potential Bibhisan within the Ravana, the dormant human instinct within the acquired scientific power. Finally, the former triumphs over the latter.

The King is weighed down by the fatigue that accumulates through the failure to reconcile science with life. This is the cause of his attraction towards Nandini, and the consequent jealousy against Ranjan. It is the longing of one who is exhausted by machine for the pure free life.

How the machine, by absorbing all the energy, leads to stagnation instead of dynamism can be seen in the predicament of the king. Though ceaseless activity is going on in the place, the King, who is supposed to be the centre of all these activities, is himself fixed/static behind the net of his own making. Thus the machine, which was manufactured to enhance man's activity, eventually robs him of the dynamic energy, and imprisons him. It is only after breaking through the net that he recovers his own initiative.

Tagore writes: "In my Pala (a folkform of play in India) there is a king. In this modern age I could not dare to give him more than one head and two arms. I would if I had the kind of confidence enjoyed by the prime poet; indeed thanks to the power of science the count of man's limbs and head has invisibly multiplied. There are hints in the play to suggest that the king of my Pala grabs and possesses by means of that very excess of strength" (my translation).

Tagore's King, however, is more complex than Ravana in the sense that he includes within himself the traits of Bibhishana too, the brother of Ravana in the epic who had rejected Ravana's ways and deserted his camp. It is a subtler and profounder concept that the King manifests in the play. If the King is a modern version of Ravana, then the Bibhishana, his other self, resides not outside, but within him; it had been dormant so long, and now wakes up at the call of Nandini, her repeated knockings on his iron net. Ultimately a time comes when he tears the net apart and comes out to declare rebellion against the lifeless crushing system created by himself.

Tagore writes: "There was no dearth of space in the seven Books of the First poet; therefore he had allotted separate places/roles to Ravana and Bibhishana. But he had also left the hint that they were the same, they were siblings. Inside the same nest sin and its lethal destructor have been nurtured. In my slim play the present incarnation of Ravana is both Ravana and Bibhishana in the same person. He defeats but himself…".

This King, like two other kings of Tagore's two other plays, *Arūpratan* and *Dākghar*, remains invisible though his voice is audible. He hides himself in the darkness or behind the curtain of iron net. Like the other two, this king also becomes visible at the end. But unlike the other two he has been terrifying; and when he finally emerges,—breaking the door open, tearing the net apart—he has rebelled against the system of his own making. This process of self-concealment eventually ending in self-revelation has been identified by Ashrukumar Sikdar as a common motif in Rabindranath's play.

However, the King continues to be apprehensive of his other self since the beginning of the play; he is afraid to come outside; he cannot relate himself to the earth, the corn, the golden light. Nandini calls out to him: "You too come out, King!—out into the fields." The 'Voice' floats out: "Fields! What could I do there?" He has lost the skill of doing simple things, as he moans, "It is the simple which is impossible for me. A lake cannot run out dancing, like a frolicsome waterfall..." (8).

Yet he commands amazing strength which fascinates Nandini; as she explains: "The day you let me into your storehouse the blocks of gold did not surprise me,—what amazed me was the immense strength with which you lifted and arranged them" (8).

There is, again, a subtle connection between the King and Ranjan. Ranjan is youth incarnate. The King too had once built up the huge system with the strength of his youth, which attracts Nandini. But she wants that enormous strength of the King to be engaged to create new living civilization instead of piling up dead wealth and erecting a dead system.

In the final analysis the King emerges as a human individual; once he had youth but now it is gone. His pain, his anger, his confusion all together make him a living individual in spite of his endless mystery. The King's progress in the play can be understood in the light of Tagore's observation in another context: "Man grows gigantic by the appropriation of everything for himself: he attains harmony by giving himself up" (*EWT* 5:20).

King and Nandini

This attainment, however, would not have been possible without the intervention of Nandini. When Nandini speaks of the 'curse' involved in rending the earth's bosom, the king seems not to understand; he seems to be rather proud and even boastful of his strength. "But we bring up strength. Does not my strength please you Nandini?" (8). The King has acquired this strength; yet he does not seem satisfied. He is annoyed by 'the mystery' of Nandini's beauty which he fails to grasp. This is the limitation of science; it can measure, weigh, analyze but cannot feel. "I want to pluck you out of it (evasion), to grasp you within my closed fist, to handle you, scrutinize you,—or else to break you to pieces." Hence his restiveness, his anger: "Why can't I strain out the tint of your oleanders and build a dream out of it to keep before my eyes? Those few frail petals guard it and hinder me. Within you there is the same hindrance, so strong because so soft…" (8).

This can be read alongside Tagore's observation: "The view that we can get of her (the West), in our mutual dealings, is that of a titanic power with an endless curiosity to analyse and know; but without sympathy to understand; with numberless arms to coerce and acquire, but no serenity of soul to realise and enjoy" (Appendix i).

Apparently, prior to meeting Nandini, the King had not been aware of his extreme fatigue, which seems to have suddenly flashed upon him with overpowering effect, and stirs Nandini's awe and sympathy.

> I, who am a desert, stretch out my hand to you, a tiny blade of grass, and cry: I am parched, I am bare, I am weary. The flaming thirst of this desert licks up one fertile field after another, only to enlarge itself,—it can never annex the life of the frailest of grasses. (9-10)

He again adds, as if in a self-absorbed slow interior monologue, looking into a mirror:

> One day, Nandini, in a far off land, I saw a mountain as weary as myself. I could not guess that all its stones were aching inwardly. One night I heard a noise, as if some giant's evil dream had moaned and moaned and suddenly snapped asunder. Next morning I found the mountain had disappeared in the chasm of a yawning earthquake. That made me understand how overgrown power crushes itself inwardly by its own weight. (10)

It is through this fatigue that he perceives in Nandini what he lacks himself, in spite of all his wealth,—"the dance rhythm of the All" (10). The 'Voice' of the invisible King here gets conflated by the voice of the poet of *Gitanjali*, as he defines the 'rhythm':

> The rhythm that lightens the enormous weight of matter. To that rhythm the bands of stars and planets go about dancing from sky to sky, like so many minstrel boys. It is that rhythm, Nandini, that makes you so simple, so perfect. How small you are compared to me, yet I envy you. (10)

In course of, his enterprise "to plunder the world's big treasure-houses", he has been self-alienated from this 'rhythm of all', and would still greedily long for the mystery of the rhythm. He can guess there are gifts that Nandini's "little flower-like fingers can easily reach, but not all the strength" of his body,—"gifts hidden in God's closed hand". He still hopes to possess it by means of force,—"That hand I must force open some day". He would implore Nandini for just a touch of her little hand, and then again lapse back to his drudgery, his schedule of "busy time, overloaded with work, dragged along against obstruction." He seems to know somehow this 'time' is not fit for receiving Nandini. The above dialog between the 'Voice' and Nandini, which discloses the erosion that has already undermined the King's stability, also carries hints of a forthcoming crisis in which the strong façade of the King's nature will collapse. It becomes clear at this stage that the King suffers from a sense of frustration, which makes him fly into sudden spurts of anger, and again relapse into sadness, almost into bleak despair of a beggar, and again getting bitter and demonic in his envy of Ranjan.

King and Ranjan: Contrast and Connection

During his talk with Nandini across the network, the King says rather resentfully, "In me there is only strength, in Ranjan there is magic." As the play starts, a conflict has already set in the king; he boasts of his power, yet it seems he does not enjoy thus amassing strength. Already he has a glimpse of the futility of his acquirements: "All I possess is so much dead weight"

(9). He feels tired (which he expresses in images of a desert, a sinking mountain). He does not want to force Nandini into subjection, yet he would occasionally lapse into the show of strength. Perhaps once he had youth, but now that youth is missing; instead what remains is strength, only strength. So he envies Ranjan. Even after Nandini admits his strength "makes my heart dance within me", the King must know if it is the same feeling that Ranjan stirs in her. As Nandini says, "that dance rhythm is different, you won't understand", the King would insist like some willful child, 'I will, I must understand' (9). He must know if Nandini likes him 'the same as Ranjan'.

The King is envious of Ranjan's youth, but fails to understand the secret of his youth, his magic, which resides in his connection with the rhythm of the universe. He has already identified his own lack, but that makes him only more resentful and fretful. "No increase of power can ever come up to youth. I can only guard by force"; it is at this point that he keenly feels inferior to Ranjan: "If I had Rañjan's youth I could leave you free and yet hold you fast. My time is spent in knotting the binding rope, but, alas, everything else can be kept tied, except joy" (9).

Ranjan

Ranjan and the King are connected by some mysterious thread of affinity. Nandini loves Ranjan, and yet feels a strange attraction for the King as well, though this is not exactly love. Ranjan is the essence of youth, held high above material and machine. On the other hand, the King is one whose essence has been caught and controlled by the machine; hence he has become unreal, which is epitomized by his invisibility behind iron net. Nandini, who manifests the exuberance of life, can love only Ranjan, the essential free man; she can have amazement, even a mild infatuation for the King; but her pure, eager, flowing love is reserved for Ranjan alone. So when the King reaches out for her flowers she refuses, because "Some one loves red oleanders and calls me by that name". She makes it clear—"It is in remembrance of him that I wear these flowers" (26), an answer that annoys and angers the King. At the end, it is to Ranjan that she sends her bangle of Raktakarabi.

In answer to the King's query—how does she love Ranjan, Nandini says, "I love Ranjan as the rudder in the water might love the sail in the sky, answering its rhythm of wind in the rhythm of waves" (23). If Nandini is beauty Ranjan is joy. Etymologically, the name suggests color and joy. Therefore he is irresistible like the wild stream. He can restore life into the realm of death. He is the laughter of God. His joy gets manifest in the exuberant energy of life. As Nandini describes—which is also a way of defining the mystery of his charm—

> ...he [Ranjan] holds an oar in each hand and ferries me across the stormy waters; he catches wild horses by the mane and rides with me through the woods; he shoots an arrow between the eyebrows of the tiger on the spring, and scatters my fear with loud laughter. As he jumps into our Nagai river and disturbs its current with his joyous splashing, so he disturbs me with his tumultuous life. Desperately he stakes his all on the game and thus has he won me. (21)

Whereas Nandini is the eternal primordial strength of life which finds expression through woman, Ranjan, symbolizes youth, which gives dynamism, motivation, inspiration to all human activity.

The Rulers and the Ruled

A common theme of Tagore's plays is that discipline is necessary; but when it becomes more hindrance than help in the blossoming of life then a crisis becomes imminent. Then the structure needs to be pulled down. But nothing else than the surge of life itself is adequate for the job. The same paradigm holds in *Muktadhārā* and *Acalāyatan*. In *Muktadhārā*, Prince Abhijit sacrifices his own life to release the waterfall from the bondage of machine.

Most of the minor personae in *Red Oleanders* are either completely under the rule of discipline, or they subscribe to the ideology of this autocracy and actively work for it; indeed they are the establishment of this domain.

Governor

Firstly, we can consider the Governors; again, even amongst the Governors, who enjoy a position of power in the total hierarchy of the autocratic system, there is yet another hierarchy, wheels within wheels, by which they are fixated in their specific positions—as the Governor, the Deputy Governor, and the Assistant Governor. These Governors are supposed to be efficient and competent persons. It is thanks to their alert administration that the Yaksha Town smoothly rolls along to unbroken prosperity. They run the place through the King. They serve to uphold and maintain the system. It is because of their ruthless service that the autocracy rules over the Yakshapuri. The system has dehumanized them and they in turn work hard to maintain and further strengthen the system. Thus they make a vicious coterie. They enjoy such tremendous power that once they get hold of something or someone even the King cannot loosen their bite.

> *Chandra.* Why, he[Governor] seems to be so nice and—
>
> *Bishu.* Yes, nice and polished, like the crocodile's teeth, which fit into one another with so thorough a bite that the King himself cannot unlock the jaw, even if he wants to. (16)

The Governors have used science and have become more powerful than science itself. They are extremely mischievous as one never knows how they would start mischief against whom, and under what pretext. Bishu says, "This place is dark with the Governor's shadow, it is everywhere" (23). [One can immediately recall the famous catch-phrase of Orwell's *1984*—'Big brother is watching you'.] Nandini says about the Governor, "I have never seen anything so lifeless,—like a cane stick cut from the cane bush,—no leaves, no roots, no sap in the veins" (23). Bishu follows with his rejoinder: "Cut off from life, he spends himself in repressing life" (23).

He is furthermore a dirty manipulator who can use any trick to trap and finish anyone. The thrashed wrestler is furious about the Governor, whose 'lying tongue' he would like to tear off. He knows what a mean schemer the Governor is,—set to destroy even the remnant of strength in a human. "They only feel safe when they rob the whole world of strength" (35). Therefore, although the wrestler had never wanted to fight, this Governor had egged him on, and now he says it is the former's fault. He mutters in impotent anger: 'If only once...I could fasten my teeth for once in the Governor's throat" (35). But actually he has no power to avenge himself over this man.

The Governor has no inhibition against selling absolute lies as truth. He sends message to Ranjan that the King has reduced Nandini to the status of royal concubine. Previously he had provoked Gajju the wrestler to challenge the King by means of some such falsehood. The Governor even cheats the King, as the King discovers at the end: "Deceived! These traitors have deceived me,—perdition take them! My own machine refuses my sway! Call the Governor—bring him to me handcuffed—" (47). But the Governor has his hand on the machine button; so even before the King can set out along with the rushing crowd of diggers set to break the prison, the Governor's troop can be heard approaching. The crashing noise can be heard above the charged atmosphere of the last scene.

Phagulal. King, do you hear the tumult?

King. There comes the Governor with his troops. How could he be so quick about it? He must have been prepared beforehand. They have used my power against me. (50)

Governor has absolutely no sense of guilt; he can glibly justify his wrongdoing by scientific analogies, and thus shirk off his responsibility in a crime he commits. To Nandini's anxious query, where has he taken Bishu, Governor replies callously:

> Who am I that I should take him? The wind carries off the clouds,—if you think that to be a crime, make enquiries as to who is behind the wind. (37)

Gosain

Chandra is taken in by the façade of Governor, the deceitful man,—'How he smiles every time he talks!' (18). But there is another around, who can beat even Governor in suave deceit; he is Gosain. Tagore wrote in *Nāṭyaparicay*: "Besides, there is one Gosainji. He takes the name of God, but he takes the food from the Governor. He contributes a lot to the well-being of the Yaksha Town" (trans. Present author). Gosain is also another Governor in disguise; he is part of this vicious establishment and perhaps the most obnoxious of the set of rulers, because of his cultivated hypocrisy. Deputy Governor tries to define the evasive Gosain:

> The poor man is really two in one, clumsily joined,—Priest on the skin, Governor at the marrow. He has to take precious care to prevent the Governor part of him coming up to the surface, lest it should clash too much with his telling of the beads. (43)

He is the religious man supposed to impart spiritual lessons to the diggers here. But his religious teachings are shaped so as to serve the interest of the autocratic establishment. It seems the two,—Governor and Gosain—are shrewdly acting rehearsed parts; the Governor informs the diggers, "I have sent for our High Preacher, Kenaram Gosain…to give moral talks to the men…", and at once Gosain enters the stage, as if he had been just waiting by the wings for the hint to drop in; Governor instantly starts ovation to a man who is but his employee, and can be 'sent for'. An obvious element of artificiality hangs low over their rehearsed conversation, carrying hints of a grim covert meaning under cover of the absurd pep-talk. One is reminded of the 'double-speak' of the *1984* Newspeak language nuances.

> *Governor*. Your Holiness, I do you reverence. These workmen of ours sometimes feel disturbed in their weak minds. Deign to whisper in their ears some texts of peace. The need is urgent.
>
> *Gosain*. These people? Are they not the very incarnation of the sacred Tortoise of our scripture, that held up the sinking earth on its back? Because they meekly suppress themselves underneath their burden, the upper world can keep its head afloat. The very thought sends a thrill through my body!

The hypocrite rolls on glibly:

> Just think of it, friend 47 V, yours is the duty of supplying food to this mouth which chants the holy

> name. With the sweat of your brow have you woven this wrap printed with the holy name, which exalts this devoted body. Surely that is no mean privilege. May you remain for ever undisturbed, is my benediction....
>
> My friends, repeat aloud the holy name of Hari, and all your burdens will be lighted.... (17)

Gosain is cynical in prostituting his 'religion' and oratory to the service of the oppressive establishment. Religion is not his goal; it is used as a clever ploy, an ideological devise, to justify the oppression. Like the sardars, he is just another guard of the system, only meaner and cleverer than others, showing the unholy alliance between 'Caesar and Church'. He is the parasite too: "Their votive fees will pay for his upkeep".

The man is characterized by an abominable innate vulgarity. Even as the wrestler lies broken in front of all he goes on talking about Nandini's garland of 'kund' flowers, as if the wounded man didn't exist. He mentions the garland with an overt vulgar thrust: "Ah indeed! The gift of a pure heart! God's own white kunda flowers! Their beauty remains unsullied even in the hands of a man of the world..." (36). To Nandini's urgent appeal to do something for the poor wrestler, Gosain says, "The Governor is sure to keep him as much alive as it is necessary for him to be. But, my child, these discussions will become your lips" (36). One feels disgusted, what gives him the right to speak in this tone to Nandini? Nandini is revolted at the suggestion of 'calculated apportioning of life'; but Gosain has no qualms to justify the evil system in God's own name: "Our class of people have their great burden to bear, therefore we have to claim a larger portion of life's sustenance for our share. That's according to Almighty God's own decree" (36). This anticipates the curious logic of the 'pigs' in Orwell's *Animal Farm* (1945) to justify their parasitic and exclusive consumption of the milk and apples, instead of sharing it with all the other animals,—and all this in the name of the 'cause': "We pigs are brain-workers. The whole management and organization of this farm depend on us. Day and night we are watching your welfare. It is for *your* sake that we drink that milk and eat those apples" (Orwell 22).

Assistant Governor

As he enters the stage for the first time, Governor calls out to him, rather brusquely, "Where are you going?" It seems Governor keeps his officers too under tight control, and they are answerable to him in this regimented hierarchical society. He proudly says, 'to arrest Ranjan', (an assignment initially given to Deputy Governor), as if this should be counted enough cause for bravado. Assistant Governor seems to be a familiar type who would not miss a chance for backbiting his colleague or immediate boss to the higher authority. So his answer is ready to the expected query from Governor, "Where is the Deputy Governor?" "He is so much amused… etc." This small touch adequately brings out the man, his personal ambition, his pettiness, meanness. He is a Governor out and out. So he would tactfully use the Deputy's sympathy for Ranjan as a handle against him and take this chance to further his own ambition.

Deputy Governor

The Assistant Governor's shrewd and mean undercutting of the Deputy helps us to understand the Deputy's nature and the man's temperamental difference from the other governors/rulers.

> He is so much amused by this fellow that he doesn't want to lay hands on him. He says the man's laugh shows what queer creatures we governors have grown into. (30)

That he can still respond to the charm of Ranjan shows his humanity has not yet withered up like the rest of the ruling coterie.

As soon as the Deputy Governor enters the stage one has the impression that he is somewhat different from the rest of the rulers. While entering he announces he has 'just sent' the dancing girls and musicians to the garden, where the rulers' families will join a feast. Governor asks him conspiratorially about "that little matter about Ranjan". The following dialogue brings out the man's character in relief against the unmitigated cynical cruelty of Governor; at the same time it sheds light on Governor, Headman and Assistant Governor who can sink to any level of sadism and even enjoy it; furthermore, it discloses in grim flashes the kind of detestable conspiracy that is executed by these men—unspoken things, as indicated by the hyphens, make the terror only the more horrifying:

> *Deputy Governor.* That kind of work is not in my line. The Assistant Governor has taken it upon himself to do the job. By this time his—
>
> *Governor.* Does the King—?
>
> *Deputy Governor.* The King can't possibly have understood. Some lie told by our men has goaded Ranjan to frenzy, and he's rushing to the usual fate of—*I detest the whole business.* Moreover, I don't think it right to deceive the King like this.
>
> *Governor.* That responsibility is mine. Now then, that girl must be—
>
> *Deputy Governor.* Don't talk of all that to me. The Headman who has been put on duty is the right man,—he doesn't shrink at any dirtiness whatever. (43; emphasis added)

Perhaps he would have been happy if he could dissociate himself from these criminal plans; but cannot, possibly because he is not a challenging rebel but only an escapist who wants to be exempted from an unpleasant job. Governor has rightly sized him up: "My friend, I see the instinct of the Ruler doesn't seem to match with the colour of your own blood..." and the Deputy replies with caustic bitterness, which is directed more at himself than the addressee, "There's hope still. Human blood is fast drying up" (43). Is he also a trapped man, waiting for the worst tragedy, the tragedy of dehumanization of self? No wonder, this schismatic person 'can't stomach' No. 321, i.e. the Headman. One wonders why did Tagore introduce such varied shades of personalities as counterpoints within the counterpoint?

Headman

The Headman is an example of unmixed servile evil. He is one of the henchmen of the system, the Governor's own team —who keep the machine of an oppressive system oiled and rolling.

With their brief appearance on the stage these small people leave a distinct impression upon the spectator. As Governor entrusts him with a 'duty' which is in no way official—to help his wife changing post near the Headman's village—he is disgustingly eager to oblige: "There is a plague on the cattle of our parish, and not a single ox can be had to draw the car. Never mind, we can press the diggers into service" (40). The suggestion brings out in a sudden grim flash the rulers' dehumanizing attitude and treatment of the diggers. Indeed, these crude henchmen of brutal power have no qualms in treating fellow humans as beasts, dragging them along the road, chained like a beast; as Bishu, under arrest, says fearlessly: "They have a big beast inside them, that's why their heads are not lowered by the indignity of man, rather the inner brute's tail swells and wags with pride at man's downfall" (39).

And all the time Headman is busy promoting some personal interest or undermining another's security, the typical reptilian creature fawning on the vestige of the powerful, a quite familiar figure to all of us. Governor makes no attempt to conceal his contempt, but the base creature does not mind. The Deputy Governor's estimate of the Headman throws adequate light on the latter's baseness,—"he doesn't stick at any dirtiness whatever" (43). It is with the eager service of such people that an oppressive system thrives.

Doctor

Doctor is another small but useful spoke in this wheel of unholy power. Like the religious man the medical man too prostitutes his vocation in the service of the system. He does not work towards curing illness and saving human life; his role is to preserve the bodies so as to provide the necessary work-force. He works at the instance of Governor, apparently he is Governor's instrument towards keeping a man "as much alive as it is necessary for him to be" (36); Governor does not trust the king; therefore, he has employed Doctor as a spy to keep watch upon the king. From his brief conspiratorial exchange with Governor, "I've seen him. I find the King" (40), one has a wiry hunch that these people are hatching some plan against the King.

Professor

The Professor is an intellectual by profession, whose intellect has been surrendered in the service of the system of the Yakshapuri. Yet he is not like the Doctor. In a way, Professor is also a digger as Nandini perceives: 'You who burrow day and night in a mass of yellow pages, like your diggers in the bowels of the earth' (4). Even so, he has not been completely eclipsed by it like Governor, Gosain or Doctor. This becomes apparent when we notice his response to Nandini, which reflects a kind of honest surprise. He first appears on the stage while addressing Nandini:

> Why do you come and startle one, now and again, and then pass by? Since you awaken a cry in our hearts, what harm if you stop a moment in answer to it? Let us talk a little. (4)

In answer to Nandini's question why he wonders at her, the Professor explains: "The sunlight gleaming through the forest thickets surprises nobody, but the light that breaks through a cracked wall is quite a different thing. In Yaksha Town, you are this light that startles..." (4). The Professor explains to the Antiquarian, who is a newcomer in the place, and as yet not quite conversant with its ways:

> She has for her mantle the green joy of the earth. That is our Nandini. In this Yaksha Town there are governors, headmen, tunnel-diggers, scholars like myself; there are policemen, executioners, and undertakers,—altogether a beautiful assortment! Only *she* is out of element. Midst the clamour of the market place she is a tuned-up lyre. (31)

He further admits how he is distracted by this phenomenon called Nandini: "There are days when the mesh of my studies is torn by the sudden breeze of her passing by, and through that rent my attention flies away swish, like a bird" (31).

The Professor seems to speak in the slightly mocking tone of a benign grandfather. Yet there is also a hidden resentful, bitterness which bursts through the seams of his apparently pleasant talk, though his oblique critique is presented in the garb of humor, it is nevertheless an acid humor. As Nandini says, it puzzles her to see a whole city thrusting its head underground, groping for dead wealth, the Professor explains, smilingly of course, though his words are dripping bitterness: "The *Jinn* of that dead wealth we invoke. If we can enslave him the whole world lies at our feet", and adds like a rejoinder, "As the ghost of our dead wealth is fearfully potent so is our ghostly royalty, made hazy by this net, with its inhuman power to frighten people" (4).

This is his way of protesting against the way of life in Yaksha Town. The sharpness of his mind flashes up at moments, as in his quick repartee to Nandini's charge that all he says is "a kind of made-up talk": "Of course made-up. The naked is without a credential, it's the made-up clothes that define us" (4). But sometimes he can barely retain the mask of humor, and a tragic seriousness casts shadow, as he says, "Yaksha Town is a city under eclipse"; or wonders why should the girl pick up the oleander from all flowers for her ornament, "Do you know we often choose our own fate thus, without knowing it!" (6).

Professor represents the typical confusion and conflict of the elite in this society. He is simultaneously attracted and repulsed by the system. Yet secretly in his innermost heart there is hope for a 'time': "When the time comes for showing us out, the great ones themselves will point the way…" (33). To Nandini's question, "Does it at all make for their well-being thus to keep watch and ward over these man-traps night and day?", Professor makes his sardonic comment: "Well-being! There's no question of 'well' in it at all—only 'being'. That *being* of theirs has expanded so terribly that, unless millions of men are pressed into service, who's going to support its weight…. They must exist, you see" (34). We come to know that he had 'told' (friendly warning?) Gajju at the outset that no 'show of heroics' will be allowed here for a moment, whereas Governor had provoked the wrestler into the encounter and thus crushed him.

Thus Professor appears to have retained at least some humanity in spite of the dehumanization all around; therefore, it does not seem unexpected or anachronistic when at the end the elderly man too leaves his cell and joins the diggers in their onward march to pull down the prison.

The Commoners

(i) Ordinary

Sometimes it has been wrongly assumed that Tagore could not perceive or portray commoners. The novels and the plays bear ample evidence to Tagore's power of observation—sometimes amused, sometimes compassionate—which is often brought out by means of sharp flashes, and minute cute touches of a casual stroke of brush.

Phagulal and Chandra

Phagulal and Chandra, the digger couple, represent the countless disempowered commoners, victims of the establishment in Yaksha Town. Though they have become accustomed to the place they still feel a kind of longing for the home village they had left behind for coming here. During the harvest season they want to go home. But they have been made distinct individuals with very different responses to people and things; whereas Phagulal is stirred by Nandini's vibrancy and ultimately he will follow Nandini to join the rebels, Chandra is jealous of her. Chandra is an instance of the very real portraits of common men and women that Tagore could do so effectively with just a few brush-strokes. She is vivid with her petty jealousy and limited vision. With her limited mind she fails to summon any sympathy for the girl, and mentions her as witch instead. As Bishu enters absorbed in his own song, she comments:

> He's been possessed by Nandini.... The witch is up to all kinds of tricks, and is sure to bring misfortune. (12)

A little later she adds:

> To see her flaunting her prettiness all over the place makes me sick. (12)

Chandra, again, is easily won over by the priest's hypocritical oratory, whereas Phagulal can see through him. Incidentally, Chandra is also taken in by Governor's artificial smile, by the 'gorgeous array' of the procession of Governors and their wives on the occasion of Flag worship.

Gokul

Tagore never draws his world in black-and-white. Though the diggers are victims of the system, individually they are not all angels. Gokul is a digger who has been vividly individualized with just a few brush-strokes. He is rude, sadist and suspicious by nature. Tagore is adept in doing such small people with their habitual meanness and limitations. For instance, one can recall the long pageant of ordinary people in *Gorā*—from Baradasundari to Harimohini, from Kailash to Mahim, from Krishnadayal to Haranbabu, from Mahim's wife to Labanya, and from the reptilian Madhab Chatterjee to the vulturish police inspector, the arrogant magistrate Brownlow, the brute policemen—amusingly/revoltingly small and mean. They are, however, no less vivacious and entertaining. These flashes adequately show that Tagore could be as realistic as any of the valorized realistic writers (Saratchandra, for instance); like Gulliver holding the Liliputians on his palm, Tagore could at ease pick these small people up for instantaneous playful observation and then leave them indifferently on the roadside to go ahead with his main characters.

Gokul is by nature suspicious, a potential sadist, given to spurts of violence. He is by temperament inclined to faultfinding with others. One can imagine him talking in loud metallic voice. Gokul is a very limited person, and he wants to understand a thing clearly in his own limited way; he is suspicious of what he fails to understand, and his failure makes him aggressive towards the object. "I don't trust what I can't understand", he says in so many words; hence his aggressive rudeness towards Nandini, whom he cannot understand.

Like Chandra, Gokul too thinks of her suspiciously as a witch. Although Chandra's motivation is jealousy, Gokul is prompted by fear of what he, in his blunt insensitivity, fails to grasp. Even Gokul, who has been dehumanized under the system, feels a kind of uneasiness at the presence of Nandini. Gokul cannot understand her, therefore cannot trust her either. He is like the blunt fascist activist/muscleman of an autocratic political party. He bluntly confronts Nandini:

> *Gokul.* Turn this way, woman! Who are you? I've never yet been able to understand you....

I don't trust what I can't understand....

....

I don't believe you, one bit!...Oh, you terrible, terrible witch! (7)

At the same time Gokul also feels a strange attraction, though this attraction only stirs up fear and violence within him: "You know some spell, I'm sure. You're snaring everybody here. You're a witch! Those who are bewitched by your beauty will come to their death" (7). Towards the end this innate violence finds its grim expression as Gokul is about to hack her with his heavy club.

At the end when all are set, including the King, for breaking the prison Gokul and Chandra are found missing. Phagulal says: "She has gone with her tears and prayers to the Governor, accompanied by Gokul. I am afraid Gokul is seeking to take up service with the Governor. He will betray us" (49). Perhaps this would have been the right placement for people like Gokul all along; persons like Chandra, with their limited minds, readily fall for them.

The Commoners

(ii) Extraordinary

Kishor

Kishor and Bishu, both slaves of the system, yet represent an extraordinary spirit of resilience, which they achieve through love. Kishor is a very young digger who has not been here long. Kishor is not only the name. He is Kishor in age too; so he can speak of his feelings without hesitation. Kishor epitomizes the pure innocence of a boy; so he can recognize beauty and also respond to it spontaneously without inhibition. He intuitively knows beauty and its worth. Kishor has no greed for the dough of gold.

Because the Yaksha Town has not yet swallowed him up, he can turn to Nandini with the love of his eager innocent mind; it is owing to this love that he procures red oleanders for her at considerable risk. The play starts with Kishor, excitedly entering the stage; he is excited at discovering a plant of red oleanders. He is happy that the flowers, which Nandini said she must have, are not easily available in this place. He tells Nandini: "I am glad they're hard to find in this place".

He does not fear or worry about punishment; that means physical pain does not affect his mind.

Nandini. But it breaks my heart to know that those brutes punish you.

Kishor. It makes these flowers all the more preciously mine. They come from my pain. (3)

Again, in a later scene, when Bishu is led in chains Kishor wants to persuade the guards to take him in exchange: "Punishment won't hurt me. I am young. I shall bear it with joy" (39). Significantly, it is Kishor, a mere boy, who is assigned the "dangerous work" (39)—the challenging task of finding out Ranjan in this huge Gulag. It is adolescence which is sent to search out endangered youth. And Kishor dies while carrying out the mission; but prior to death he has done his duty—he has handed over the bunch of red oleanders to Ranjan. This is what he had dreamt of as he said to Nandini on his first appearance: "I dream of dying one day for your sake" (3). This avowal flashes upon Nandini as she notices the flower in the dead hand of Ranjan. As she challenges, the King informs, Kishor has disappeared like a bubble, because the poor boy, with a woman's charming face and strange haughty words, had dared to take on the King. "He burst himself against me, like a bubble" (48).

Kishor can be placed in line with Uttiya in Tagore's dance-drama *Shyāmā*, who is mentioned as *bālak kiśôr* (*a young boy*), and who sacrifices his life for the sake of the woman he loves; or Amulya in *Ghare-Bāire* (*The Home and the World*), the teenage boy who takes great risk to help Bimala, whom he adores. The innocence and nobility of this selfless love of a boy for an older woman recurs in Tagore's oeuvre as a repeated motif, which can be examined from the perspective of psychological criticism.

Bishu

Bishu is called Bishu the madcap—derisively by some, lovingly by Nandini. There had been a time when Bishu was part of this autocratic establishment. But eventually he was got rid of. Now he is a misfit in the Yaksha Town, and generally passes off as the mad one. This is again a recurring feature of Tagore's plays; a madman, or a grandpa, or a Baul singer,—somebody outside the pale of the common run of life, and thereby lending a special dimension and perspective to the play. Bishu is to Nandini what Dhananjoy Bairagi is to the Prince Abhihit in *Free Water*—a musical inspiration and support. In answer to the King's anxious and annoyed query, "Nandini, what is this man to you?", she replies: "He's my partner in music. My heart soars in his voice, my pain cries in his tunes, that's what he tells me" (25). Indeed, the 'partnership' between Nandini and Bishu, a long-lost and recently found friend, has touched a special altitude. Whereas Kishor supplies flowers Bishu brings his gift of songs for Nandini.

Bishu had started work in Yaksha Town with the job of a spy for the establishment. It was a 'comfortable job' by any standard, but he could not stick to it, and eventually gave up. But he cannot break away from the place. It is apparent that Bishu is not liked much by the Governor, who holds him in suspicion, and naturally. He is certainly intriguing for this man who cannot make out why the man rejected position and status (his wife used to receive calls for joining the Governors' wives at their card-game) and chose to come down among the diggers instead; a shrewd materialistic mind cannot but conclude that he has some design up his sleeves.

Obviously Bishu is not an average digger; he has a depth of mind, a sweet disposition, and above all a sensitive decent mind which retains the capacity to soar. Nandini says, "In this closed fort a bit of sky survives only between you and me..." (20). He has looked into his own heart and has known, "The pain of desire for the near belongs to the animal, the sorrow of aspiration for the far belongs to man. That far away flame of my eternal sorrow is revealed through Nandini" (20). If Ranjan is joy, Bishu is sorrow. Joy and sorrow together make life rich. He is the obverse side of Ranjan. Seeing Bishu by Nandini's side the King's voice asks brusquely: "Who is that with you? A pair to Ranjan?" Bishu steps forward to reply: "No, King, I am the obverse side of Ranjan, on which falls the shadow" (25). When

Chandra asks Bishu, "Tell me, Bishu, what does she charm you with?", Bishu says, "The charm of sorrow", and then further explains: "She reminds me that there are sorrows, to forget which is the greatest sorrow" (20). It is "the charm of sorrow" (20) that binds him to Nandini. In one of his songs he addresses Nandini as 'O waker of my grief!' (21). Through the dialog between Nandini and Bishu we can guess they knew each other before coming to the place, possibly Bishu loved her, but did not stake his claim; subsequently, he was brought to Yaksha Town by 'a woman', like a bird brought to the dust by a chance arrow. Yet Bishu has no anger or resentment against his wife as he mentions the event.

Before Nandini came to this place Bishu just maintained the average digger's life, although his refusal to do the job of spying was a way of protest. But as a digger he maintained a low profile so that the Governor spared him "out of sheer contempt". But with the arrival of Nandini, and their renewed friendship, Bishu gets over his fear by degrees. He explains the change: "I felt as if they had pounded me.... Then you came and looked into my face in a way that made me sure some light could still be seen through me" (20). He tells Nandini, "when I am with you my mind scorns to be cautious" (24). The proof follows immediately; in reply to the Governor's query about the subject of his talk he says point-blank, "We are discussing how to escape from this fortress of yours". The Governor can barely hide his astonishment: "Really? So recklessly, that you don't even mind confessing it?" (24). Towards the end, after being arrested for "speaking out the truth...at last", Bishu says, "at last I am free" (38), "these chains will bear witness to the truth of my freedom" (39).

No Children

Children frequently figure in Tagore's plays and take dominant roles. Here, however, Tagore has carefully kept children out of his dramatic space, but the presence of couples is indicated—Phagulal-Chandra, Bishu-his wife, the governors and their wives. Why? Is it because the environment is so dead and cruel that children would have been misfits here, and it would have been too cruel to bring them into the dark arena of the Yaksha Town, in the suffocating grim concentration camp where trigger-happy guards come down upon bent-backed people in chains forced to dig in darkness for dead gold?

Technique

(i) Pālā

Tagore himself described the play as *Pālā*—a popular folk form of theatre in India. Pala is usually based upon some very well-known legendary story—outline. *Pālā* means the oral/written text/script of *Jatra*, a traditional and very popular form of folk theatre in Bengal. *Pālā* also means a long narrative—usually unsophisticated, and drawing from a common pool of public memory for its subject—either sung or performed on stage with a lot of songs and dances—both being of folk-origin.

At the same time Tagore makes a most fine use of symbols which were of course not the way of the age-old *Pālā*. Tagore in this play shows an interesting twining of the ancient folk-form with *avante-garde* dramaturgy.

(ii) Symbols

(a) *Gold*

Tagore wrote in the Preface to the play: "that agriculture has forgotten itself under the pull of a demonic avarice—in order to convey this message in a covert manner in the *Tretāyug* the magical gold deer had been introduced. Isn't it the lure of the magical gold deer of the Rakshasa that the Sitas of today fall easy prey to the demon; otherwise why should the peasants abandon their villages under the cool shadow of the big sprawling trees to embrace the deadly life at the Titagarh jute mills? All these came about in later times than Valmiki's…" (my translation).

Shambhu Mitra interprets this as not mineral gold "just as Hanuman too did not burn down a Lanka of mineral gold"; he would rather hold it as the "fossil fuel, which the earth had kept buried for long ages", and further argues, "this thoughtless greedy use of natural resources is a major feature of this machine age" (Mitra 27; my translation).

There are also hints of another kind of gold; this is conveyed through the music that wafts in at intervals from the distant fields. While the diggers of the Yaksha Town are delving deep into the bowels of the earth, and coming up with heaps of gold, music resonates across the fields far away—music about the gold of sunlight spreading over the earth, a music that stirs in the diggers a longing for their village home in the lap of open nature, so much that they even think of asking for leave to go home.

Two kinds of gold are counterpoised through the text: the dead gold on the one hand, and on the other the gold of life gleaming in the light of the sun, the colour of the ripe corn, the beauty of Nandini. The dead wealth of tangible gold is associated with darkness, with the underworld which is the mythic domain of death, whereas the epitomes of intangible gold belong to the realm of light and life. Early in the play the Professor highlights this counterpoint as he tells Nandini:

> In this Yaksha Town all our treasure is of gold, the secret treasure of the dust. But the gold which is you, beautiful one, is not of the dust, but of the light which never owns any bond. (4)

Perhaps that is why this gold fails to attract Nandini. Nandini makes it clear to the King, that her admiration for the King is not stirred by his gold, but by his strength with which he handles the gold. She unambiguously points the lack, the dearth in this dead treasure:

> The day you let me into your store-house the blocks of gold did not surprise me,—what amazed me was the immense strength with which you lifted and arranged them. But can blocks of gold ever answer to the swinging rhythm of your arms in the same way as fields of corn? (8)

Then she asks the King, "Are you not afraid, King, of handling the dead wealth of the earth?" She explains the 'fear': "The living heart of the earth gives itself up in love and life and beauty, but when you rend its bosom and disturb the dead, you bring up with your booty the curse of its dark demon, blind and hard, cruel and envious. Don't you see everybody here is either angry, or suspicious, or afraid?" (8).

The gold is not a thing of necessity for the King, but it is obsession; Bishu says, in conclusion to his penetrating discourse on drink: "These nuggets are the drink—the solid drink—of our Gold King" (15). Still the dead weight of amassed gold cannot yield one facet of a touchstone. Even as the play opens, the King has already begun to realize that all he possesses is only "so much dead weight. No increase of gold can create a particle of a touchstone" (9).

The symbol of gold also tangentially foregrounds several counterpoints as follows:

1. The 'dead' gold and the golden light of the autumnal sun; the gold of the ripe corn-sheaf.
2. The deadly power of gold and the vibrant youth of Ranjan.
3. "The stolen wine of the prison house", the "wine of death" in Bishu's song, which "flushes all emptiness with laughter" (13), and the "boundless tavern, underneath the blue canopy". (13)
4. The dark tunnels leading to the dark mines underground and the open corn-fields flooded with sunlight.
5. The golden spires of the palace and the sunset clouds. Bishu describes how he had drifted to Yaksha Town in terms of contrapuntal images of gold which highlights his basic difference from his wife.

   "One day, while I was gazing at the sunset clouds, she had her eye upon the golden spire of the Governor's palace. Her glance challenged me to take her over there. In my foolish pride I vowed to do so. When I did bring her here, under the golden spire, the spell was broken." (22)
6. Diggers and Tillers; Nandini charges the Professor as another 'digger' into dead things.

(b) *The Iron Net*

The King remains invisible behind a net. The Antiquarian, new to the place, is stunned by the information, "There's no means of meeting him. You'll have to talk to him from outside this network" (31).

The play opens with the direction: "The curtain rises on a window covered by a network of intricate pattern in front of the Palace." In parenthetic stage direction it is denoted as a window—(Nandini [knocking at the window]. Do you hear?...) (25), and also mentioned just as 'network'—(Nandini [shaking the network violently]. Open the door...) (47).

It is across this netting that the dialog between Nandini and the King is carried on. Nandini implores him to come out from behind the net: "come out into the light, step on the ground, let the earth be glad" (8). But the King fails to respond.

Tagore mentions this as "cover of an intricate network—the scientific system".

> It is an organized passion of greed that is stalking abroad in the name of European civilization.... Such an objectified passion lacks the true majesty of human nature; it only assumes a terrifying bigness, its physiognomy blurred through its cover of an intricate net-work,—the scientific system. It barricades itself against all direct human touch with barriers of race pride and prestige of power.

Nandini asks Professor: "...you hide your King behind a wall of netting. Is it for fear of people finding out that he's a man?" (4). Professor answers in his characteristic tone of mild mockery: "As the ghost of our dead wealth is fearfully potent so is our ghostly royalty, made hazy by this net, with its inhuman power to frighten people" (4). At a climactic moment in the play Nandini desperately knocks and pushes at the network, crying, "Listen, listen, listen!" Gosain asks, with his typical touch of sardonic vulgarity, whom is she 'prodding' like that; Nandini bursts out: "That boa-constrictor of yours, who remains in hiding and swallows men" (44). It is only towards the end that the King comes out of his net to join his own rebellious people (47).

Does the net signify a convenient device installed and maintained by the Governors who run the place in the name of the King? So that the 'Big Brother' (*à la* Orwell) remains inaccessible to common people, so that the common individuals can establish no connection with him, the King has been kept separated from the rest behind a net. It is also deliberately meant to create confusion, like a mist; during a moment of exasperation Nandini says, "That King of yours, shrouded in his mist of netting." It is the obstacle put up to preclude communication, as well as clarity.

The net suggests the inaccessibility and abstraction of modern power as well as "the panoptic modality of power" (*à la* Foucault 211) at all levels; one can find a correspondence to this idea in Foucault's argument: "The state is superstructural in relation to a whole series of networks...these networks stand in a conditioning-conditioned relationship to a kind of 'metapower' which is structured essentially around a certain number of great prohibition functions" (Foucault 64). The network in the play is an instrument in the hands of the oppressors; the net serves their vested interest. Therefore the net can be ever-spreading instead of being a fixed size and shape. Its scope can be all-encompassing like the power of a totalitarian state. To Nandini's agonized question at seeing the torture perpetrated upon her village neighbors, Professor says: "Well-being! There's no question of 'well' in it at all,—only 'being'. That *being* of theirs has expanded so terribly that, unless millions of men are pressed into service, who's going to support its weight? So *the net is spreading farther and farther*" (34; emphasis added), in order to ensure their existence. The netted window thus also becomes a paradigm for the entire place which is but an extended and inescapable concentration camp, a paradigm for the entire system which is an all-pervasive and all-powerful labyrinthine prison, an epitome of what Foucault calls "the regular extension, the infinitely minute web of panoptic techniques" (Foucault 213). The Professor's comment on the Antiquarian's futile attempt at escaping Yaksha Town sends a shudder down the spine:

> You see how our Antiquarian has quietly slipped off, thinking he'll fly and save himself. After going a few steps, he'll soon discover that there's a wire network stretched from post to post, from country to country. (33-34)

Again, the net in front of the King seems to guard an exclusive and exclusivist space behind it. Thus it becomes a net within the net, as it were. The King says he wants to see Nandini and Ranjan together. Nandini points out the hindrance to 'see'-ing : "You won't be able to see from behind your net" (25). The 'Voice' says, "I shall let you sit inside my room", simply because he wants to 'know' them. Once one is allowed inside the net, one becomes the object, and ceases to be the subject of the sentence—object of voyeurism, of 'knowing'—that is mechanical analysis, and at the worst—of torture and annihilation. However, the one occasion on which Nandini had been allowed inside, the King did not try to 'know', but surrendered to the moment instead, and so Nandini did not find the King fearsome there, he appeared rather like some great mythical type instead.

But this must have been a very rare moment; significantly this has not been presented, but only reported instead. Otherwise the King remains a mysterious disembodied 'Voice', invisible, inaccessible, and frequently intractable in his own exclusive space behind the net, which continues to send hints of a terrible operation going on inside. Once, from behind the net the King throws a dead frog outside; later we find dead/squeezed humans (the left-over of the King) being churned out.

Seen from the perspective of Tagore's dramatic oeuvre, the net can call up a cluster of associated symbols, like the solid wall of *Acalāyatan*, or the dam of *Free Water*. Like the wall symbolizing the stagnated mind of man, or the dam metaphorizing the force that stops the flow of love, the net too semiotizes the imprisonment of dynamic living energy which has been made inert by some deadening mechanical power.

Bhattacharya draws attention to a running motif in Tagore's symbolic-allegoric plays: it is the stagnation/ entrapment/imprisonment of the human soul and his subsequent release from the obstruction. The net can also be considered in this light. The obstacle can come from within, or be posed from outside; through the blinding ego of man, or through obscurantist constraining systems of society/religion. Thus Sudarsana (*Rājā*) is entrapped by her addiction to external beauty and desire; Mahapanchak (*Acalāyan*) is confined within the prison of obscurantist, ritualistic religion; Amal (*Post-Office*) is kept imprisoned by scriptural strictures, by society, by family; the King (*Fālguṇī*) is entrapped by his own lust and fear of senility; King Ranajit (*Muktadhārā*) is obsessed by the power of science and the lust for imperial power.

In line with the above, the King in *Red Oleanders* is imprisoned by his own avarice for unlimited wealth, his pride of material power, and the mechanical system he has installed. The net symbolizes this imprisonment. Though it seems self-opted, yet it is also obsessive for him. It is only at the end when he can realize his mistake that he can come out from behind this net. But in course of the play the 'Voice' behind the net grows increasingly fretful, and Nandini wonders, "It is you who entangle yourself in your own net, then why keep on fretting?" (220). Ultimately in the clash between the iron net and the red oleander flower, paradoxically it is the flower that wins, while the net collapses.

On one occasion the Professor admits his own scholarship to be a 'net' of defence behind which he hides like the King hiding behind his own net. "Do you know Nandini", he says, "I too live behind a net-work of scholarship. I am an unmitigated scholar just as our King is an unmitigated king." (5). Of course he seems to say this in an unmistakable tone of self-mockery.

(c) *The Frog*

On one occasion, the King, from behind the invisibility of the network, stretches out his hand and drops a dead frog outside, on the stage. Nandini shudders. The Voice rolls on in monotone (presumably):

> Once upon a time this frog got into a hole in a stone, and in that shelter it existed for three hundred years. I have learnt from it the secret of continuing to exist, but to live it does not know. To-day I felt bored and smashed its shelter. I've thus saved it from existing forever. Isn't that good news? (25)

The petty and unpleasant detail acquires symbolic dimension in the context of the basic counterpoint posed by the play between non-living and living, death-in-life existence and buoyant vibrancy of real life; this also carries a hint of the King's grim search for power and his boredom with the same, which gives a clue to his growing restiveness.

(d) *The Floral Symbol: /Title: /Signifier[Signiflower]*

Tagore said he would refuse to take the responsibility for any debacle that might be caused by the critics' search for meaning supposed to have lain hidden between the petals of the flower. Yet the flower, mention of which lies interspersed through the text, and which constitutes the very title, indeed emerges as a loaded image in the course of the play, which was first titled as *Yakshapuri*, then it was changed to *Nandini* and finally *Nandini* was replaced by *Raktakarabi*.

The very opening is signaled by a bunch of the flower,—as Kishor rushes in with some red oleander flowers, excited at his success in getting them at considerable personal risk. Just because Nandini said, she "*must* have red oleanders" Kishor has staked a lot to gather it; he is 'glad' that "they're hard to find in this place", because that poses a challenge for him. "Only one tree I discovered after days of search, nearly hidden away behind a rubbish heap". Incidentally, Kishor's description of the location of the plant closely corresponds to a personal experience of the author. Pramathanath Bishi cites from a letter, written to him by Pandit Kshitimohan Senshastri, in which Senshastri refers to Tagore's mention of the flowers in the play just a few days prior to his death "Close to my room there was a garbage heap of scrap iron things. A small Karabi sapling had been buried under it. When it first fell under the garbage I did not notice; afterwards the scraps were removed but the little sapling could not be traced. After a certain time suddenly one day I caught the sight of a delicate graceful Karabi-branch had sprung up above the iron rubbish, holding one red flower in its bosom. As if showing its heart's blood spouting up at a cruel blow, it came to greet lovingly with sweet smile. It said, "See, I didn't die! You couldn't nip me, could you?" This revelation then stirred my mind with pain. Prior to this I had entitled the play variously as 'Yakshapuri', 'Nandini', etc, but I was not happy with any of these names; so now I conferred it the name, 'Raktakarabi'" (my translation). In the play too there is only one plant of Raktakarabi (Red Oleander), and that has come up untended, unnoticed, by the garbage heap at one end of the Yakshapuri. Indeed the system of the Yakshapuri is not supposed to accommodate flower shrubs.

For Kishor the flowers are 'preciously' his own, because, as he claims, "they come from my pain"; he has to gather the flowers with great difficulty and at considerable risk. Thus from the very start the flower ceases to be a mere flower, and in course of the play becomes increasingly a signifier. For Kishor the flowers are his 'homage' to Nandini, and in the bitter ignominy of his life in Yaksha Town at last he has found a 'triumph', that has made him bold. To Nandini's anxious admonition, he says, "No, no, I shall be rash and defy their blows. My homage shall be my daily triumph."

On the other hand, the Professor who yearns for one flower in the garland Nandini is weaving, lets out his uneasy intuition about her floral choice in an unguarded moment: "How often have I thought that there is some omen in these ornaments of yours." As Nandini says she knows no omen, the Professor murmurs in a serious note of apprehension: "Perhaps your fate knows. In that red there is not only beauty, but also the fascination of fear." It is interesting that the very same flower which inspires Bishu to defy 'fear', stirs the Professor to respond to 'the fascination of fear'; he wonders why the girl opted for this particular flower in preference to all others. So he mutters almost to himself, "I don't know what event you have come to write with that crimson tint", and adds, "Do you know, we often choose our own fate thus, without knowing it!" (6). Nandini explains her preference in romantic articulation. "Ranjan sometimes calls me Red Oleander. I feel that the colour of his love is red,—that red I wear on my neck, on my breast, on my arms" (6). [Incidentally, allusions to the scarlet or vermilion of spring flowers run through the countless spring songs and poems of Tagore; for instance, his famous spring song, "Oh, look there, Spring has burst out like a red fire in the forests".] Professor would beg for "just one of those flowers" from her, though in the same breath he adds in a tone of self-mockery: "let me try to understand the meaning of its colour" (6); as if he remembers his limitation. To the Professor's cool, cynical wisdom, the flowers are a sign of desperate defiance which is bound to be futile, howsoever charming it may look. So he tries to play down, albeit with a barely suppressed sadness, Nandini's honest anger against the crushing system as "the wild cry of red oleander" (35). In his perception by degrees Nandini becomes identified with the flowers which belong to the realm of light and air, in contrast to the dark underground which rules life here; hence his appeal to her: "My sweet Red Oleander, don't try to probe our secrets in the depths of their dust. Be for us swaying in the air above, that we may gaze upwards to see you" (36). Through this half-serious appeal Professor actually makes a semiotic gesture in which Nandini gets merged with the flower.

The habitually suspicious Gokul on the other hand, who does not trust what he cannot understand, must have the 'meaning' of the 'dangling' thing over her forehead; Nandini's indifferent answer that it has no meaning, sends him into a frenzy of fear, so much that he abuses her as a 'terrible witch' and an 'ominous torch'. Thus for Gokul also the flower presents a sign—the sign of the 'ominous torch' indicating a dangerous witch.

The King, at another level, feels no less uneasy about the soft petals which he cannot possess. "Why can't I strain out the tint of your oleanders and build a dream out of it to keep before my eyes? Those few frail petals guard it and hinder me" (8). But not even the King can have them, since Nandini's oleander flowers are exclusively meant for Ranjan. The King's complex attitude of mistrust and longing, jealousy and love is foregrounded by his ambivalent response of synchronic longing and violence regarding the flowers. So he would angrily turn out Nandini, and immediately implore her, "No, no, wait a little. Give me that tassel of red oleanders which hangs from your hair." Yet when Nandini asks what he would do with it, he says:

> When I look at those flowers it seems to me as if the red light of my evil star has appeared in their shape. At times I want to snatch them from you and tear them to

> pieces. Again I think that if Nandini were ever to place that spray of flowers on my head, with her own hands, then—... Then perhaps I might die in peace.

Nandini. Some one loves red oleanders and calls me by that name. It is in remembrance of him that I wear these flowers.

Voice. Then, I tell you, they're going to be *his* evil star as well as *mine.* (26)

The flower thus serves as a motif to draw out the working of the troubled mind of a split personality which is curiously torn between the sadism of fierce possessiveness and the peace of loving surrender.

Towards the end when Kishor is sent by Bishu to find out Ranjan, Nandini hands over the 'tassel of red oleanders' from her hair (39). The flower thus again becomes a sign/code, her insignia, her encrypted eloquent message for Ranjan. Finally, at the end when all the workers and prisoners are rushing out to join the fight with the Governor's force, Phagulal notices something: "Here is her wristlet of red oleanders. She has bared her arm today,—and left us." Bishu bends low and tenderly picks it up in a gesture of great sorrow, great humility: "Once I told her I would not take anything from her hand. I break my word and take this. Come along!" With their departure the play ends while the music of autumn reverberates in the distance.

The bunch of red oleander flowers can be considered the floral symbol of what Nandini manifests as a human figure. The flower is a pure imagistic form of what Nandini is in actuality. According to Bishi, Nandini is the essence of life's vibrancy; the flower is the essence of Nandini. It is Nandini in abstraction, isolated from specific, circumstantial detail, evoking the irrepressible power of life above all forces of death. Like Nandini the flower too bursts out amidst all-round repression, and springs up like the fountain. It is the indomitable, undefeatable spirit of life which refuses to die.

Again, it is only Kishor, a boy in his teens, who knows its location. He has recognized the essence of Nandini through his loving vision; perhaps that is why the flower has revealed its presence only to the boy.

The oleander finally denotes a vision of hope. In the letter of Senshastri to Bishi (mentioned earlier) we find, Tagore said: "Have no worry about life. The *Upanisad* says life is the true thing, it has no death; so the fear was for the inorganic. Now science claims, a thing made by nature also has no death. What die are the man-made artificial, untrue things. I have said this in *Raktakarabī*. Who has ever succeeded in killing life, even after tying it up with a thousand shackles, burying it over hundreds of times?" (trans. Present writer). At the end of the play we have a brief glimpse of Ranjan, lying dead, with the bunch of red oleanders on his bosom. As if he too is saying "See, I didn't die! You couldn't nip me, could you?". The flower symbolizes the irrepressible force of life which cannot be crushed, whose freedom cannot be robbed whatever bondage or shackles may have been applied to put it down. This is the subtext of the title.

The garland of red oleanders that Nandini makes is meant exclusively for Ranjan alone. At the same time there is mention of another flower, the white 'kunda'. Nandini offers a garland of white kunda flowers to Governor in return to his 'message of hope' that she will see Ranjan this very day. The Governor says, albeit sardonically, because he knows already his machinery for finishing Ranjan has been set in motion,—"Why throw away the garland thus, and not keep it for Ranjan?"

> *Nandini*. There is a garland for him.

Governor responds in a half-sardonic half-serious tone:

> *Governor*. Aha, I thought so! I suppose it's the one hanging round your neck. The garland of victory may be of *kunda* flowers, the gift of the hand; but the garland of welcome is of red oleanders, the gift of the heart. Well, let's be quick in accepting what comes from the hand, for that will fade; as for the heart's offering, the longer it waits the more precious it grows. (24)

Does the gift affect even the hardened man ever so slightly? At least he cannot resist being conscious of it; so the next time Nandini confronts him, he says, rather flippantly: "Hallo, Nandini, is that you? I shall wear your kunda chain late in the evening. When three-quarters of me can hardly be seen for the dark, then perchance a flower garland might become even me" (32). Again, on his re-entry, the first thing he mentions is the Gosain's surprise at seeing the garland in his room (36). Gosain, however, in tune with his mean nature, is suspicious of even this flower, but he hides his suspicion under the smooth garb of false velvet talks which still fail to hide the stink of vulgar pretence which is in his nature. "Ah indeed! The gift of a pure heart! God's own white *kunda* flowers! This is what gives one faith in the power of virtue, and hope for the sinners' redemption" (36). What right does he have to comment like this, with the air of a superior, on *her* gift to another? People like this assume the right to vulgarly interfere and control lives by means of glib hypocrisy. Thus the white flower draws out the blackness of the person.

At a climactic point towards the end the two flowers are thrown into a superb counterpoint; the King has already joined the rebels and the Governor is seen coming down with his soldiers. Nandini cries out: "He has swung up my garland of *kunda* flowers on his spear-head. I will dye that garland the colour of my oleanders with my heart's blood...Victory to Ranjan!" (50). Thus at this point the oleanders become synonym for the 'heart's blood', extreme daring, sacrifice, martyrdom, something like the 'rosa mystica' in Hopkins's poem, 'Rosa Mystica', which also shows the metamorphosis of a white rose into a red one through suffering and martyrdom. This is the last glimpse we get of Nandini, after which she rushes out, possibly to meet her death.

It seems interesting to note that both the flowers chosen by Nandini, red oleander as well as white kunda, are without fragrance. Why?

(iii) Music

Music has been frequently thematized in Tagore's plays through 'intermedial transposition' or 'intermedial reference'. Here music is 'contrapuntal' (*ā la* Said). The lost way of life close to nature, has been evoked at frequent intervals through intangible music floating in from some distance, or the impalpable nostalgic memory of the diggers; but this is never shown onstage.

(a) *The Harvesting Song*

The song of harvesting, which apparently wafts in, from distant fields, has been used as the 'prelude' and 'coda' in the play. This is the theme song. Sometimes it can be heard; sometimes it is inaudible, submerged under the harsh noise. Whenever there is a pause in the grinding, grating, rumbling sound of the machines of the Yaksha Town one can hear the song in the distance. But actually it is running through the space, the texture, the mood, and thus pervades the play, percolating through and seeping into every seam of the text, lending thereby to an additional thematic overtone as well as leading to an extraordinary aesthetic effect.

It is clearly a choric song, and not a solo one, although it is repeatedly made to overlap with Nandini's speech. The tune is very simple, like some folk-song, sung by common rural people. Nandini ignores Gokul's abusive speech as the song floats in.

Hark, 'tis Autumn calling:
'Come, O come away!'—
Her basket is heaped with corn.

At this point Nandini speaks out, as if to herself, to any and everybody, including those in the audience, "Don't you see the September sun is spreading the glow of the ripening corn in the air?" (7).

During this utterance, we can imagine the music has not stopped, but continues in the distance; the moment she stops we can at once hear the song rising like the open wind over the fields.

Drunken with the perfumed wine of the wind,
the sky seems to sway among the shivering corn,
its sunlight trailing on the fields.

Nandini calls out to the 'Voice' behind the net, "You too come out, King!—out into the fields" (7). All the while the song wafts in as the singers pass by in the distance. Again and again, at regular intervals the song, quite a part, or in snatches, can be heard rhythmically, sometimes coming closer, and sometimes receding in the distance until at the end it takes over.

While clearly indicating the season, the song, further, presents a counterpoint to the dead gold under the earth, by means of celebrating the golden sunlight rippling over the earth, embracing the golden ears of the ripe corn. Of course few here can hear the song. This music does not seem to reach the ears of the bulk of Yaksha Town population, who have imbibed the system heart and soul. The King cannot hear the song initially. When Nandini draws his attention he hears it at last, but he does not know what he would do in response, or if he could at all go out to the cornfields in case. Fagulal and Chandra can also hear the song, and they are visibly disturbed; they are pulled by a strong nostalgia for their lost village home and past.

The governors and the diggers do not hear the song. Even if it chances to reach their ears they would prefer to hold it out as an unnecessary nuisance. This insensitivity to the simple folk-song of harvest joys shows how alienated they have become from nature, its seasonal beauty, the ripe cornfield, its association of joy and pure abandon.

At the end we again hear the song in Bishu's voice:

Hark 'tis Autumn calling,—
Come, O come away!
The earth's mantle of dust is filled with ripe corn!
O the joy! the joy!

At this point the song seems to indicate a kind of fulfillment to be attained through sorrow, that the mantle of dust too is filled with golden corn; though the pity of the waste,—the ripe corn scattered on the dust, cannot be ignored either.

Shantikumar Dasgupta perceptively points out about the harvest song in *Red Oleanders* that it is the expression of the longing of all the people here who had been formerly tillers, but now reduced to numbers. Indeed, it is evocative of their yearning for the free, sunny, fulfilling life above the surface of the earth from under the dark-cramping-imprisoning life inside the bowel of the earth. It is the longing for the absent from the heart of the present. And the sadness emanating from that longing bursts forth through the song.

(b) *Other Songs*

Nandini sings an exuberant song, 'I love, I love'; but this annoys the king, and he disappears in the midst of the song, leaving a dead frog on the road under his window. Nandini guesses: "He is afraid of songs" (28).

Bishu sings several other songs to Nandini apart from his beautiful song addressed to his 'waker of grief' (21),—and the 'song of waiting' prior to the final catastrophe (29).

(c) *Latent Music*

Sambhu Mitra offers a finely sensitive discussion of the latent music in the play which, he feels, has been projected through the sequence of varied voices:

> ...I would like to draw attention to a special feature. The play is set off with the voice of a young boy, a fresh young voice. Next enters the voice of an elderly person. His scale is different. Next follows the metallic voice of Gokul. It is sound on a high pitch. Then comes the King's voice: 'Fields! What could I do there?'—a deep bass voice. And all the while Nandini's voice can be heard alongside. Four different relationships between Nandini and these four characters are expressed. Her instrument seems to play duet with four different instruments. It is like some wonderful orchestration. It is in this way that Rabindranath's musical talent has found expression in his play. When this orchestration is built up in course of acting, the spectators are not conscious as their attention has already been absorbed by the dialogue and characters. Yet through that very unconsciousness this musical artistry creates effect upon their senses. These are fine attributes of art.... (Mitra 25; my translation)

(d) *Anti-music*

The horrifying anti-music of Yaksha Town presents a contrast to the simple, charming song of the tillers in the field. The Antiquarian, a fresher to the place, is understandably shocked by this anti-music.

Antiquarian. I say what is this infernal noise going on inside?

... It sounds like big pillars crashing down one after another. (31)

(iv) Dance rhythm

(a) *Rhythm of nature*

The King sees in Nandini his opposite, which he identifies as 'the dance rhythm' of the universe. Indeed Nandini is connected with the earth, the air, the light, from which the King has become disconnected. He does not know what he can do in the fields. Shambhu Mitra interprets this 'dance rhythm' as the rhythm of nature, its eco-system: that man must understand and follow the rhythm of nature for his survival; if he seeks to plunder nature indiscriminately that will perpetrate his own destruction. Indeed "like a seer Rabindranath had apprehended a crisis of this civilization through his extraordinary foresight and had imagined a way of survival" (Mitra 36; my translation).

(b) *Diggers' dance*

The Headman reports to Governor how Ranjan had instilled joy even in the diggers at their drudgery: "He cheered them up, and asked them to have a diggers' dance...". The absence of drums was compensated by beating the spades. As the Headman thundered Ranjan said, "I have unbound the work.... It won't have to be dragged out by force any more, it will run along of itself, dancing" (30). Tagore held that when man works in joy, work can give him a kind of freedom. In this machine-ruled civilization work means compulsion and drudgery, it carries no release, no joy. The diggers' dance offers a tentative solution to the crisis of today when the worker is alienated from his work and reduced to compulsive drudgery. But the rulers of Yaksha Town are not only impercipient to the idea, they are scared of it as well. So they issue the opinion, 'the fellow is mad'.

(v) The Stage

(a) A written script and the play-on-stage are certainly not the same thing. Shambhu Mitra, the eminent script-writer and actor, who is also known for his famous stage-production of *Raktakarabī*, explained how on-stage performance brings out a living manifestation of dynamic reality simultaneously at multiple layers. And when a novelist or a story-writer turns to play-writing, even a writer like Rabindranath with his peerless command of expression, the author looks for this assistance from the performance of the play.

(b) Rabindranath did not leave many detailed instructions in parenthetic notes like many a dramatist before and after him. He preferred to leave it to the creative imagination of sympathetic actors and directors.

(c) Tagore was against the use of drop-scene; he held that in order to indicate the change of act or scene, it could be sufficient if you just switched off the light once, and then switched it on again.

(d) Tagore was against crude imitation of reality in the stage-setting on the ground that an excessive adherence to realistic detail proved a hindrance to the free play of imagination in the spectator's mind; furthermore a fixed backdrop/screen at the back of the stage did not tally with the dynamism of the action. He thought this concern with creating optical illusion amounted to a kind of injustice to literature and a device suitable only for children's distraction. He also claimed that this was not the practice in ancient India or Greece where the actors and the spectators focused their attention upon the literary and dramatic core/content of the play.

Tagore wrote in the Preface to his play *Tapatī*:

> In the stage-planning of modern European drama the scene[backdrop] has entered as a kind of disturbance. This is childishness. This is the effort to dazzle the vision. This is a gate-crasher in the realm of literature and dramaturgy.... The idea of the tapovan in Sakuntala is given in the poetry itself. That is sufficient. That it has not been over-specified through a painting is

> itself congenial for the spectator's mind which can move freely. The drama makes its demands upon the spectator's imagination; the painting would have belittled it, and the loss would have been on the spectators' part. Acting is a dynamic, vibrant thing; the backdrop is its opposite. After making its unrightful entry into the dynamism it remains dumb, dull, and inert. By putting up a fixed fence before the spectator's view it keeps the vision constrained within limits. Where the mind should have taken its own space, a picture is imposed to bid farewell to the mind. This has been introduced in this era of mechanical devices; it was not so in the past. (my translation)

Tagore refers to the traditional folkforms of India, the *Yātrāpālā*, where no such delimiting scene constricts the vision and mind. In this context we can mention the return to folkform in Girish Karnad and Shambhu Mitra among major Indian dramatists of the post-Tagorean era. Tagore insisted about half a century before either Mitra or Karnad on the removal of so-called realistic appliances from the stage:

> It is for this very reason that wherever I have some control over the stage management I don't allow this childish practice of drawing up and dropping down the screen every now and then. This mocks the truth of reality and hinders the truth of imagination.

This applies to all his later plays.

(e) In *Red Oleanders*, in particular, only one scene provides the backdrop for the entire play. This is largely like *Yātrāpālā* or folk theatre, or Sanskrit theatre, in which all gather and disperse at the same open space. Everything goes on within the open space in front of the net of King, including even the supposedly confidential exchange between Governor and his men. The spectator knows and understands. Thus Tagore proves himself to be the foremost avant-garde theatrical practitioner of his time as he uses the age-old heritage of folkforms to articulate the most modern message/subject. Thus by saying

> little he can suggest a lot as he ensures the creative co-operation of the spectator in imaginatively conferring elasticity to the stage—telescoping or stretching distances between characters. The play validates Tagore's opinion that the theatre-stage does not require the realistic scene and backdrop of the movie.

It may be noted that the play was not staged during Tagore's lifetime.

(vi) Costume

While preparing for the stage presentation of *Raktakarabī* Shambhu Mitra had felt a bit intrigued about the appropriate costume of the King, because the old sign of thunder which used to be in currency in ancient India as the royal insignia might not be understood by the present-day audience. Then Nandalal Basu, the famous artist and ashramic of Shantiniketan, suggested the idea of using toothed wheel as a sign on the tunic, which he held to be an international item in today's world. The idea of a King is immediately associated in our mind with long sword, grand headgear, and other such gorgeous equipage. But Nandalal Basu instantly dismissed the idea, as he thought this 'King' represented modern man's scientific mind. Mitra's troupe 'Bahurupi' took special care in simultaneously disclosing and concealing the King towards the end when he would break through the net.

> In our theatre even when the King came out towards the end, no light was cast upon him. Only the gleam of a faint reflection of all the other lights cast on other people and items fell on the King. Only once a very faint light fell in a slant upon his back; it showed up distinctly the toothed wheel on his shirt back. The King's face was never seen; even his body too was seen only indistinctly as a shadow. (Mitra; my translation)

On the other hand the diggers, including Bishu, were given the dress of laborers; they were shown drinking liquor on-stage. Gosain must be unmistakable with his identity trade-mark of one who trades religion,—the white dhoti, scarf and sandalpaste-smeared forehead. Nandini's special costume is of course defined by the text itself, complete with her rice-coloured sari, and floral ornaments of red oleander; thus as soon as she appears on the stage she stands apart from the rest.

The Mythical Dimension

The spatial backdrop, the time-frame, the characters, anonymous as well as individualized, various allusions and touches in the script, including occasional fine details, relate to and stir up a range of mythic evocations/associations/signs—and all this together lend a mythical dimension to the play.

(i) In order to describe Ranjan, or 'youth' which floods over all barriers of rules with its dynamic force, the playwright uses the analogies of rowing across the turbulent river during cyclone, riding the wild horse through the forest by holding the mane, shooting the arrow at the exact midpoint between the eyebrows of the springing tiger, churning the strong current of the fast flowing hilly rivulet—these seem to be pictures restored from a hoary mythic world. Yet the author claims it to be a play about the modern times. Mitra wonders if these have been gleaned from Sanskrit literature, or from our old legends? These seem to have an affinity with our folklore. "The myths in currency in various parts of India in the folklores of various languages since ancient times—including the community tales of primitive tribes like the Kol, Bhil, Santhal—these images have been gleaned from the mines of that folk-memory to suggest an archetype of youth which refuses to surrender, which destroys to renew again and again." (Mitra 47-48; my translation)

(ii) Characters like Ranjan, Nandini, King, who are also archetypes, are presented side by side with distinct individuals like Phagulal-Chandra-Gokul. This can remind us of a very old tradition in our *Yātrāpālā*, in which 'Bibek' (conscience incarnate) used to move about on the stage perfectly at ease with royalties and villagers. Later figures representing 'Bharatmata', 'Niyati'(fate), etc., also appeared on our theatre stage and took part in the action even during the decade when *Raktakarabi* was written.

Thus the play seems to anticipate "a unique modern form of Indian dramatic tradition—a form in which the deepest and most complex thoughts of today can be projected by means of a distinct Indian idiom. It is not by imitating the structure of some Sanskrit play, or by adapting the frame of some folk theatre" (Mitra 48; trans. Present author).

Indeed Rabindranath here seems to show the way how to present in dramatic form, the crisis of civilization, the cruelty of the depersonalized system that have come up at the cost of personal relationships, and is bent on repressing life, on destroying youth,—in short the fascinating tale of the Yaksha Town at an apocalyptic time. He seems to reconcile the solid specificity of the stage with the impalpable but deeply stirring evocations from our racial memory, the collective memory of our folklore, and thus achieves a spectacular effect by means of stirring deep chords within us.

(iii) Some of the characters are simultaneously real human beings at one level, and symbols at another—not realistic but true. For instance, one can cite Nandini's description of King to Bishu:

> Like a man from the epics,—his forehead like the gateway of a tower, his arms the iron bolts of some inaccessible fortress.... A falcon was sitting on his left wrist. (22)

Again,

> It was as if he were a thousand-year-old banyan tree, and I a tiny little bird.... (23)

Rabindranath seems to move at ease between these different layers of realism and myth, and thus touches deep layers within our mind in flashes. The mythic evocation ushers in crowded emotions and associations which enrich our response.

(iv) Some other details also suggest the telescoping of times which is natural in the magic realism of myths; for instance, although it is a city of machines, Governor's wife rides a car drawn by bullocks, and when bullocks are unavailable the diggers are pressed into service. One is reminded of Kafka's surreal castle-village in his novel *The Castle*, where there is telephone link as well as man-driven sledge.

(v) Professor explains to Nandini, "The *Jinn* of that dead wealth we invoke. If we can enslave him the whole world lies at our feet" (4); this seems to evoke the legendary past of the *1001 Arabian Nights*.

(vi) Again, he says, the Yaksha Town is under eclipse; "The Shadow Demon, who lives in the gold caves, has eaten into it" (6). Here is a conflation of the ancient Hindu myths about the empirical phenomenon of eclipse and the fractured swallowing ways of the dark town; whereas eclipse takes place on the open space of the sky, here paradoxically it is an underground process carried on in darkness. Eclipse itself was considered inauspicious and ominous by the ancient people. Hence the effectiveness of the evocation.

(vii) The labyrinth that takes one further and further inwards—"as soon as one enters the maw of Yaksha Town, its jaws shut fast, and the one road that remains open leads withinwards" (14)—seems to carry the echo of so many legends and folklores across the world, registering the terror and confusion embedded in the racial memory regarding some mysterious power. One can also recall the Argentine writer J.L. Borges's magic realistic evocation of a 'labyrinth' as an archetypal symbol of frustrating bafflement and enigma in his story 'The Immortals', written nearly half-a-century after *Red Oleanders*.

> I have said that the city was founded on a stone plateau. ...in the rear was a pit, in the pit a stairway which sank down abysmally into the darkness below. I went down; through a chaos of

> sordid galleries I reached a vast circular chamber, scarcely visible. There were nine doors in this cellar; eight led to a labyrinth that treacherously returned to the same chamber (through another labyrinth). (Borges, J.L. 139)

(viii) The song that permeates the action is also part of age-old harvesting rituals—one of those rituals which generated the great myths of mankind. In this connection, it may be pointed out that certain ritual aspects of theatre have been increasingly appearing in the avant-garde drama in India, particularly since the '70s, which Victor Turner would have called 'performing ethnography' (63). In his essay "Are there Universals of Performance in Myth, Ritual and Drama?" Turner, who had first hand experience of Indian drama, discusses the "developmental relationship from ritual to theatre" and maintains that "both ritual and theatre crucially involve liminal events and processes and have an important aspect of social metacommentary" (Turner 63). In this context Turner also rightly points out that theatre is the inheritor of that great multifaceted system of preindustrial ritual which embraces ideas and images of cosmos and chaos, interdigitates clowns and their foolery with gods and their solemnity, and uses all the sensory codes to produce symphonies in more than music: the intertwining of dance, body languages of many kinds, song, chant, architectural forms, incense, offerings, ritualized feasting and drinking, body painting, as also the enacting of mythic and heroic plots drawn from oral traditions (Turner 65). Tagore can be considered a trend-setter for modern Indian drama in this regard.

(ix) Bishu's narrating of the lure of golden spires—seems to resonate with the collective memory of so many folklores.

(x) The feather of the blue bird (28) floats in from the treasure of European myths from which Materlink took his 'blue bird'; again the blue-throated bird is also to be found in the dream-studded folklore of rural Bengal, which has been poignantly used by contemporary Bengali novelist Atin Bandyopadhya in his epic novel of partition,—*Nīlkaṇtha Pākhīr Sandhāne* (In search of the blue-throated bird).

(xi) Worship of the Flag and Weapons (11) also carries trace from ancient myths and rituals, once common and perhaps not entirely obsolete even today, though Tagore applies in the specific context of the play only.

Nandini. "Your God of the Flagstaff—he will never unbend". (44)

Finally, the King breaks the flagstaff while inviting Nandini 'to tear its banner' (48). Thus together they challenge and reject the myth installed by Yaksha Town.

The King, declaring war against his own prison emerges as the supreme mythical conclusion of a play resonating with so many mythical echoes.

(xii) The allusion to Lakshmi and Kuber in order to highlight the contrast between beautiful wealth and ugly accumulation can be traced back to an essay written just a few years before the play. In this essay written in 1328 Tagore made a differentiation between Lakshmi and Kuber, the deity of wealth and the deity of accumulation:

> For seven months at a stretch I had been in America, the demonic citadel of wealth. There I have seen the face of consumerism, but not joy. I do not use the term demon (*dānab*) in any derogatory sense; had I been writing in English perhaps I would have said, titanic wealth, that is such wealth power is immense, whose volume is huge. Everyday I used to sit by the window in my hotel room under the frown of thirty/thirty-five floor buildings, and said to myself, Lakshmi is one and Kuber is another—a world of difference lies between them. The essential message of Lakshmi is benediction, by which wealth acquires beauty. The principle of Kuber is accumulation

> by which treasure multiplies. But sheer multiplication has no absolute meaning. Whosoever has been caught in this ceaseless race of acquiring more and more, becomes obsessed, dizzied, and rushes on inebriated with the addiction.... Sitting in the concrete jungle on the other side of the Atlantic my mind shrieked in pain, Where is the music amidst all this endless noise? I must have more and more and more—this message cannot acquire the melody of creation.
>
> ('Sikşhar Milan'. *Kālāntar*; my translation)

Real and True

Tagore wrote in 1925 about *Red Oleanders*: "this book, which, being a mere translation, can have no pretension to a permanent place as literature in a language not the author's own". Yet Tagore had also claimed that this play was based on 'truth'. And truth, as we know, ensures its own perennial position and universal appeal. Is this the truth of facts, actuality, realism, or the truth of authentic perception inferred from the essence of human predicament? It is perhaps for the reader/audience to decide.

References

Barthes. *S/Z*. Trans. Richard Miller. N.Y.: Hill and Wang, 1974.

Bhattacharya, Upendranath. *Rabīndranātya Parikramā*. Kolkata: Orient Book Company, 1379 (Bengali Year).

Bishi, Pramathanath. *Rabīndranātyaprabāha* (1966). Kolkata: Orient Book Company, 1988.

Bloom, H. *The Anxiety of Influence* (1973). London: OUP Paperback, 1975.

Borges, J.L. "The Immortal", *Labyrinths*. (1964). N.Y.: Penguin Books, 1987.

Dasgupta, Shantikumar. *Rabīndranāther Rūpak Nātya*. Kolkata: Bharati Prakashani, 1392 (Bengali Year).

Foucault, M. *The Foucault Reader* (ed. Paul Rabinow). London: Penguin Books, 1991.

Mitra, Shambhu. *Nāṭak Raktakarabī*. Kolkata: M.C. Sarkar & Sons Pvt. Ltd., 1992. rpt. 2004.

Orwell, George. *Animal Farm* (1945). Orient Longman Limited (Indian Edition), 1995.

Sikdar, Ashrukumar. *Rabīndranāṭya: Rūpāntar O Oikya*. Kolkata: Grantha Nilay, 1374 (Bengali Year).

Tagore, Rabindranath. *The English Writings of Rabindranath Tagore*, (Vol. 3-Vol. 7). New Delhi: Atlantic Publishers & Distributors, 2007. [mentioned as *EWT*]

Turner, Victor. "Are there Universals of Performance in Myth, Ritual and Drama?". *Modern Theories of Drama* [Ed. G.W. Brandt]. Oxford: Clarendon Press, 1998.

Rama Kundu

Red Oleanders

A DRAMA IN ONE ACT

The curtain rises on a window covered by a network of intricate pattern in front of the Palace.

[Nandini and Kishôr, *a digger boy, come in.*]

Kishôr. Have you enough flowers, Nandini? Here, I have brought some more.

Nandini. Run away, Kishôr, do,—back to your work, quick! You'll be late again.

Kishôr. I must steal some time from my digging and digging of nuggets to bring out flowers to you.

Nandini. But they'll punish you, my boy, if they know.

Kishôr. You said you *must* have red oleanders. I am glad they're hard to find in this place. Only one tree I discovered after days of search, nearly hidden away behind a rubbish heap.

Nandini. Show it me. I'll go and gather the flowers myself.

Kishôr. Don't be cruel, Nandini. This tree is my one secret which none shall know. I've always envied Bishu, he can sing to you songs that are his own. From now I shall have flowers which you'll have to take only from my hands.

Nandini. But it breaks my heart to know that those brutes punish you.

Kishôr. It makes these flowers all the more preciously mine. They come from my pain.

Nandini. It pains me to accept anything which brings you hurt.

Kishôr. I dream of dying one day for your sake, Nandini.

Nandini. Is there nothing I can give you in return?

Kishôr. Promise that you will accept flowers only from me every morning.

Nandini. I will. But do be careful.

Kishôr. No, no, I shall be rash and defy their blows. My homage shall be my daily triumph. [*Goes.*]

[Professor *comes in.*]

Professor. Nandini!

Nandini. Yes, Professor!

Professor. Why do you come and startle one, now and again, and then pass by? Since you awaken a cry in our hearts, what harm if you stop a moment in answer to it? Let us talk a little.

Nandini. What need have you of me?

Professor. If you talk of need, look over there!—You'll see our tunnel-diggers creeping out of the holes like worms, with loads of things of need. In this Yaksha Town all our treasure is of gold, the secret treasure of the dust. But the gold which is you, beautiful one, is not of the dust, but of the light which never owns any bond.

Nandini. Over and over again you say this to me. What makes you wonder at me so, Professor?

Professor. The sunlight gleaming through the forest thickets surprises nobody, but the light that breaks through a cracked wall is quite a different thing. In Yaksha Town, you are this light that startles. Tell me, what d'you think of this place?

Nandini. It puzzles me to see a whole city thrusting its head underground, groping with both hands in the dark. You dig tunnels in the underworld and come out with dead wealth that the earth has kept buried for ages past.

Professor. The *Jinn* of that dead wealth we invoke. If we can enslave him the whole world lies at our feet.

Nandini. Then again, you hide your king behind a wall of netting. Is it for fear of people finding out that he's a man?

Professor. As the ghost of our dead wealth is fearfully potent so is our ghostly royalty, made hazy by this net, with its inhuman power to frighten people.

Nandini. All you say is a kind of made-up talk.

Professor. Of course made-up. The naked is without a credential, it's the made-up clothes that define us. It delights me immensely to discuss philosophy with you.

Nandini. That's strange! You who burrow day and night in a mass of yellow pages, like your diggers in the bowels of the earth,—why waste your time on me?

Professor. The privilege of wasting time proves one's wealth of time. We poor drudges are insects in a hole in this solid toil, you are the evening star in the rich sky of leisure. When we see you, our wings grow restless. Come to my room. For a moment allow me to be reckless in my waste of time.

Nandini. No, not now. I have come to see your king, in *his* room.

Professor. How can you enter through the screen?

Nandini. I shall find my way through the net-work.

Professor. Do you know, Nandini, I too live behind a net-work of scholarship. I am an unmitigated scholar, just as our king is an unmitigated king.

Nandini. You are laughing at me, Professor. But tell me, when they brought me here, why didn't they bring my Rañjan also?

Professor. It's their way to snatch things by fractions. But why should you want to drag your life's treasure down amongst this dead wealth of ours?

Nandini. Because I know he can put a beating heart behind these dead ribs.

Professor. Your own presence is puzzling enough for our governors here; if Rañjan also comes they will be in despair.

Nandini. They do not know how comic they are,—Rañjan will bring God's own laughter in their midst and startle them into life.

Professor. Divine laughter is the sunlight that melts ice, but not stones. Only the pressure of gross muscle can move our governors.

Nandini. My Rañjan's strength is like that of your river, Sankhini,—it can laugh and yet it can break. Let me tell you a little secret news of mine. I shall meet Rañjan to-day.

Professor. Who told you that?

Nandini. Yes, yes, we shall meet. The news has come.

Professor. Through what way could news come and yet evade the Governor?

Nandini. Through the same way that brings news of the coming Spring.

Professor. You mean it's in the air,—like the rumours which flush in the colour of the sky, or flutter in the dance of the wind?

Nandini. I won't say more now. When Rañjan comes you'll see for yourself how rumours in the air come down on earth.

Professor. Once she begins to talk of Rañjan there's no stopping Nandini's mouth! Well, well, I have my books, let me take my shelter behind them,—I dare not go on with this. [*Coming back after going a little way.*] Nandini. Let me ask you one thing. Aren't you frightened of our Yaksha Town?

Nandini. Why should I feel afraid?

Professor. All creatures fear an eclipse, not the full sun. Yaksha Town is a city under eclipse. The Shadow Demon, who lives in the gold caves, has eaten into it. It is not whole itself, neither does it allow any one else to remain whole. Listen to me, don't stay here. When you go, these pits will yawn all the wider for us, I know,—yet I say to you, fly; go and live happily with Rañjan where people in their drunken fury don't tear the earth's veil to pieces. [*Going a little way and then coming back.*] Nandini, will you give me a flower from your chain of red oleanders?

Nandini. Why, what will you do with it?

Professor. How often have I thought that there is some omen in these ornaments of yours.

Nandini. I don't know of any.

Professor. Perhaps your fate knows. In that red there is not only beauty, but also the fascination of fear.

Nandini. Fear! Even in me?

Professor. I don't know what event you have come to write with that crimson tint. There was the gardenia and the tuberose, there was white jasmine,—why did you leave them all and choose this flower? Do you know, we often choose our own fate thus, without knowing it!

Nandini. Rañjan sometimes calls me Red Oleander. I feel that the colour of his love is red,—that red I wear on my neck, on my breast, on my arms.

Professor. Well, just give me one of those flowers,—a moment's gift,—let me try to understand the meaning of its colour.

Nandini. Here, take it. Rañjan is coming to-day,—out of my heart's delight I give it to you. [Professor *goes.*]

[Gôkul, *a digger, comes in.*]

Gôkul. Turn this way, woman! Who are you? I've never yet been able to understand you.

Nandini. I'm nothing more than what you see. What need have you to understand me?

Gôkul. I don't trust what I can't understand. For what purpose has the King brought you here?

Nandini. Because I serve no purpose of his.

Gôkul. You know some spell, I'm sure. You're snaring everybody here. You're a witch! Those who are bewitched by your beauty will come to their death.

Nandini. That death will not be yours, Gôkul, never fear! You'll die digging.

Gôkul. Let me see, let me see, what's that dangling over your forehead?

Nandini. Only a tassel of red oleanders.

Gôkul. What does it mean?

Nandini. It has no meaning at all.

Gôkul. I don't believe you, one bit! You're up to some trickery. Some evil will befall us before the day is out. That's why you have got yourself up like this. Oh you terrible, terrible witch!

Nandini. What makes you think me so terrible?

Gôkul. You're looking like an ominous torch.

Nandini. The autumn song:

Hark, 'tis Autumn calling:
'Come, O, come away!'—
Her basket is heaped with corn.

Don't you see the September sun is spreading the glow of the ripening corn in the air?

Drunken with the perfumed wine of wind,
the sky seems to sway among the
shivering corn,
its sunlight trailing on the fields.

You too come out, King!—out into the fields.

Voice. Fields! What could I do there?

Nandini. The work there is much simpler than your work in Yaksha Town.

Voice. It's the simple which is impossible for me. A lake cannot run out dancing, like a frolicsome waterfall. Leave me now, I have no time.

Nandini. The day you let me into your store-house the blocks of gold did not surprise me,—what amazed me was the immense strength with which you lifted and arranged them. But can blocks of gold ever answer to the swinging rhythm of your arms in the same way as fields of corn? Are you not afraid, King, of handling the dead wealth of the earth?

Voice. What is there to fear?

Nandini. The living heart of the earth gives itself up in love and life and beauty, but when you rend its bosom and disturb the dead, you bring up with your booty the curse of its dark demon, blind and hard, cruel and envious. Don't you see everybody here is either angry, or suspicious, or afraid?

Voice. Curse?

Nandini. Yes, the curse of grabbing and killing.

Voice. But we bring up strength. Does not my strength please you, Nandini?

Nandini. Indeed it does. Therefore I ask you, come out into the light, step on the ground, let the earth be glad.

Voice. Do you know, Nandini, you too are half-hidden behind an evasion,—you mystery of beauty! I want to pluck you out of it, to grasp you within my closed fist, to handle you, scrutinise you,—or else to break you to pieces.

Nandini. Whatever do you mean?

Voice. Why can't I strain out the tint of your oleanders and build a dream out of it to keep before my eyes? Those few frail petals guard it and hinder me. Within you there is the same hindrance, so strong because so soft. Nandini, will you tell me what you think of me?

Nandini. Not now, you have no time. Let me go.

Voice. No, no, don't go. Do tell me what you think of me.

Nandini. Have I not told you often enough? I think you are wonderful. Strength swelling up in your arms, like rolling clouds before a storm,—it makes my heart dance within me.

Voice. And when your heart dances to see Rañjan, is that also—

Nandini. Let that be,—you have no time.

Voice. There is time,—for this; only tell me, then go.

Nandini. That dance rhythm is different, you won't understand.

Voice. I will, I must understand.

Nandini. I can't explain it clearly. Let me go.

Voice. Tell me, at least, whether you like me.

Nandini. Yes, I like you.

Voice. The same as Rañjan?

Nandini. Again the same question! I tell you, you don't understand these things.

Voice. I *do* understand, a little. I know what the difference is between Rañjan and me. In me there is only strength, in Rañjan there is magic.

Nandini. What d'you mean by magic?

Voice. Shall I explain? Underground there are blocks of stone, iron, gold,—there you have the image of strength. On the surface grows the grass, the flower blossoms,—there you have the play of magic. I can extract gold from the fearsome depths of secrecy, but to wrest that magic from the near at hand I fail.

Nandini. You have no end of things, yet why always covet?

Voice. All I possess is so much dead weight. No increase of gold can create a particle of a touchstone, no increase of power can ever come up to youth. I can only guard by force. If I had Rañjan's youth I could leave you free and yet hold you fast. My time is spent in knotting the binding rope, but, alas, everything else can be kept tied, except joy.

Nandini. It is you who entangle yourself in your own net, then why keep on fretting?

Voice. You will never understand. I, who am a desert, stretch out my hand to you, a tiny blade of grass, and cry: I am parched, I am bare, I am weary. The flaming thirst of this desert licks up one fertile field after another, only to enlarge itself,—it can never annex the life of the frailest of grasses.

Nandini. One would never think you were so tired.

Voice. One day, Nandini, in a far off land, I saw a mountain as weary as myself. I could not guess that all its stones were aching inwardly. One night I heard a noise, as if some giant's evil dream had moaned and moaned and suddenly snapped asunder. Next morning I found the mountain had disappeared in the chasm of a yawning earthquake. That made me understand how overgrown power crushes itself inwardly by its own weight. I see in you something quite opposite.

Nandini. What is it you see in me?

Voice. The dance rhythm of the All.

Nandini. I don't understand.

Voice. The rhythm that lightens the enormous weight of matter. To that rhythm the bands of stars and planets go about dancing from sky to sky, like so many minstrel boys. It is that rhythm, Nandini, that makes you so simple, so perfect. How small you are compared to me, yet I envy you.

Nandini. You have cut yourself off from everybody and so deprived yourself.

Voice. I keep myself apart, that it may become easy for me to plunder the world's big treasure-houses. Nevertheless there are gifts that your little flower-like fingers can easily reach, but not all the strength of my body,—gifts hidden in God's closed hand. That hand I must force open some day.

Nandini. When you talk like that, I don't follow you. Let me go.

Voice. Go then; but here, I stretch out this hand of mine from my window, place your hand on it for a moment.

Nandini. Only a hand, and the rest of you hidden? It frightens me!

Voice. Everybody flies from me because they only see my hand. But if I wished to hold you with all of me, would you come to me, Nandini?

Nandini. Why talk like this when you wouldn't even let me come into your room?

Voice. My busy time, overloaded with work, dragged along against obstruction, is not for you. On the day when you can arrive, full sail before the wind, into the bosom of my full.

Phágulal. Isn't it our holiday? Yesterday was the feast day of the War Goddess. To-day they worship the Flag.

Chandrá. Must you drink just because it's a holiday? In our village home, on feast days, you never—

Phágulal. Freedom itself was enough for the holidays in our village. The caged bird spends its holiday knocking against the bars. In Yaksha Town holidays are more of a nuisance than work.

Chandrá. Let's go back home, then.

Phágulal. The road to our home is closed for ever.

Chandrá. How's that?

Phágulal. Our homes don't yield them any profit.

Chandrá. But are we closely fitted to their profits only,—like husks to grains of corn,—with nothing of us left over?

Phágulal. Our mad Bishu says: to remain whole is useful only for the lamb itself; those who eat it prefer to leave out its horns and hooves, and even object to its bleating when butchered.

[*There's the madcap, singing as he goes.*]

Chandrá. It's only the last few days that his songs have burst forth.

Phágulal. That's true.

Chandrá. He's been possessed by Nandini. She draws his heart and his songs too.

Phágulal. No wonder.

Chandrá. Indeed! You'd better be careful. She'll next be bringing out songs from *your* throat,—which would be rough on our neighbours. The witch is up to all kinds of tricks, and is sure to bring misfortune.

Phágulal. Bishu's misfortune is nothing recent, he knew Nandini long before coming here.

Chandrá [*calling out*]. I say, Bishu, come this way. Maybe you'll find somebody here also to listen to your singing,—it won't be altogether thrown away.

[Bishu *comes in, singing.*]

Bishu [*sings*].

Boatman of my dreams,
The sail is filled with a boisterous breeze
and my mad heart sings
to the lilt of the rocking of thy boat,
at the call of the far away landing.

Chandrá. I know who the boatman of your dreams is.

Bishu. How should you know from outside? You haven't seen from inside my boat.

Chandrá. Your boat is going to get wrecked one of these days, let me tell you,—by that pet Nandini of yours.

[Gôkul, *the digger, comes in.*]

Gôkul. I say, Bishu, I don't quite trust your Nandini.

Bishu. Why, what has she done?

Gôkul. She does nothing, that's the rub. I don't understand the way she goes on.

Chandrá. To see her flaunting her prettiness all over the place makes me sick.

Gôkul. We can trust features that are plain enough to understand.

Bishu. I know the atmosphere of this place breeds contempt for beauty. There must be beauty even in hell; but nobody there can understand it, that's their cruellest punishment.

Chandrá. Maybe we are fools, but even our Governor here can't stand her—d'you know that?

Bishu. Take care, Chandrá, lest you catch the infection of our Governor's eyes—then perhaps yours too will redden at the sight of us. What say you, Phágulal?

Phágulal. To tell you the truth, brother, when I see Nandini, I feel ashamed to think of myself. I can't utter a word when she's there.

Gôkul. The day will come when you'll know her to your cost,—perhaps too late. [*Goes.*]

Phágulal. Bishu, your friend Chandrá wants to know why we drink.

Bishu. God in his mercy has everywhere provided a liberal allowance of drink. We men with our arms supply the output of our muscles, you women with yours supply the wine of embraces. In this world there is hunger to force us to work; but there's also the green of the woods, the gold of the sunshine, to make us drunk with their holiday-call.

Chandrá. You call these things *drink?*

Bishu. Yes, drinks of life, an endless stream of intoxication. Take my case. I come to this place; I am set to work burgling the underworld; for me nature's own ration of spirits is stopped; so my inner man craves the artificial wine of the market place. [*Sings.*]

My life, your sap has run dry,
Fill then the cup with the wine of death,
That flushes all emptiness with its laughter.

Chandrá. Come, brother, let us fly from here.

Bishu. To that boundless tavern, underneath the blue canopy? Alas, the road is closed, and we seek consolation in the stolen wine of the prison house. No open sky, no leisure for us; so we have distilled the essence of all the song and laughter, all the sunlight of the twelve hours' day into one draught of liquid fire. [*Sings.*]

Thy sun is hidden amid a mass of murky cloud.
Thy day has smudged itself black in dusty toil.
Then let the dark night descend
the last comrade of drunken oblivion,
Let it cover thy tired eyes with the mist
that will help thee desperately to lose thyself.

Chandrá. Well, well, Bishu, you men have gone to the dogs in Yaksha Town, if you like, but we women haven't changed at all.

Bishu. Haven't you? Your flowers have faded, and you are all slavering for gold.

Chandrá. No, never!

Bishu. I say, yes. That Phágulal toils for hours over and above the twelve,—why? For a reason unknown to him, unknown even to you. But I know. It's your dream of gold that lashes him on to work, more severely than the foreman's whip.

Chandrá. Very well. Then why don't we fly from here, and go back home?

Bishu. Your Governor has closed the way as well as the will to return. If you go there to-day you will fly back here to-morrow, like a caged bird to its cage, hankering for its drugged food.

Phágulal. I say, Bishu, once upon a time you came very near spoiling your eyesight poring over books; how is it they made you ply the spade along with the rest of us stupid boors?

Chandrá. All this time we've been here, we haven't got from Bishu the answer to this particular question.

Phágulal. Yet we all know it.

Bishu. Well, out with it then!

Phágulal. They employed you to spy on us.

Bishu. If you knew that, how is it you let me off alive?

Phágulal. But, we knew also, that game was not in your line.

Chandrá. How is it you couldn't stick to such a comfortable job, brother?

Bishu. Comfortable job? To stick to a living being like a carbuncle on his back?

I said: 'I must go home, my health is failing.'

'Poor thing,' said the Governor, 'how can you go home in such a state? However, there's no harm in your trying.'

Well, I did try. And then I found that, as soon as one enters the maw of Yaksha Town, its jaws shut fast, and the one road that remains open leads withinwards. Now I am swamped in that interior without hope and without light, and the only difference between you and me is, that the Governor looks down upon me even worse than upon you. Man despises the broken pot of his own creation more than the withered leaf fallen from the tree.

Phágulal. What does that matter, Bishu? You have risen high in our esteem.

Bishu. Discovery only means death. Where you favour falls there falls the Governor's glance. The more noisily the yellow frogs welcome the black toad, the sooner their croaking points him out to the boa-constrictor.

Chandrá. But when will your work be finished?

Bishu. The calendar never records the last day. After the first day comes the second, after the second the third. There's no such thing as getting finished here. We're always digging—one yard, two yards, three yards. We go on raising gold nuggets,—after one nugget another, then more and more and more. In Yaksha Town figures follow one another in rows and never arrive at any conclusion. That's why we are not men to them, but only numbers.—Phágu, what's yours?

Phágulal. I'm No. 47 V.

Bishu. I'm 69 Ng.

Chandrá. Brother, they've hoarded such heaps of gold, can't they stop digging now?

Bishu. There's always an end to things of need, no doubt; so we stop when we've had enough to eat. But we don't need drunkenness, therefore there's no end to it. These nuggets are the drink—the solid drink—of our Gold King. Don't you see?

Chandrá. No, I don't.

Bishu. Cups in hand, we forget that we are chained to our limits. Gold blocks in hand, our master fancies he's freed from the gravitation of the commonplace, and is soaring in the rarest of upper heights.

Chandrá. In this season the villages are preparing for their harvest festival. Let's go home.

Phágulal. Don't worry me, Chandrá. A thousand times over have I told you that in these parts there are high roads to the market, to the burning ground, to the scaffold,—everywhere except to the homeland.

Chandrá. If we were to go to the Governor, and just tell him—

Bishu. Hasn't your woman's wit seen through the Governor yet?

Chandrá. Why, he seems to be so nice and—

Bishu. Yes, nice and polished, like the crocodile's teeth, which fit into one another with so thorough a bite that the King himself can't unlock the jaw, even if he wants to.

Chandrá. There comes the Governor.

Bishu. Then it's all up with us. He's sure to have overheard—

Chandrá. Why, we haven't said anything so very—

Bishu. Sister, we can only say the words,—they put in the meaning.

[*The* Governor *comes in.*]

Chandrá. Sir Governor!

Governor. Well, my child?

Chandrá. Grant us leave to go home for a little.

Governor. Why, aren't the rooms we have given you excellent, much better than the ones at home? We have even kept a state watchman for your safety.

Hullo, 69 Ng, to see you amongst these people reminds one of a heron come to teach paddy birds how to cut capers.

Bishu. Sir, your jesting does not reassure me. Had my feet the strength to make others dance, would I not have run away from here, first thing? Especially after the striking examples I've seen of the fate that overtakes dancing masters in this country. As things are, one's legs tremble even to walk straight.

Chandrá. Give us leave, Sir Governor, do give us leave. Let us go just for once, and see our waving fields of barleycorn in the ear, and the ample shade of our banian tree with its hanging roots. I cannot tell you how our hearts ache. Don't you see that your men here work all day in the dark, and in the evening steep themselves in the denser dark of drunkenness? Have you no pity for them?

Governor. My dear child, surely you know of our constant anxiety for their welfare. That is exactly why I have sent for our High Preacher, Kenarám Gosain himself, to give moral talks to the men. Their votive fees will pay for his upkeep. Every evening the Gosain will come and—

Phágulal. That won't do, sir! Now, at worst, we get drunk of an evening, but if we are preached to every night, there'll be manslaughter!

Bishu. Hush, hush, Phágulal.

[*Preacher* Gosain *comes in.*]

Governor. Talk of the Preacher and he appears. Your Holiness, I do you reverence. These workmen of ours sometimes feel disturbed in their weak minds. Deign to whisper in their ears some texts of peace. The need is urgent.

Gosain. These people? Are they not the very incarnation of the sacred Tortoise of our scripture, that held up the sinking earth on its back? Because they meekly suppress themselves underneath their burden, the upper world can keep its head aloft. The very thought sends a thrill through my body!

Just think of it, friend 47 V, yours is the duty of supplying food to this mouth which chants the holy name. With the sweat of your brow have you woven this wrap printed with the holy name, which exalts this devoted body. Surely that is no mean privilege. May you remain for ever undisturbed, is my benediction, for then the grace of God will abide with you likewise.

My friends, repeat aloud the holy name of Hari, and all your burdens will be lightened. The name of Hari shall be taken in the beginning, in the middle, and at the end,—so say the scriptures.

Chandrá. How sweet! It's long since I have heard such words! Give, oh give me a little dust off your feet!

Phágulal. Stop this waste of money, Governor. If it's our offerings you want, we can stand it, but we're fairly sick of this cant.

Bishu. Once Phágulal runs amok it's all over with the lot of you. Hush, hush, Phágulal!

Chandrá. Are you bent on spoiling your chances both in this world and the next, you wretched man? You were never like this before. Nandini's ill wind has blown upon you,—and no mistake.

Gosain. What charming naiveté, Sir Governor! What's in their heart is always on their lips. What can we teach them?—it's they who'll teach us a lesson. You know what I mean.

Governor. I know where the root of the trouble is. I'll have to take them in hand myself, I see. Meanwhile, pray go to the next parish and chant them the holy name,—the sawyers there have taken to grumbling, somewhat.

Gosain. Which parish did you say?

Governor. Parish T-D. No. 71 T is headman there. It ends to the left of where No. 65 of Row M lives.

Gosain. My son, though Parish T-D may not yet be quieted, the whole Row of M's have lately become steeped in a beautiful spirit of meekness. Still it is better to keep an extra police force posted in the parish some time longer. Because, as you know our scripture says,—pride is our greatest foe. After the strength of the police has helped to conquer pride, then comes our turn. I take my leave.

Chandrá. Forgive these men, Your Holiness, and give them your blessing, that they may follow the right path.

Gosain. Fear not, good woman, they'll all end thoroughly pacified. [*The* Gosain *goes.*]

Governor. I say, 69 Ng, the temper of your parish seems to be somewhat strained.

Bishu. That's nothing strange. The Gosain called them the incarnation of the Tortoise. But, according to scripture, incarnations change; and, when the Tortoise gave place to the Boar, in place of hard shell came out aggressive teeth, so that all-suffering patience was transformed into defiant obstinacy.

Chandrá. But, Sir Governor, don't forget my request.

Governor. I have heard it and will bear it in mind. [*He goes.*]

Chandrá. Ah now, didn't you see how nice the Governor is? How he smiles every time he talks!

Bishu. Crocodile's teeth begin by smiling and end by biting.

Chandrá. Where does his bite come in?

Bishu. Don't you know he's going to make it a rule not to let the workmen's wives accompany them here.

Chandrá. Why?

Bishu. We have a place in their account book as numbers, but women's figures do not mate with figures of arithmetic.

Chandrá. O dear! but have they no women-folk of their own?

Bishu. Their ladies are besotted with the wine of gold, even worse than their husbands.

Chandrá. Bishu, you had a wife at home,—what's become of her?

Bishu. So long as I filled the honoured post of spy, they used to invite her to those big mansions to play cards with their ladies. Ever since I joined Phágulal's set, all that was stopped, and she left me in a huff at the humiliation.

Chandrá. For shame! But look, brother Bishu, what a grand procession! One palanquin after another! Don't you see the sparkle of the jewelled fringes of the elephant-seats? How beautiful the out-riders on horseback look, as if they had bits of sunlight pinned on the points of their spears!

Bishu. Those are the Governor's and Deputy Governor's ladies, going to the Flag-worship.

Chandrá. Bless my soul, what a gorgeous array and how fine they look!

I say, Bishu, if you hadn't given up that job, would you have gone along with that set in this grand style?—and that wife of yours surely—

Bishu. Yes, we too should have come to just such a pass.

Chandrá. Is there no way going back,—none whatever?

Bishu. There is,—through the gutter.

A Distant Voice. Bishu, my mad one!

Bishu. Yes, my mad girl!

Phágulal. There's Nandini. There'll be no more of Bishu for us, for the rest of the day.

Chandrá. Tell me, Bishu, what does she charm you with?

Bishu. The charm of sorrow.

Chandrá. Why do you talk so topsy-turvy?

Bishu. She reminds me that there are sorrows, to forget which is the greatest of sorrow.

Phágulal. Please to speak plainly, Bishu, otherwise it becomes positively annoying!

Bishu. The pain of desire for the near belongs to the animal, the sorrow of aspiration for the far belongs to man. That far away flame of my eternal sorrow is revealed through Nandini.

Chandrá. Brother, we don't understand these things. But one thing I do understand and that is,—the less you men can make out a girl, the more she attracts you! We simple women,—our price is not so high, but we at least keep you on the straight path. I warn you, once for all, that girl with her noose of red oleanders will drag you to perdition.

[Chandrá *and* Phágulal *go.*]

[Nandini *comes in.*]

Nandini. My mad one, did you hear their autumn songs this morning?

Bishu. Is my morning like yours that I should hear singing? Mine is only a swept-away remnant of the weary night.

Nandini. In my gladness of heart I thought I'd stand on the rampart and join in their song. But the guards would not let me, so I've come to you.

Bishu. I am not a rampart.

Nandini. You are *my* rampart. When I come to you I seem to climb high, I find the open light.

Bishu. Ever since coming to Yaksha Town the sky has dropped out of my life. I felt as if they had pounded me in the same mortar with all the fractions of men here, and rolled us into a solid lump.

Then you came and looked into my face in a way that made me sure some light could still be seen through me.

Nandini. In this closed fort a bit of sky survives only between you and me, my mad one.

Bishu. Through that sky my songs can fly towards you.

[*Sings.*]

You keep me awake that I may sing to you,
O Breaker of my sleep!
And so my heart you startle with your call,
O Waker of my grief!
The shades of evening fall,
the birds come to their nest.
The boat arrives ashore,
yet my heart knows no rest,
O Waker of my grief!

Nandini. The waker of your grief, Bishu?

Bishu. Yes, you are my messenger from the unreachable shore. The day you came to Yaksha Town a gust of salt air knocked at my heart.

Nandini. But I never had any message of this sorrow of which you sing.

Bishu. Not even from Rañjan?

Nandini. No, he holds an oar in each hand and ferries me across the stormy waters; he catches wild horses by the mane and rides with me through the woods; he shoots an arrow between the eyebrows of the tiger on the spring, and scatters my fear with loud laughter. As he jumps into our Nagai river and disturbs its current with his joyous splashing, so he disturbs me with his tumultuous life. Desperately he stakes his all on the game and thus has he won me.

You also were there with us, but you held aloof, and at last something urged you one day to leave our gambling set. At the time of your parting you looked at my face in a way I could not quite make out. After that I've had no news of you for long. Tell me where you went off to then.

Bishu. My boat was tied to the bank; the rope snapped; the wild wind drove it into the tackles unknown.

Nandini. But who dragged you back from there to dig for nuggets here in Yaksha Town?

Bishu. A woman. Just as a bird on the wing is brought to the ground by a chance arrow, so did she bring me down to the dust. I forgot myself.

Nandini. How could she touch you?

Bishu. When the thirsty heart despairs of finding water it's easy enough for it to be deluded by a mirage, and driven in barren quest from desert to desert.

One day, while I was gazing at the sunset clouds, she had her eye upon the golden spire of the Governor's palace. Her glance challenged me to take her over there. In my foolish pride I vowed to do so. When I did bring her here, under the golden spire, the spell was broken.

Nandini. I've come to take you away from here.

Bishu. Since you have moved even the king of this place, what power on earth can prevent you? Tell me, don't you feel afraid of him?

Nandini. I did fear him from outside that screen. But now I've seen him inside.

Bishu. What was he like?

Nandini. Like a man from the epics,—his forehead like the gateway of a tower, his arms the iron bolts of some inaccessible fortress.

Bishu. What did you see when you went inside?

Nandini. A falcon was sitting on his left wrist. He put it on the perch and gazed at my face. Then, just as he had been stroking the falcon's wings, he began gently to stroke my hand. After a while he suddenly asked: 'Don't you fear me, Nandini?'

'Not in the least,' said I.

Then he buried his fingers in my unbound hair and sat long with closed eyes.

Bishu. How did you like it?

Nandini. I liked it. Shall I tell you how? It was as if he were a thousand-year-old banyan tree, and I a tiny little bird; when I lit on a branch of his and had my little swing, he needs must have felt a thrill of delight to his very marrow. I loved to give that bit of joy to that lonely soul.

Bishu. Then what did he say?

Nandini. Starting up and fixing his spear-point gaze on my face, he suddenly said: 'I want to know you.'

I felt a shiver run down my body and asked: 'What is there to know?—I am not a manuscript!'

'I know all there is in manuscripts,' said he, 'but I don't know you.' Then he became excited and cried: 'Tell me all about Rañjan. Tell me how you love him.'

I talked on: 'I love Rañjan as the rudder in the water might love the sail in the sky, answering its rhythm of wind in the rhythm of waves.'

He listened quietly, staring like a big greedy boy. All of a sudden he startled me by exclaiming: 'Could you die for him?'

'This very moment,' I replied.

'Never,' he almost roared, as if in anger.

'Yes, I could,' I repeated.

'What good would that do you?'

'I don't know,' said I.

Then he writhed and shouted: 'Go away from my room, go, go at once, don't disturb me in my work.'

I could not understand what that meant.

Bishu. He gets angry when he can't understand.

Nandini. Bishu, don't you feel pity for him?

Bishu. The day when God will be moved to pity for him, he will die.

Nandini. No, no, you don't know how desperately he wants to live.

Bishu. You will see this very day what his living means. I don't know whether you'll be able to bear the sight.

Nandini. There, look, there's a shadow. I am sure the Governor has secretly heard what we've been saying.

Bishu. This place is dark with the Governor's shadow, it is everywhere. How do you like him?

Nandini. I have never seen anything so lifeless,—like a cane stick cut from the cane bush,—no leaves, no roots, no sap in the veins.

Bishu. Cut off from life, he spends himself in repressing life.

Nandini. Hush, he will hear you.

Bishu. He hears even when you are silent, which is all the more dangerous. When I am with the diggers I am careful in my speech, so much so that the Governor thinks I'm the sorriest of the lot, and spares me out of sheer contempt. But, my mad girl, when I am with you my mind scorns to be cautious.

Nandini. No, no, you must not court danger. There comes the Governor.

[*The* Governor *comes in.*]

Governor. Hallo, 69 Ng! you seem to be making friends with everybody, without distinction.

Bishu. You may remember that I began by making friends even with you, only it was the distinction that stood in the way.

Governor. Well, what are we discussing now?

Bishu. We are discussing how to escape from this fortress of yours.

Governor. Really? So recklessly, that you don't even mind confessing it?

Bishu. Sir Governor, it doesn't need much cleverness to know that when a captive bird pecks at the bars it's not in the spirit of caress. What does it matter whether that's openly confessed or not?

Governor. The captives' want of love we were aware of, but their not fearing to admit it has become evident only recently.

Nandini. Won't you let Rañjan come?

Governor. You will see him this very day.

Nandini. I knew that; still, for your message of hope I wish you victory. Governor, take this garland of *kunda* flowers.

Governor. Why throw away the garland thus, and not keep it for Rañjan?

Nandini. There is a garland for him.

Governor. Aha, I thought so! I suppose it's the one hanging round your neck. The garland of victory may be of *kunda* flowers, the gift of the hand; but the garland of welcome is of red oleanders, the gift of the heart. Well, let's be quick in accepting what comes from the hand, for that will fade; as for the heart's offering, the longer it waits the more precious it grows. [*The* Governor *goes.*]

Nandini [*knocking at the window*]. Do you hear? Let me come into your room.

Voice [*from behind the scenes*]. Why always the same futile request? Who is that with you? A pair to Rañjan?

Bishu. No, King, I am the obverse side of Rañjan, on which falls the shadow.

Voice. What use has Nandini for you?

Bishu. The use which music has for the hollow of the flute.

Voice. Nandini, what is this man to you?

Nandini. He's my partner in music. My heart soars in his voice, my pain cries in his tunes,—that's what he tells me. [*Sings.*]

> *'I love, I love,'— 'Tis the cry that breaks out*
> *from the bosom of earth and water.*

Voice. So that's your partner! What if I dissolved your partnership this very minute?

Nandini. Why are you so cross? Haven't you any companion yourself?

Voice. Has the mid-day sun any companion?

Nandini. Well, let's change the subject. What's that? What's that in your hand?

Voice. A dead frog.

Nandini. What for?

Voice. Once upon a time this frog got into a hole in a stone, and in that shelter it existed for three thousand years. I have learnt from it the secret of continuing to exist, but to live it does not know. To-day I felt bored and smashed its shelter. I've thus saved it from existing for ever. Isn't that good news?

Nandini. Your stone walls will also fall away from around me to-day,—I shall meet Rañjan.

Voice. I want to see you both together.

Nandini. You won't be able to see from behind your net.

Voice. I shall let you sit inside my room.

Nandini. What will you do with us?

Voice. Nothing, I only want to know you.

Nandini. When you talk of knowing, it frightens me.

Voice. Why?

Nandini. I feel that you have no patience with things that cannot be known, but can only be felt.

Voice. I dare not trust such things lest they should play me false. Now go away, don't waste my time.—No, no, wait a little. Give me that tassel of red oleanders which hangs from your hair.

Nandini. What will you do with it?

Voice. When I look at those flowers it seems to me as if the red light of my evil star has appeared in their shape. At times I want to snatch them from you and tear them to pieces. Again I think that if Nandini were ever to place that spray of flowers on my head, with her own hands, then—

Nandini. Then what?

Voice. Then perhaps I might die in peace.

Nandini. Some one loves red oleanders and calls me by that name. It is in remembrance of him that I wear these flowers.

Voice. Then, I tell you, they're going to be *his* evil star as well as *mine.*

Nandini. Don't say such things for shame! I am going.

Voice. Where?

Nandini. I shall go and sit near the gate of your fort.

Voice. Why?

Nandini. When Rañjan comes he'll see I am waiting for him.

Voice. I should like to tread hard on Rañjan and grind him in the dust.

Nandini. Why pretend to frighten me?

Voice. Pretend, you say? Don't you know I am really fearsome?

Nandini. You seem to take pleasure in seeing people frightened at you. In our village plays Srikantha takes the part of a demon; when he comes on the stage, he is delighted if the children are terrified. You are like him. Do you know what I think?

Voice. What is it?

Nandini. The people here trade on frightening others. That's why they have put you behind a network and dressed you fantastically. Don't you feel ashamed to be got up like a bogeyman?

Voice. How dare you!

Nandini. Those whom you have scared all along will one day feel ashamed to be afraid. If my Rañjan were here, he would have snapped his fingers in your face, and not been afraid even if he died for it.

Voice. Your impudence is something great. I should like to stand you up on the top of a heap of everything I've smashed throughout my life. And then—

Nandini. Then what?

Voice. Then, like a squeezed bunch of grapes with its juice running out from between the gripping fingers, if I could but hold you tight with these two hands of mine,—and then—go, go, run away, at once, at once!

Nandini. If you shout at me so rudely, I'll stay on, do what you will!

Voice. I long savagely to prove to you how cruel I am. Have you never heard moans from inside my room?

Nandini. I have. Whose moaning was it?

Voice. The hidden mystery of life, wrenched away by me, bewails its torn ties. To get fire from a tree you have to burn it. Nandini, there is fire within you too, red fire. One day I shall burn you and extract that also.

Nandini. Oh, you are cruel!

Voice. I must either gather or scatter. I can feel no pity for what I do not get. Breaking is a fierce kind of getting.

Nandini. But why thrust out your clenched fist like that?

Voice. Here, I take away my fist. Now fly, as the dove flies from the shadow of a hawk.

Nandini. Very well, I will go, and not vex you any more.

Voice. Here, listen, come back, Nandini!

Nandini. What is it?

Voice. On your face, there is the play of life in your eyes and lips; at the back of you flows your black hair, the silent fall of death. The other day when my hands sank into it they felt the *soft calm of dying.* I long to sleep with my face hidden inside those thick black clusters. You don't know how tired I am!

Nandini. Don't you ever sleep?

Voice. I feel afraid to sleep.

Nandini. Let me sing you the latest song that I've learnt.

[*Sings.*]

'I love, I love' is the cry that breaks out from
the bosom of earth and water.
The sky broods like an aching heart, the horizon is
tender like eyes misted with tears.

Voice. Enough! Enough! stop your singing!

Nandini [*sings on*].

A lament heaves and bursts
on the shore of the sea.
The whispers of forgotten days
are born in new leaves to die again.

See, Bishu, he has left the dead frog there and disappeared. He is afraid of songs.

Bishu. The old frog in his heart yearns to die when it hears singing, that's why he feels afraid. My mad girl, why is there a strange light on your face to-day, like the glow of a distant torch in the sky?

Nandini. News has reached me, Rañjan is coming to-day.

Bishu. How?

Nandini. Let me tell you. Every day a pair of blue-throats come and sit on the pomegranate tree in front of my window. Every night, before I sleep, I salute the pole star and say: Sacred star of constancy, if a feather from the wings of the blue-throats finds its way into my room, then I will know my Rañjan is coming. This morning, as soon as I woke, I found a feather on my bed. See, here it is under my breast-cloth. When I meet him I shall put this feather on his crest.

Bishu. They say blue-throats' wings are an omen of victory.

Nandini. Rañjan's way to victory lies through my heart.

Bishu. No more of this; let me go to my work.

Nandini. I shan't let you work to-day.

Bishu. What must I do then.

Nandini. Sing that song of waiting.

Bishu [*sings*].

He who ever wants me through the ages,—
is it not he who sits to-day by my wayside?
I seem to remember a glimpse I had of his face,
in the twilight dusk of some ancient year.
Is it not he who sits to-day by the wayside?

Nandini. Bishu, when you sing I cannot help feeling that I owe you much, but have never given anything to you.

Bishu. I shall decorate my forehead with the mark of your never-giving, and go my way. No little-giving for me, in return for my song! Where will you go now?

Nandini. To the wayside by which Rañjan is coming.

[*They go.*]

[*The* Governor *and a* Headman *come in.*]

Governor. No, we can't possibly allow Rañjan to enter this parish.

Headman. I put him to work in the tunnels of Vajragarh.

Governor. Well, what happened?

Headman. He said he was not used to being made to work. The Headman of Vajragarh came with the police, but the fellow doesn't know what fear is. Threaten him, he bursts out laughing. Asked why he laughs, he says solemnity is the mask of stupidity and he has come to take it off.

Governor. Did you set him to work with the diggers?

Headman. I did, I thought that pressure would make him yield. But on the contrary it seemed to lift the pressure from the diggers' minds also. He cheered them up, and asked them to have a digger's dance!

Governor. Digger's dance! What on earth is that?

Headman. Rañjan started singing. Where were they to get drums?—they objected. Rañjan said, if there weren't any drums, there were spades enough. So they began keeping time with the spades, making a joke of their digging up of nuggets.

The Headman himself came over to reprimand them. 'What style of work is this?' he thundered.

'I have unbound the work,' said Rañjan. 'It won't have to be dragged out by main force any more, it will run along of itself, dancing.'

Governor. The fellow is mad, I see.

Headman. Hopelessly mad. 'Use your spade properly,' shouted I. 'Much better give me a guitar,' said he, smiling.

Governor. But how did he manage to escape from Vajragarh and come up here?

Headman. That I do not know. Nothing seems to fasten on to him. His boisterousness is infectious. The diggers are getting frisky.

Governor. Hallo, isn't that Rañjan himself,—going along the road, thrumming on an old guitar? Impudent rascal! He doesn't even care to hide.

Headman. Well, I never! Goodness alone knows how he broke through the wall!

Governor. Go and seize him instantly! He must not meet Nandini in this parish, for anything.

[*Enters* Assistant Governor.]

Governor. Where are you going?

Assistant Governor. To arrest Rañjan.

Governor. Where is the Deputy Governor?

Assistant Governor. He is so much amused by this fellow that he doesn't want to lay hands on him. He says the man's laugh shows us what queer creatures we governors have grown into.

Governor. I have an idea. Don't arrest Rañjan. Send him on to the King's sanctum.

Assistant Governor. He refuses to obey our call, even in the King's name.

Governor. Tell him the King has made a slave-girl of his Nandini.

Assistant Governor. But if the King—

Governor. Don't you worry. Come on, I'll go with you myself.

[*They go.*]

[*Enter* Professor *and* Antiquarian.]

Antiquarian. I say, what is this infernal noise going on inside?

Professor. The King, probably in a temper with himself, is engaged in breaking some of his own handiwork.

Antiquarian. It sounds like big pillars crashing down one after another.

Professor. There was a lake, at the foot of our hill over there, in which the waters of this Sankhini river used to gather. One day, suddenly, the rock to its left gave way, and the stored-up water rushed out laughing like mad. To see the King now-a-days, it strikes me that his treasure lake has grown weary of its rock wall.

Antiquarian. What did you bring me here for, Professor?

Professor. Latterly he has begun to get angry with my science. He says it only burgles through one wall to reveal another behind it, and never reaches the inner chamber of the Life spirit. I thought that, perhaps in the study of antiquity, he might explore the secret of Life's play. My knapsack has been rifled empty, now he can go on pocket-picking history.

Antiquarian. A girl wearing a grass-green robe.

Professor. She has for her mantle the green joy of the earth. That is our Nandini. In this Yaksha Town there are governors, foremen, headmen, tunnel-diggers, scholars like myself; there are policemen, executioners, and undertakers,—altogether a beautiful assortment! Only *she* is out of element. Midst the clamour of the market place she is a tuned-up lyre. There are days when the mesh of my studies is torn by the sudden breeze of her passing by, and through that rent my attention flies away *swish,* like a bird.

Antiquarian. Good heavens, man! Are even your well-seasoned bones subject to these poetic fits?

Professor. Life's attraction, like the tidal wave, tears away mind from its anchorage of books.

Antiquarian. Tell me, where am I to meet the King.

Professor. There's no means of meeting him. You'll have to talk to him from outside this network.

Antiquarian. We're to converse with this net between us?

Professor. Not the kind of whispered talk that may take place through a woman's veil, but solidly concentrated conversation. Even the cows in his stall don't dare to give milk, they yield their butter straight off.

Antiquarian. Admirable! To extract the essential from the diluted, is what scholars aim at.

Professor. But not what God in His creation aims at. He respects the fruit stones that are hard, but rejoices in the pulp that is sweet.

Antiquarian. Professor, I see that your grey science is galloping fast towards grass-green. But I wonder how you can stand this King of yours.

Professor. Shall I tell you the truth? I love him.

Antiquarian. You don't mean to say so?

Professor. He is so great that even what is wrong with him will not be able to spoil him.

[*The* Governor *comes in.*]

Governor. I say, man of science, so this is the person you volunteered to bring here. Our King flew into a passion at the very mention of his special subject.

Antiquarian. May I ask why?

Governor. The King says there is no age of history which may be called old. It is always an eternal extension of the present.

Antiquarian. Can the front exist without the back?

Governor. What he said was: 'Time proceeds by revealing the new on his front; but the men of learning, suppressing that fact, will have it that Time ever carries the burden of the old on his back.'

[Nandini *comes in hurriedly.*]

Nandini. What is happening? Who are they?

Governor. Hallo, Nandini, is that you? I shall wear your *kunda* chain late in the evening. When three-quarters of me can hardly be seen for the dark, then perchance a flower garland might become even me.

Nandini. Look over there—what a piteous sight! Who are those people, going along with the guards, filing out from the backdoor of the King's apartments?

Governor. We call them the King's leavings.

Nandini. What does that mean?

Governor. Some day you too will know its meaning; let it be for today.

Nandini. But are these men? Have they flesh and marrow, life and soul?

Governor. Maybe they haven't.

Nandini. Had they never any?

Governor. Maybe they had.

Nandini. Where then is it all gone now?

Governor. Man of science, explain it if you can, I'm off.

[*He goes.*]

Nandini. Alas, alas! I see amongst these shadows faces that I know. Surely that is our Anup and Upamanyu?

Professor, they belong to our neighbouring village. Two brothers as tall as they were strong. They used to come and race their boats in our river on the fourteenth day of the moon in rainy June. Oh, who has brought them to this miserable plight?

See, there goes Shaklu,—in sword play he used to win the prize garland before all the others. Anu-up! Sha-klu-u! look this way; it's I, your the principle underlying all rise to greatness.

Nandini. It's a fiendish principle!

Professor. It's no use getting annoyed with a principle. Principles are neither good nor bad. That which happens *does* happen. To go against it, is to knock your head against the law of being.

Nandini. If this is the way of man's being, I refuse to *be,* I want to depart with those shadows,—show me the way.

Professor. When the time comes for showing us out, the great ones themselves will point the way. Before that, there's no such nuisance as a way at all! You see how our Antiquarian has quietly slipped off, thinking he'll fly and save himself. After going a few steps, he'll soon discover that there's a wire network stretched from post to post, from country to country.

Nandini, I see, your temper is rising. The red oleanders against your flaming cheek are beginning to look like evening storm clouds gathering for a night of terror.

Nandini [*knocking at the net window*]. Listen, listen!

Professor. Whom are you calling?

Nandini. That King of yours, shrouded in his mist of netting.

Professor. The door of the inner room has been closed. He won't hear you.

Nandini [*calling out*]. Bishu, mad brother mine!

Professor. What d'you want with *him?*

Nandini. Why hasn't he come back yet? I feel afraid.

Professor. He was with you only a little while ago.

Nandini. The Governor said he was wanted to identify Rañjan. I tried to go with him, but they wouldn't let me. Whose groaning is that?

Professor. It must be that wrestler of ours.

Nandini. What wrestler?

Professor. The world-famous Gajju, whose brother, Bhajan, had the bravado to challenge the King to a wrestling match, since when not even a thread of his loin cloth is anywhere to be seen. That put Gajju on his mettle, and he came on with great sound and fury. I told him at the outset that, if he wanted to dig in the tunnels underneath this kingdom, he was welcome,—he could at least drag on a dead and alive existence for some time. But if he wanted to make a show of heroics, that would not be tolerated for a moment.

Nandini. Does it at all make for their well-being thus to keep watch and ward over these man-traps night and day?

Professor. Well-being! There's no question of 'well' in it at all,—only 'being'. That *being* of theirs has expanded so terribly that, unless millions of men are pressed into service, who's going to support its weight? So the net is spreading farther and farther. They must exist, you see.

Nandini. Must they? If it is necessary to die in order to live like men, what harm in dying?

Professor. Again that anger, the wild cry of red oleander? It is sweet, no doubt, yet what is true is true. If it gives you pleasure to say that one must die to live, well, say so by all means; but those who say that others must die that they themselves may live,—it's only they who are actually alive. You may cry out that this shows a lack of humanity, but you forget, in your indignation, that this is what humanity itself happens to be. The tiger does not feed on the tiger, it's only man who fattens on his fellow-man.

[*The* Wrestler *totters in.*]

Nandini. Oh poor thing, see how he comes, staggering. Wrestler, lie down here. Professor, do see where he's hurt.

Professor. You won't see any outward sign of a wound.

Wrestler. All-merciful God, grant me strength once more in my life, if only for one little day!

Professor. Why, my dear fellow?

Wrestler. Just to wring that Governor's neck!

Professor. What has the Governor done to you?

Wrestler. It's he who brought about the whole thing. I never wanted to fight. Now, after egging me on, he goes about saying it's my fault.

Professor. Why, what interest had he in your fighting?

Wrestler. They only feel safe when they rob the whole world of strength. Lord of Mercy, grant that I may be able to gouge his eyes out some day, to tear asunder his lying tongue!

Nandini. How do you feel now, Wrestler?

Wrestler. Altogether hollowed out! These demons know the magic art of sucking away not only strength but hope.

If only once I could somehow,—O good God, but once,—everything is possible to Thy mercy,—if only I could fasten my teeth for once in the Governor's throat!

Nandini. Professor, help me to raise him.

Professor. That would be a crime, Nandini, according to the custom of this land.

Nandini. Wouldn't it be a crime to let the man perish?

Professor. That which there is none to punish may be a sin, but never a crime. Nandini, come away, come right away out of this. The tree spreads its root-fingers and does its grabbing underground, but there it does not bring forth its flowers. Flowers bloom on the branches which reach towards the light. My sweet Red Oleander, don't try to probe our secrets in the depths of their dust. Be for us swaying in the air above, that we may gaze upwards to see you.

There comes the Governor. He hates to see me talk to you. So I must go.

Nandini. Why is he so dead against me?

Professor. I can guess. You have touched his heart-strings. The longer it takes to tune them up, the more awful the discord meanwhile.

[*The* Professor *goes, the* Governor *comes in.*]

Nandini. Sir Governor!

Governor. Nandini, when our Gosain saw that *kunda* garland of yours in my room, both his eyes,—but here he comes—[*The* Gosain *comes in.*]

Your Holiness, accept my reverence. That garland was given to me by our Nandini here.

Gosain. Ah indeed! the gift of a pure heart! God's own white *kunda* flowers! Their beauty remains unsullied even in the hands of a man of the world. This is what gives one faith in the power of virtue, and hope for the sinners' redemption.

Nandini. Please do something for this man, Your Reverence. There's very little life left in him.

Gosain. The Governor is sure to keep him as much alive as it is necessary for him to be. But, my child, these discussions will become your lips.

Nandini. So in this kingdom you follow some calculation in apportioning life?

Gosain. Of course,—for mortal life has its limits. Our class of people have their great burden to bear, therefore we have to claim a larger portion of life's sustenance for our share. That's according to Almighty God's own decree.

Nandini. Reverend Sir, may I know what good God has so heavily charged you to do to these people?

Gosain. The life that is unlimited gives no provocation to fight for its distribution. We Preachers have the charge of turning these people towards this unlimited life. So long as they remain content with that, we are their friends.

Nandini. Let me come over to the Headman's quarters to help you.

Wrestler. No. Don't add to my troubles, I beg of you.

[*The* Wrestler *goes.*]

Nandini. Governor, stay, tell me, whither have you taken my Bishu?

Governor. Who am I that I should take him? The wind carries off the clouds,—if you think that to be a crime, make enquiries as to who is behind the wind.

Nandini. Dear me, what an awful place! You are not men, and those you drive are not men, either,—you are winds and they are clouds!

Reverend Gosain, I am sure, *you* know where my Bishu is.

Gosain. I know, for sure, that wherever he is, it's for the best.

Nandini. For whose best?

Gosain. That you won't understand—

Oh, I say, leave off, let go of that, it's my rosary.—Hallo, Governor, what wild girl is this you have—

Governor. The girl has somehow managed to ensconce herself in a niche, safe from the laws of this land, and we can't lay hands on her. Our King himself—

Gosain. Good heavens, now she'll tear off my wrap of the Holy Name too. What unspeakable outrage!

[*The* Gosain *flies.*]

Nandini. Governor, you *must* tell me where you have taken Bishu.

Governor. They have summoned him to the court of judgement. That's all that there is to tell you. Let me go.

Nandini. Because I am a woman, you are not afraid of me? God sends His thunderbolt through His messenger, the lightning spark—that bolt I have borne here with me; it will shatter the golden spire of your mastery.

Governor. Then let me tell you the truth before I go. It's you who have dragged Bishu into danger.

Nandini. I?

Governor. Yes, you! He was so long content to be quietly burrowing away underground like a worm. It's you who taught him to spread the wings of death. O fire of the gods, you'll yet draw forth many more to their fate.—Then at length will you and I come to our understanding, and that won't be long.

Nandini. So may it be. But tell me one thing before you go. Will you not let Rañjan come and see me?

Governor. No, never.

Nandini. Never, you say! I defy you to do your worst. This very day I am sure, absolutely sure, that he and I will meet!

[Governor *goes.*]

Nandini [*knocking and tugging at the network*]. Listen, listen, King! Where's your court of judgement? Open its door to me. [Kishôr *comes in.*]

Who is that? My boy, Kishôr! Do you know where Bishu is?

Kishôr. Yes, Nandini, be ready to see him. I don't know how it was, the Chief of the Guard took a fancy to my youthfulness and yielded to my entreaties. He has consented to take him along by this path.

Nandini. Guard! Take him along? Is he then—

Kishôr. Yes, here they come.

Nandini. What! Handcuffs on your wrists? Friend of my heart, where are they taking you like that?

[Bishu *comes in under arrest.*]

Bishu. It's nothing to be anxious about!—Guards, please wait a little, let me say a few words to her.—My wild girl, my heart's joy, at last I am free.

Nandini. What do you mean, Singer of my heart? I don't understand your words.

Bishu. When I used to be afraid, and try to avoid danger at every step, I seemed to be at liberty; but that liberty was the worst form of bondage.

Nandini. What offence have you committed that they should take you away thus?

Bishu. I spoke out the truth to-day, at last.

Nandini. What if you did?

Bishu. No harm at all!

Nandini. Then why did they bind you like this?

Bishu. What harm in that either? These chains will bear witness to the truth of my freedom.

Nandini. Don't they feel ashamed of themselves to lead you along the road chained like a beast? Aren't they men too?

Bishu. They have a big beast inside them, that's why their heads are not lowered by the indignity of man, rather the inner brute's tail swells and wags with pride at man's downfall.

Nandini. O dear heart! Have they been hurting you? What are these marks on your body?

Bishu. They have whipped me, with the whips they use for their dogs. The string of that whip is made with the same thread which goes to the stringing of their Gosain's rosary. When they tell their beads they don' t remember that; but probably their God is aware of it.

Nandini. Let them bind me like that too, and take me away with you, my heart's joy! Unless I share some of your punishment I shan't be able to touch food from to-day.

Kishôr. I'm sure I can persuade them to take me in exchange for you. Let me take your place, Bishu.

Bishu. Don't be silly!

Kishôr. Punishment won't hurt me. I am young. I shall bear it with joy.

Nandini. No, no, do not talk like that.

Kishôr. Nandini, my absence has been noticed, their bloodhounds are after me. Allow me to escape the indignity awaiting me by taking shelter in a punishment I joyfully accept.

Bishu. No, it won't do for you to be caught—not for a while yet. There's work for you, dear boy, and dangerous work too. Rañjan has come. You must find him out.

Kishôr. Then I bid you farewell, Nandini. What is your message when I meet Rañjan?

Nandini. This tassel of red oleanders. [*Hands it to him.*]

[Kishôr *goes.*]

Bishu. May you both be united once again.

Nandini. That union will give me no pleasure now. I shall never be able to forget that I sent you away empty-handed. And what has that poor boy, Kishôr, got from me?

Bishu. All the treasure hidden in his heart has been revealed to him by the fire you have lighted in his life. Nandini, I remind you, it's for you to put that blue-throat's feather on Rañjan's crest.—There, do you hear them singing the harvest song?

Nandini. I do, and it wrings my heart, to tears.

Bishu. The play of the fields is ended now, and the field-master is taking the ripe corn home. Come on, Guards, let's not linger anymore. [*Sings*.]

> *Mow the corn of the last harvest,*
> *bind it in sheaves.*
> *The remainder, let it return*
> *as dust unto the dust.*

[*They go*.]

[*The* Governor *and a* Doctor *come in*.]

Doctor. I've seen him. I find the King.

Governor. My wife will be driving out to-day. The post will be changed near your village, and you must see that she's not detained.

Headman. There's a plague on the cattle of our parish, and not a single ox can be had to draw the car. Never mind, we can press the diggers into service.

Governor. You know where you have to take her? To the garden-house, where the feast of the Flag-worship is to be held.

Headman. I'll see to it at once, but let me tell you one thing before I go. That 69 Ng, whom they call mad Bishu,—it's high time to cure his madness.

Governor. Why, how does he annoy you?

Headman. Not so much by what he says or does, as by what he implies.

Governor. There's no need to worry about him any further. You understand!

Headman. Really! That's good news, indeed! Another thing. That 47 V, he's rather too friendly with 69 Ng.

Governor. I have observed that.

Headman. Your Lordship's observation is ever keen. Only, as you have to keep an eye on so many things, one or two may perchance escape your notice. For instance, there's our No. 95, a distant connection of mine by marriage, ever ready to make sandals for the feet of Your Lordship's sweeper out of his own ribs,—so irrepressibly loyal is he that even his wife hangs her head for very shame,—and yet up to now—

Governor. His name has been entered in the High Register.

Headman. Ah, then his lifelong service will at last receive its reward! The news must be broken to him gently, because he gets epileptic fits, and supposing suddenly—

Governor. All right, we'll see to that. Now be off, there's no time.

Headman. Just a word about another person,—though he's my own brother-in-law. When his mother died, my wife brought him up with her own hands; yet for my master's sake—

Governor. You can tell me about him another time. Run away now.

Headman. There comes His Honour the Deputy Governor. Please speak a word to him on my behalf. He doesn't look upon me with favour. I suspect that when 69 Ng used to enjoy the favour of free entry into the palace, he must have been saying things against me.

Governor. I assure you, he never even mentioned your name.

Headman. That's just his cleverness! What can be more damaging than to suppress the name of a man, whose name is his best asset? These schemers have their different ways. No. 33 of our parish has an incurable habit of haunting Your Lordship's private chamber. One is always afraid of his inventing goodness knows what calumnies about other people. And yet if one knew the truth about his own—

Governor. There's positively no time to-day. Get away with you, quick!

Headman. I make my salute. [*Coming back.*] Just one word more lest I forget. No. 88 of our neighbouring parish started work on a miserable pittance, and before two years are out his income has run into thousands, not to speak of extras! Your Lordship's mind is like that of the gods—a few words of hypocritical praise are enough to draw down the best of your boons.

Governor. All right, all right,—that can keep for to-morrow.

Headman. I'm not so mean as to suggest taking away the bread from his mouth. But Your Lordship should seriously consider whether it's wise to keep him on at the Treasury. Our Vishnu Dutt knows him inside out. If you send—

Governor. I shall send for him this very day. But begone,—not another word!

Headman. Your Lordship, my third son is getting to be quite a big boy. He came the other day to prostrate himself at your feet. After two days of dancing attendance outside, he had to go away without gaining admission to you. He feels it very bitterly. My daughter-in-law has made with her own hands an offering of sweet pumpkin for Your Lordship—

Governor. Oh confound you! Tell him to come day after to-morrow, he will be admitted. *Now, will you—*

[Headman *goes. The* Deputy Governor *comes in.*]

Deputy Governor. I've just sent on the dancing girls and musicians to the garden.

Governor. And that little matter about Rañjan,—how far—?

Deputy Governor. That kind of work is not in my line. The Assistant Governor has taken it upon himself to do the job. By this time his—

Governor. Does the King—?

Deputy Governor. The King can't possibly have understood. Some lie told by our men has goaded Rañjan to frenzy, and he's rushing to the usual fate of—I detest the whole business. Moreover, I don't think it right to deceive the King like this.

Governor. That responsibility is mine. Now then, that girl must be—

Deputy Governor. Don't talk of all that to me. The Headman who has been put on duty is the right man,—he doesn't stick at any dirtiness whatever.

Governor. Does that man Gosain know about this affair?

Deputy Governor. I'm sure he can guess, but he's careful not to know for certain.

Governor. What's his object?

Deputy Governor. For fear of there being no way left open for saying: 'I don't believe it.'

Governor. But what makes him take all this trouble?

Deputy Governor. Don't you see? The poor man is really two in one, clumsily joined,—Priest on the skin, Governor at the marrow. He has to take precious care to prevent the Governor part of him coming up to the surface, lest it should clash too much with his telling of beads.

Governor. He might have dropped the beads altogether.

Deputy Governor. No, for whatever his blood may be, his mind, in a sense, is really pious. If only he can tell his beads in his temple, and revel in slave-driving in his dreams, he feels happy. But for him, the true complexion of our God would appear too black. In fact, Gosain is placed here only to help our God to feel comfortable.

Governor. My friend, I see the instinct of the Ruler doesn't seem to match with the colour of your own blood, either!

Deputy Governor. There's hope still. Human blood is fast drying up. But I can't stomach your No. 321 yet. When I'm obliged to embrace him in public, no holy water seems able to wash out the impurity of his touch.

[*Here comes* Nandini.]

Governor. Come away, I don't trust you. I know the spell of Nandini has fallen on your eyes.

Deputy Governor. I know that as well as you do. But you don't seem to know that a tinge of her oleanders has got mixed with the colour of duty in *your* eyes too—that's what makes them so frightfully red.

Governor. That may be. Fortunately for us, our mind knows not its own secret. Come away. [*They go.*]

[Nandini *comes in.*]

Nandini [*knocking and pushing at the network*]. Listen, listen, listen!

[Gosain *comes in.*]

Gosain. Whom are you prodding like that?

Nandini. That boa-constrictor of yours, who remains in hiding and swallows men.

Gosain. Lord, lord! When Providence wishes to destroy the small, it does so by putting big words into their little mouths.

See here, Nandini, believe me when I tell you that I aim at your welfare.

Nandini. Try some more real method of doing me good.

Gosain. Come to my sanctuary, let me chant you the Holy Name for a while.

Nandini. What have I to do with the name?

Gosain. You will gain peace of mind.

Nandini. Shame, shame on me if I do! I shall sit and wait here at the door.

Gosain. You have more faith in men than in God?

Nandini. Your God of the Flagstaff,—he will never unbend. But the man who is lost to sight behind the netting, will he also remain bound in his network for ever? Go, go. It's your trade to delude men with words, after filching away their lives. [Gosain *goes.*]

[*Enter* Phágulal *and* Chandrá.]

Phágulal. Our Bishu came away with you, where is he now? Tell us the truth.

Nandini. He has been made prisoner and taken away.

Chandrá. You witch, you must have given information against him. You are their spy.

Nandini. You don't really believe that!

Chandrá. What else are you doing here?

Phágulal. Every person suspects every other person in this cursed place. Yet I have always trusted you, Nandini. In my heart I used to—However, let that pass. But to-day it looks very very strange, I must say.

Nandini. Perhaps it does. It may really be even as you say. Bishu has got into trouble for coming with me. He used to be quite safe in your company, he said so himself.

Chandrá. Then why did you decoy him away, you evil-omened creature?

Nandini. Because he said he wanted to be free.

Chandrá. A precious kind of freedom you have given him!

Nandini. I could not understand all that he said, Chandrá. Why did he tell me that freedom could only be found by plunging down to the bottom of danger?—Phágulal, how could I save him who wanted to be free from the tyranny of safety?

Chandrá. We don't understand all this. If you can't bring him back, you'll have to pay for it. I'm not to be taken in by that coquettish prettiness of yours.

Phágulal. What's the use of idle bickering? Let's gather a big crowd from the workmen's lines, and then go and smash the prison gate.

Nandini. I'll come with you.

Phágulal. What for?

Nandini. To join in the breaking.

Chandrá. As if you haven't done quite enough breaking already, you sorceress!

[Gôkul *comes in.*]

Gôkul. That witch must be burnt alive, before everything else.

Chandrá. That won't be punishment enough. First knock off that beauty of hers, with which she goes about ruining people. Weed it out of her face as the grass is weeded with a hoe.

Gôkul. That I can do. Let this hammer just have a dance on her nose tip—

Phágulal. Beware! If you dare touch her—

Nandini. Stop, Phágulal. He's coward; he wants to strike me because he's afraid of me. I don't fear his blows one bit.

Gôkul. Phágulal, you haven't come to your senses yet. You think the Governor alone is your enemy. Well, I admire a straightforward enemy. But that sweet-mouthed beauty of yours—

Nandini. Ah, so you too admire the Governor, as the mud beneath his feet admires the soles of his shoes!

Phágulal. Gôkul, the time has at length come to show your prowess, but not by fighting a girl. Come along with me. I'll show you what to fight.

[Phágulal, Chandrá, *and* Gôkul *go.*]

[*A band of* Men *come in.*]

Nandini. Where are you going, my good men?

First Man. We carry the offering for the Flag-worship.

Nandini. Have you seen Rañjan?

Second Man. I saw him once, five days ago, but not since. Ask those others who follow us.

Nandini. Who are they?

Third Man. They are bearing wine for the Governors' feast.

[*The first batch goes, another comes in.*]

Nandini. Look here, red-caps, have you seen Rañjan?

First Man. I saw him the other day at the house of Headman Sambhu.

Nandini. Where is he now?

Second Man. D'you see those men taking the ladies' dresses for the feast? Ask them. They hear a lot of things that don't reach our ears.

[*Second batch goes, a third come in.*]

Nandini. Do *you* know, my men, where they have kept Rañjan?

First Man. Hush, hush!

Nandini. I am sure you know. You *must* tell me.

Second Man. What enters by our ears doesn't come out by our mouths, that's why we are still alive. Ask one of the men who are carrying the weapons.

[*They go, others come in.*]

Nandini. Oh do stop a moment and listen to me. Tell me, where is Rañjan?

First Man. The auspicious hour draws near. It's time for the King himself to come for the Flag-worship. Ask him about it when he steps out. We only know the beginning, not the end. [*They go.*]

Nandini [*shaking the network violently*]. Open the door. The time has come.

Voice [*behind the scenes*]. But not for you. Go away from here.

Nandini. You must hear *now* what I have to say. It cannot wait for another time.

Voice. You want Rañjan, I know. I have asked the Governor to fetch him at once. But don't remain standing at the door when I come out for the worship, for then you'll run great risk.

Nandini. I have cast away all fear. You can't drive me away. Happen what may, I'm not going to move till your door is opened.

Voice. To-day's for the Flag-worship. Don't distract my mind. Get away from my door.

Nandini. The gods have all eternity for their worship, they're not pressed for time. But the sorrows of men cannot wait.

King. Deceived! These traitors have deceived me,—perdition take them! My own machine refuses my sway! Call the Governor—bring him to me handcuffed—

Nandini. King, they all say you know magic. Make him wake up for my sake.

King. My magic can only put an end to waking.—Alas! I know not how to awaken.

Nandini. Then lull me to sleep,—the same sleep! Oh, why did you work this havoc? I cannot bear it any more.

King. I have killed youth. Yes, I have indeed killed youth,—all these years, with all my strength. The curse of youth, dead, is upon me.

Nandini. Did he not take my name?

King. He did,—in such a way that every vein in my body was set on fire.

Nandini [*to* Rañjan]. My love, my brave one, here do I place this blue-throat's feather in your crest. Your victory has begun from today, and I am its bearer. Ah, here is that tassel of my flowers in his hand. Then Kishôr must have met him—

But where is he? King, where is that boy?

King. Which boy?

Nandini. The boy who brought these flowers to Rañjan.

King. That absurd little child! He came to defy me with his girlish face.

Nandini. And then? Tell me! Quick!

King. He burst himself against me, like a bubble.

Nandini. King, the Time is indeed now come!

King. Time for what?

Nandini. For the last fight between you and me.

King. But I can kill you in no time,—this instant.

Nandini. From that very instant that death of mine will go on killing you every single moment.

King. Be brave, Nandini, trust me. Make me your comrade to-day.

Nandini. What would you have me do?

King. To fight against me, but with your hand in mine. That fight has already begun. There is my flag. First I break the Flagstaff,—thus! Next it's for you to tear its banner. Let your hand unite with mine to kill me, utterly kill me. That will be my emancipation.

Guards [*rushing up*]. What are you doing, King? You dare break the Flagstaff, the holiest symbol of our divinity? The Flagstaff which has its one point piercing the heart of the earth and the other that of heaven! What a terrible sin,—on the very day of the Flag-worship! Comrades, let us go and inform our Governors. [*They run off.*]

King. A great deal of breaking remains to be done. You will come with me, Nandini?

Nandini. I will.

[Phágulal *comes in.*]

Phágulal. They won't hear of letting Bishu off. I am afraid, they'll—Who is this? The King!

Oh you wicked witch,—conspiring with the King himself! O vile deceiver!

King. What is the matter with you? What is that crowd out for?

Phágulal. To break the prison gate. We may lose our lives, but we shan't fall back.

King. Why should you fall back? I too am out for breaking. Behold the first sign—my broken Flagstaff!

Phágulal. What! This is altogether beyond us simple folk.

Be merciful, Nandini, don't deceive me. Am I to believe my eyes?

Nandini. Brother, you have set out to win death. You have left no chance for deception to touch you.

Phágulal. You too come along with us, our own Nandini!

Nandini. That is what I'm still alive for, Phágulal. I wanted to bring my Rañjan amongst you. Look there, he has come, my hero, braving death!

Phágulal. Oh, horror! Is that Rañjan lying there, silent?

Nandini. Not silent. He leaves behind him in death his conquering call. He will live again, he cannot die.

Phágulal. Ah, my Nandini, my beautiful one, was it for this you were waiting all these eager days?

Nandini. I *did* await his coming, and he *did* come. I still wait to prepare for his coming again, and he *shall* come again. Where is Chandrá?

Phágulal. She has gone with her tears and prayers to the Governor, accompanied by Gôkul. I'm afraid Gôkul is seeking to take up service with the Governor. He will betray us.

King, are you sure you don't mistake us? We are out to break your own prison, I tell you!

King. Yes, it is my *own* prison. You and I must work together, for you cannot break it alone.

Phágulal. As soon as the Governor hears of it, he will march with all his forces to prevent us.

King. Yes, my fight is against them.

Phágulal. But the soldiers will not obey you.

King. You will be on my side!

Phágulal. Shall we be able to win through?

King. We shall at least be able to die! At last I have found the meaning of death. I am saved!

Phágulal. King, do you hear the tumult?

King. There comes the Governor with his troops. How could he be so quick about it? He must have been prepared beforehand. They have used my own power against me.

Phágulal. My men have not yet turned up.

King. They will never come. The Governor is sure to get round them.

Nandini. I had my last hope that they would bring my Bishu to me. Will that never be?

King. No hope of that, I'm afraid.

Phágulal. Then come along, Nandini, let us take you to a safe place first. The Governor will see red, if he but catches sight of you.

Nandini. You want to banish me into the solitary exile of safety? [*Calling out*] Governor! Governor!—He has swung up my garland of *kunda* flowers on his spear-head. I will dye that garland the colour of my oleanders with my heart's blood.—Governor! He has seen me! Victory to Rañjan! [*Runs off.*]

King [*calling after her*]. Nandini! [*Follows her.*]

[*The* Professor *comes in.*]

Phágulal. Where are *you* hurrying to, Professor?

Professor. Some one said that the King has at last had tidings of the secret of Life, and has gone off in quest of it. I have thrown away my books to follow him.

Phágulal. The King has just gone off to his death. He has heard Nandini's call.

Professor. The network is torn to shreds! Where is Nandini?

Phágulal. She has gone before them all. We can't reach her any more.

Professor. It is only now that we shall reach her. She won't evade us any longer.

[Professor *rushes out,* Bishu *comes in.*]

Bishu. Phágulal, where is Nandini?

Phágulal. How did you get here?

Bishu. Our workmen have broken into the prison. There they are,—running off to fight. I came to look for Nandini. Where is she?

Phágulal. She has gone in advance of us all.

Bishu. Where?

Phágulal. To the last freedom. Bishu, do you see who is lying there?

Bishu. Rañjan!

Phágulal. You see the red streak?

Bishu. I understand,—then red marriage.

Phágulal. They are united.

Bishu. Now it is for me to take my last lonely journey.—Perhaps we may meet.—Perhaps she may want me to sing.—My mad girl, O my mad girl!—

Come, brother, on to the fight!

Phágulal. To the fight! Victory to Nandini!

Bishu. Victory to Nandini!

Phágulal. Here is her wristlet of red oleanders. She has bared her arm to-day,—and left us.

Bishu. Once I told her I would not take anything from her hand. I break my word and take this. Come along!

[*They go.*]

[*Song in the distance.*]

Hark 'tis Autumn calling,—
Come, O come away!
The earth's mantle of dust is filled with ripe corn!
O the joy! the joy!

Reference

English Writings of Tagore, Vol. 3, New Delhi: Atlantic Publishers and Distributors (P) Ltd., 2007, pp. 211-65

APPENDICES

Appendix I

Tagore on Red Oleanders[1]

'Red Oleanders: An Interpretation'

For those of us who are concerned with life and with the play of human forces across the stage of our daily existence, it is the underlying significance which forms the kernel of the problem. In this play there is no attempt to point a moral or to preach a sermon, but because these characters "are the abstract and brief chronicles of the time", they give us a mirror in which perhaps we may catch some glimpse of that truth to which we are so accustomed that we have forgotten all about it. The test of every great work of art, in colour, sound, form or word, is this test of significance. The artist has had something great to say and he has said it greatly, so truth is revealed. But to do this, and much modern work shows a woeful lack of consciousness in the matter, life itself must be a great work of art, so that out of significance of his life a man will draw forth that which holds the essence of truth and, with the tool over which he has the most complete mastery, will give to it artistic shape. There are those who, in perfecting their tool of craftsmanship, spend their whole lives comparing their facility of use with that of others and await with anxiety the plaudits or criticisms of their fellow craftsmen. This is not so with him who lives greatly. Out of the wealth of his experience of life and of his conviction of truth he draws that which is most truly significant and offers it to us chiseled with no doubting hand and illuminated by his own creative imagination.

In daring to sit in judgment upon *Red Oleanders*, we are not judges, we are the accused. For we stand in front of a great life, the life of one who has lived and drunk of the draft of life from foam to dregs, so that according to our judgment we shall stand judged. The figure on the canvas cannot be separated from its background, else the unity of truth is broken. The background to this play is one which needs careful attention if the characters, as they step upon the stage, are to tell their tale, and keep their significance. Divest them of this and it is so easy to be superficial, to repeat the catchwords of the modern marketplace; a poetic tirade against modern industrialism, the usual hit at Science, the national complain of the subject against oppression. But whether we will or no, the forces that we ordinarily applaud are beaten at the end. They dissolve before the close into a complete insignificance and vanish in the face of a superior force which somehow convinces us, whether we see its significance or not.

In *Red Oleanders*, there are certain underlying principles at work, principles which we can quite easily recognize in our daily existence if we choose to look for one moment under the surface. The habit of greed—greed for things, for power, for facts, with all the ramifications that greed is able to set up between man and man—is arrayed against the explosive force of human sympathy, of neighbourliness, of fellowship and of love, the force which we may term good. Good is here arrayed against the dehumanizing force of mammon, of selfishness, of evil; of that which separates us from our fellows against that which cements us together, of that which, because it divides us, is untruth, is a lie. Only in so far as he recognizes this truth, has man succeeded in reaching the peak upon which the human race now stands, whilst the tiger, a solitary wandering unit, still prowls the jungle alone.

To the gardener of a northern clime the oleander is a flowering shrub, which, because of the character of its foliage and the simple beauty of its red blossoms, well repays careful attention and its place inside the heated greenhouse. In more temperate regions the oleander finds its welcome in the open garden, and will lavish its splendour within the courts of palace or monastery, whilst in India it flourishes of its own accord over jungle and plain. It has the same flower, the same nature, the same principle of growth, but according to temperature and environment it finds devotion from one, appreciation from another, and only cursing and bitterness from the poor cultivator, who, as its roots spread from the hedgerow and invade his scanty plot, must set to work with his *kodali* and root it out. In his struggle for livelihood he is concerned with the underground ramifications of the root system, and with his eyes upon the soil he lacks either time or the energy to glance at the spray of red blossoms that hangs immediately over his head.

Into a world where men have sacrificed every simple human relationship and are grabbing for what they can get, out of each other, out of the soil, out of books or the exploitation of souls, where the beauty of human sympathy is forgotten, the oleander sheds its flower, and, with a shock, some with protest, some in anger, some in response to a deep echo within, cast away their tools and according to their several abilities realize that beauty of life which had dwelt among them, but which they had allowed to grow out of reach.

The background, then, is a world based upon the principle that each must fight the other, oppress or be oppressed, in order not merely that the ordinary simple needs of life may be satisfied, but that piles of accumulation may be set up. This is a world where, with every available means in his power, the Great King exploits the resources of the underworld, of nature, of the mind, of science and of human physique and intelligence, using all the weapons of organization and the elaborate machinery of a highly centralized bureaucracy in order to add to his wealth. This wealth he measures in gold, or in souls or in facts, or in human bodies, so that men are men no longer but numbers. The King sits fascinated as he watches this hive where everyone is busy, but no one content, where all are piling cell to cell, adding honey to honey, guarding the stores of accumulated wealth with efficient death-dealing stings, or casting out the human wastage, the drones, men who have been broken, or exploited. Into his hive flies the butterfly, armed with no sting, equipped with no power to gather or to store, but clothed in beauty, loving the light of day and life, asking all to share in her sunshine revels, kissing one here and one there with the waft of her wings, arousing a petulant anger where others are too busy even to look at her and are annoyed when she interferes with the work in hand. Like strings on an untuned instrument they respond to her touch, and though the instrument had long been thrown on one side, still here and there music and harmony come struggling forth, toils and troubles are forgotten, memories are aroused of the old scents and sounds, of the simple artistic colour and variety of nature, of the co-operative life of the village, where all were not numbers but neighbours, where there was music and beauty of life. But we have become numbers, with numbers on our doors, our telephones, our cars, our factories our restaurants, our votes and our tickets at sports or theatre. Even as worshippers we are card indexed.

Nandini then is this touch of life, the spirit of joy in life. Matched with Ranjan, the spirit of joy in work, together they embody the spirit of love; love in union, union in love, a harmony before which the discord of greed is scattered as under a spell. Linked in this harmony of beauty they walk fearlessly into this world of getting, and, being independent of it, they break down its barriers, even though in the process they are broken themselves,—but such sacrifice is the price which must always be paid in the effort to break down the wall of darkness, of untruth and to flood the world with light. In the face of this combination of simplicity, the king, enclosed in his pride of empire, in his accumulation of wealth, of things, finds a touch of that happiness that he had lost. His gold loses its luster, his scientific experiments, involving the crushing out of human life, and with it of faith and hope, no longer gives him interest. His research into elemental forces, which in his curiosity he has broken down from compounds to molecules, from molecules to atoms, is dazzled and confounded by the beams of a beauty that warms and embraces everything under its cloak of human affection and sympathy.

So it is that, when men make use of men and leave out this elemental touch of kindliness, by which alone we may live in harmony with our surroundings, they crush and mutilate not merely their victims but the humanity which is in themselves. They prefer to think in terms of empire, of organization in factory or field or workshop, in politics or church or sport, and to satisfy their craving for power or survival at the expense of their human feelings. They use every variety of machinery to fortify themselves or their selfish ends against the dissolving power of beauty and love,—the trust, the company, stocks and shares investments, machinery through which they can avoid all human connection and so cut themselves off from their fellows whilst they extract for their own benefit the very essence of the lives of their neighbours. Organizations are set up with the best of aims and ideals and of executive machinery churches, universities, and charitable institutions which, so long as their income is paid regularly, come to depend for their survival upon the denial of just that element of mutual love and trust, sympathy and friendship, which they were pledged to try and establish. In return for the bread of existence they offer a stone, the kind that holds down papers at a meeting of some far-off Board of Directors, and what wonder, when people come to them in their turn for bread, the bread of knowledge or of spiritual refreshment, they only find a stone.

In such organizations men have become mere numbers. The love which is truth and the truth which is love are violated. For to accept in theory the law of love, but to deny it in practice as impracticable today, is not to accept it at all. This is happening wherever men use men as tools, as a means to some further end in which these tools have no part, lot of interest, and where they fail to recognize in their fellow beings a common inheritance of a common humanity.

Through love, the love of a Nandini for a Ranjan, it is possible to accept any gift from man, even his death for your sake. But the moment it becomes necessary for us to depend upon men on any other basis, then it is well for us to walk with caution. We are treading upon holy ground without removing our shoes. Without our knowing what is happening the nails in our shoes grind the life under our feet to dust. We walk rough-shod over our neighbours without realizing that humanity and truth have been violated.

It is to this insensibility and to the growth in size of all ramifications of society that our misery is due. If man were wise he would set to work to discover some common denomination whereby this reduction of life by fractions into death might be prevented for ever. If his intelligence is no longer capable of facing this truth, he must be prepared to face complete entombment and disintegration under the very ramifications which he has himself set up to ward off the day of wrath.

This does not mean that it is necessary for him to cultivate friendship with every individual he meets, but rather that he should extend to all human beings with whom he has any connection, direct or indirect, that same civility and courtesy which he ordinarily reserves for strangers or servants. Civility with friends is not necessary, for, as friendship grows by mutual giving, all barriers break down. Whilst the barrier of strangeness remains, civility or courtesy, is essential. It was this courtesy which made something great of the battles of olden time, but which, now lost, has started the whole human race on a downward path. Once man disdains this courtesy towards his fellows and refuses to use it as a law, a seasoning whereby all human relationship becomes palatable, the human soul suffers torture. Misery arises and real friendship, that springs up so easily from a basis of courtesy, becomes impossible.

The sun shines upon us all and rules this material world with its light, the light that is life. Where the sun does not penetrate we light our lamp or turn the switch, but we prefer the rays of the sun, which give us a light, a life, a "sunshine" that the electric bulb can never supply. So in the world of man it is upon the light of love that we are dependent for human sunshine, for life and joy and beauty, for the "good life". There are regions in our daily life where our touch with our fellows is so meager that this light does not penetrate, and we have to fall back upon courtesy. The tip itself, handed surreptitiously to porter or waiter, is a recognition of the fact that, however efficient the machine with which we are momentarily in contact, direct human service demands direct human recognition and so it has become the civil thing to do. We do it surreptitiously because the management has warned us that their organization and remuneration are so efficient, that it has reduced to the lowest fraction the need for human contact, that such a custom is not only unnecessary but even illegal. Such is the complication of life today that most of our money, which is the measure of our power over our fellows, "changes hands" as we say, without those hands ever coming into civil much less friendly contact. We sign cheques, we drop money into slots, and we push it through pigeon holes, where a hand but no face takes charge of it. Through our failure to light the lamp of civility, where the sunshine of friendship cannot reach, we hurt ourselves at the same time as we deprive others of their self-respect, and deny to them their own human significance.

In a loveless world, a world where men have ceased ever to be civil, a world of "foreign investment", comes Nandini, the embodiment of that light that is beauty and love. She represents the highest truth in the human world, in the nature of man, a truth for which all down the ages, the great have lived, suffered and even died. She too is willing to suffer torture, a death, a mental crucifixion. In losing her lover and her own life she loses her all to save all, the truth of love, for humanity. She offers herself for Ranjan, for love has life in its keep.

So it is that, according to the measure in which we fail to reach this relationship of love in our relations with our fellow men, our life is incomplete. We suffer, we do not deserve peace, if we cannot afford to love. And thus men organize themselves for all kinds of ends, excellent in themselves, but fail to recognize this root principle of love that is truth, of truth that is love, in their politics, their worship, their education, their business, their investments, their imperialisms. Just so long will they be capable of progress, just so long will they tread the path of inevitable destruction. Nature is never so impatient as with those who would divest her of beauty for selfish ends. Without a common love, a common appreciation of all that is good in man and in the world, it is easy for some tyrant force to find entry, to assert supremacy and to overthrow the little good that remains in a general destruction.

The problem is simple, the cure is simple, so simple that we have grown clever enough not to see it. The highest goal of all is love; a love that each of us is still able to recognize and appreciate, not an abstraction and not an organization, but a spirit, a truth for which men, in all times and countries, have been willing and eager to make the supreme sacrifice, believing that behind this spirit in man, which can be felt, almost touched, lay an objective background which they termed God. To them God was love. In this God was possible and easy for all men to find a fundamental union, which was truth. Even if we do not believe in this God, or in any God, yet our experience in home, or family, or community, or country, tells us that love is truth.

The diggers, the King, the Governor, these were men who had no love for the medium in which they worked, for the soil that they were bent upon exploiting. In their efforts they never hesitated to litter the earth with their ugly piles of rubbish in the name of progress. Yet the law of love holds good in the world of nature as well as in the world of man. It is through love for the soil, and for the cherishing of it, that the soil responds to our touch. At that touch our own hurt is healed. In mutilating the soil, that source of beauty that is also wealth, we mutilate ourselves. It was the same soil that these villagers had cherished, cultivated and loved, out of which they had grown and produced their needs of livelihood, food, clothes and implements. In it they were now digging their own damnation in service to the god of greed, of profit making, but no longer to the ideal of mutual co-operation and love.

Until Nandini came they had not realized that "the times were out of joint" or that there was any more human mode of existence. They accepted their surroundings as King, Priest, Professor and Governor ordered or taught. They took for granted the perpetual domination of the strong, the continued oppression of the weak, and that, in the effort to pile up material wealth, they should, by their own fellows, be transformed from men into machineries, to the mutilation of their own humanity.

Suddenly in the face of this vision of truth, of beauty and of love, the "perfect love which casteth out fear", they realized the greatness of their deprivation. Snatched from her village and her love to satisfy the self-indulgence of the King, to be dissected into her several component parts and analyzed, her hands, her soul, her body and her brain, each with its own marketable value, each capable of being turned to some "useful" purpose in the adding up of wealth, she defeated all by spreading an atmosphere of love wherever she went, in the study of the "dry-as-on dust" Professor, lost in his maze of facts, in the office of the file-grinding Governor, even in the room where the policemen kept their thumb-mark register and their card index catalogue. There were of course some who had by long pruning lost all sensibility to love and beauty who had developed a crookedness which could only recognize love as sentiment, and beauty, as effeminacy, who had feasted their souls upon the ugly until they had become suspicious of anything so naked as the truth. Since ugliness is a lie, as lack of civility is a lie, and is a refusal to recognize that beauty is truth as well as love, so beauty itself is invincible. Had the King failed to break the flag-staff with his own hand, it would have been merely a question of time before the very foundations of his vast structure would have been sapped and brought crashing to the ground by the invincible truth of love.

Perfection of order, of law, of government, of empire, of organization in church and state, society or commerce, this is the perfection of machinery and not the creation of happiness. Like the red oleander flower happiness too must be the fruit of love, of labour that is true, that is civil, that is honest, the fruit of human sympathy and consideration, and of human sacrifice in the cause of that great unity which is truth.

Appendix II

Tagore on Red Oleanders[2]

Some criticisms of my *Red Oleanders* that have appeared in the English papers have convinced me that to a considerable portion of my readers in England this play of mine seems obscure in meaning. Such a fact, I believe, almost always comes as a surprise to an author, because generally a work of this nature springs from a vision that is vivid to himself and a feeling that belongs to his direct experience. It is not for me to discuss the literary qualities of this book, which, being a mere translation, can have no pretension to a permanent place as literature in a language not the author's own. But I think, in justice to myself, I should make it clear that it has a definite meaning which can legitimately claim literary expression.

There was a time when, in the human world, most of our important dealings with our fellow-beings were personal dealings, and the professional element in society was never hugely disproportionate to the normal constitution of its life. Therefore, naturally, in the tradition of literature, which is the ideal expression of man's life, interaction of human relationship have so long occupied the most important position.

To-day another factor has made itself immensely evident in shaping and guiding human destiny. It is the spirit of organization, which is not social in character, but utilitarian. Christian Europe no longer depends upon Christ for her peace, but upon the league of Nations, because her peace is not disturbed by forceful individuals so much as by organised Powers. Naturally, in all organizations, variation of personality is eliminated, and the individual members, in so far as they represent the combination to which they belong, give expression to a common type and very little to their uniqueness of individuality.

But the personal man is not dead, only dominated by the organised man. The world has become the world of Jack and Giant—the Giant, who is not a gigantic man, but a multitude of men turned into a gigantic system.

I am not competent to say how Europe feels about this phenomenon produced by her science. Very likely her stout-hearted Jack is already busy making breeches in the walls of this fortress. But I can say, on behalf of inarticulate Asia, what a terrible reality for us, is the West, whose relation to ourselves is so little human. The view that we can get of her, in our mutual dealings, is that of a titanic power with an endless curiosity to analyse and know; but without sympathy to understand; with numberless arms to coerce and acquire, but no serenity of soul to realise and enjoy.

It is an organized passion of greed that is stalking abroad in the name of European civilization. I know that this does not represent the whole truth as to its character, and therefore the pity of it is all the greater when mainly this aspect of it is forcibly presented to us, causing the spread of dumb sadness over a vast portion of the world and the dread of a devastation of its future into an utterly bankrupt life. Such an objectified passion lacks the true majesty of human nature; it only assumes a terrifying bigness, its physiognomy blurred through its cover of an intricate net-work,—the scientific system. It barricades itself against all direct human touch with barriers of race pride and prestige of power. The impersonal pressure which, from its aloofness, applies to our living soul is enormous ever narrowing our prospect of growth, smothering the power of initiative in our mind.

Once our people had either an Akbar or an Aurangzeb to deal with; now we have an organised avarice,—frightfully simple in its purpose, mechanically complicated in its process. Its messengers who come to us—be they Lord Birkenhead or Lord Curzon—are never for us our fellow-beings in flesh and blood, as were Julius Caesar and Antony who could easily find their immortal places in Shakespeare's drama. They are abstractions, at once far and near, and therefore awful; they are obscure to us in the dark secrecy of their political laboratory and yet grimly concrete in their grasp upon our vitals.

Therefore it should cause no surprise to anybody if a poet, belonging to a continent swallowed by the menacing shadow of Europe, gives a prominent place among the *dramatis personae* of his play to an apparition which now so powerfully occupies the imagination of a vast world consisting of non-Western races. It is not an individual, but a doom; and therefore it should never be compared to such characters as Lady Macbeth by those who wish to find a literary precedent. I am told that science has become a principal subject for some notable poets in Europe. That is natural, for science has permeated Western life; it no longer has its own cradle in the secluded cells of the learned. In a similar manner, the hungry purpose, having science for its steed, running about unchecked, trampling our life's harvest, is not an intellectual generalization unfit for imaginative literature. It is intensely real; its hot breath is upon us; its touch is all over our shrinking soul. It is the principal hero to-day in the drama of human history; and I trust I have the right to invoke it in my own play, not in the spirit of a politician, but of a poet, possibly a lyrical poet.

I am glad to find that my critics readily acknowledge that Nandini, the heroine of the play, has definite features of an individual person. She is not an abstraction, but is pursued by an abstraction, like one tormented by a ghost. And this is the drama. Nandini is a real woman who knows that wealth and power are māyā, and that the highest expression of life is in love, which she manifests in her love for Ranjan. But love-ties are ruthlessly molested by megalomaniac ambition, while an acquisitive intellect plies its psychological curiosity, probing into the elusive mystery of love through vivisection.

I can assure my readers that I never meant to use this book as propaganda. It is a vision that has come to me in the darkest hour of dismay. I have a stronger faith in the simple personality of man than in the prolific brood of machinery that wants to crowd it . This personality—the divine essence of the infinite in the vessel of the finite—has its last treasure-house in woman's heart. Her pervading influence will some day restore the human to the desolated world of man. As in the animal world the physically meek has to-day inherited the earth, woman will one day prove that the meek in soul, through the sure power of love, will rescue this world from the dominance of the unholy spirit of rapacity. The joy of this faith has inspired me to pour all my heart into painting against the background of black shadows—the nightmare of a devil's temptation—the portrait of Nandini as the bearer of the message of reality, the saviour through death.

Appendix III

Tagore's poem 'Vijayī'

Tagore's poem 'Vijayī' (The Victorious) was published in the journal *Prabāsī* in 1918, and later included in the anthology of poems, *Pūrabī*. One can trace in it some of the ideas of the play in an embryonic form. Here is a feeble paraphrase of the poem:

> They were rushing ahead then in proud pace riding their triumphal chariots./ Impatient, infatuated, they were speeding along the blood-red dust of directionless paths./ All around them it was dark night when the hours were dragging along like some tardy sleep-walker;/ the wind had fallen, the birds were dumb.
>
> Their torches flared up to pierce the bosom of darkness/ the red lotus of fiery petals burst out in fierce

arrogance,/ the silent star in the distant sky just looked on like some spell-bound bee./ The voyagers thought this their torch was not just the mirage of a flickering moment./ They thought—this was the very flame of the lodestar;/ it will go on burning alongside the stars, deathless over the vast universe./ They thought—by means of the fierce strength of this very torch they will burn down the rampart of the fort of darkness,/ will snatch up the perennial treasures by breaking open the closed gate of darkness;/ will make the earth their own concubine.

Suddenly the bell starts ringing./ Waking up with a start they find they were blinded by stupor;/ had been dreaming alas of themselves/ as occupying the throne of Yakshapuri in the royal costume studded with million gems,/ as if they had plundered God's own creation with loud laughter of derision.

The new sun rises in the sky./ Look there, its flag flies above,/ shimmering in its fresh white splendour that crushes darkness./ The ashes of the burnt down torches seek the shelter of eternal sleep./ The realm of joy has opened doors, the sky radiates the thrill of joy—/ Oh, celebrate the victory, the victory of the earth, the victory of the sky, the victory of the light. (my translation)

Appendix IV

List of Tagore's Major Plays

(1) Musical drama—*Vālmīki Prativā; Māyār Khalā.*

(2) Verse drama—*Citrāñgadā; Bidāy-Abhiśāp; Gāndhārīr Ābedan; Satī; Narakbās; Karṇa-Kuntī Sambād; Lakṣmīr Parīkṣā.*

(3) Romantic tragedy—*Rājā O Rāṇī; Bisarjan; Mālinī.*

(4) Symbolic drama—*Prakṛtir Pratiśodh; Śāradotsav; Acalāyatan; Rājā; Dākghar; Fālguṇī; Muktadhārā; Raktakarabī (Red Oleanders); Rather Raśi; Tāser Deś; Kabir Dīkṣā.*

(5) Social plays—*Prāyaścitta; Gṛhaprabeś; Śodhbodh; Naṭīr Pūjā; Candālikā; Bãśarī; Muktir Upāy.*

(6) Comedy—*Godāy Galad; Baikuṇṭher Khātā; Cirakumār Sabhā; Hāsyakautuk; Byañgakautuk.*

(7) Seasonal plays—*Śeṣbarṣaṇ; Basanta; Nabīn; Naṭarāj-Ṛturañgaśālā; Śrābaṇgāthā.*

(8) Dance drama—*Citrāñgadā; Candālikā; Shyāmā; Naṭīr Pūjā; Śāpmocan.*

Notes

1. A talk of Tagore, transcribed by L.K. Elmherst in 1924, during the poet's visit and stay in Argentina, November-December 1924; published in *The Visva-Bharati Quarterly*, Nov. 1951-Jan. 1952, under the title '*Red Oleanders*: An Interpretation'.
2. "*Red Oleanders*: Author's Interpretation", *The Visva-Bharati Quarterly*, October 1925.